# THE HISTORY OF SWANSEA
From Rover Settlement to the Restoration

**RHONDDA BOROUGH LIBRARIES**

**LENDING DEPARTMENT**

1. This book must be returned within 3 weeks of the date of issue. The loan may be renewed on personal application or by telephone if not required by another reader.

2. Overdue books will be charged at the rate enforced by the Authority at the time of issue.

3. Borrowers will be charged for lost or damaged books.

4. <u>One</u> set of tickets may be issued to a borrower. The tickets may be used at any Library except the Mobile.

5. Please notify of change of address.

6. The Librarian may suspend or cancel       of borrowers who fail to       with these regulations.

               ott, F.L.A.,
               Librarian

I
Ellis, Brenda
a'r Plant

# Contents

| | |
|---|---|
| Foreword | ix |
| Preface | xi |
| Maps and Illustrations | xiii |
| Introduction | xv |
| 1  Early Beginnings and the Medieval Town | 1 |
| 2  The Economic Pulse | 35 |
| 3  The Social Scene | 78 |
| 4  Municipal Government | 118 |
| 5  The Reformation and the Emergence of Puritanism | 158 |
| 6  Swansea during the Civil Wars | 186 |
| 7  Swansea under the Interregnum | 213 |
| Bibliography | 247 |
| Index | 251 |

# Foreword

For most people, Swansea is best known as an industrial centre whose expansion took place in the eighteenth and nineteenth centuries. But the City has a far longer history, one which extends back over a millenium. The era before the Industrial Revolution saw Swansea's formative years and was no less important than the later period. In the Dark Ages, the town was initially founded and given its name—'Sweyn's Eie'—by Viking settlers. Since its refoundation by the Normans in the early twelfth century, it never ceased to be an important centre of commerce and local administration. In the sixteenth and seventeenth centuries, it played a significant role, not just in matters relating to its immediate locality, but in the history of Wales as a whole.

For many years, Dr. Kenneth Thomas' doctoral thesis on early Swansea has been known to professional historians and has been widely referred to by them for their own researches, but it has not been available to the general public. Now, for the first time, with this edition, a revised and updated version of this important work is available to all.

Swansea City Council is ever mindful of the City's long heritage and I am therefore pleased that the Council has associated itself with the publication of Dr. Thomas' study, which, I have no doubt, will become the standard work on the early history of Swansea for many years to come.

Councillor E. Tyssul Lewis
Leader of Swansea City Council

# Preface

This book, very largely, represents the fruits of my labours as a postgraduate research student at University College, Swansea, between 1954-57, though here and there the original text has been revised and amended.

I readily embraced the history of Swansea between 1485-1660 as my particular field of specialism for several reasons: first, because a rich store of manuscript material for the period had survived locally, thanks in large measure to the unremitting and dedicated efforts of enlightened antiquaries like George G. Francis, Lewis W. Dillwyn, and W. C. Rogers; secondly, urban development was, to some degree, an uncultivated, even neglected, field in Welsh historical studies, and consequently a foray into this particular pasture could well prove both stimulating and enlightening; and finally, ever since my mother, the daughter of a small hill farmer in the upper reaches of the Swansea valley, had introduced me to the delights of a bucket and spade on the sands at Fabian's bay, I had developed a strong attachment to the town, a bond that was strengthened still further during my years as a student at the college in Singleton Park.

During those years of research, I was most fortunate to have as my tutor Emeritus Professor Glanmor Williams who, at the time, was senior lecturer in the History department. Among his many kindnesses to me, he personally effected an introduction to the mysteries and wonders of the Public Record Office and British Museum in London and, much nearer home, the National Library of Wales, Aberystwyth, and when my footsteps showed any signs of faltering, his was the steadying hand. Now I find myself even further indebted to him for he has read the present volume in typescript, and the book has benefited inestimably from his many useful and perceptive comments. Needless to say, for the errors that remain I hold myself entirely responsible.

Dr John Alban, the city archivist, who upholds the highest traditions of his office, also has a call on my gratitude for he has proved helpful in so many respects, not least in the degree of interest which he has displayed since the decision was first made to embark upon publication. I acknowledge his enthusiastic support with a considerable degree of satisfaction.

I wish to record further my warm appreciation of the significant financial support which I have received from Swansea City Council. I can only express the hope that this account of the early history of their town will not only go some way towards meeting a legitimate need, but that it will, furthermore, if only in some small degree, satisfy a few expectations.

My former colleagues at Brecon High School, Mr S. Foulkes, Dr W. Ll. Williams, and Miss Margaret Lewis, all now, like myself, in contented retirement, are also most deserving of my thanks for so readily undertaking the exacting task of reading the proof sheets. Mention, as well, must be made of Mr Denzil Hackford, until recently Principal Educational Adviser in Powys, for preparing the map on p. 20.

During the writing of this book, my wife and family were called upon to display an immense degree of tolerance, and to their constant and unfailing support and encouragement I largely owe the motivation which made its completion possible.

Finally I wish to express my appreciation to Gomer Press for undertaking the work of publication and for their sympathetic consideration throughout.

*W. S. K. Thomas*
*Brecon, October 1989*

# Maps and Illustrations

| | | |
|---|---|---|
| 1 | Viking Longship *c.* AD 800 | 2 |
| 2 | Sketch of Sweyn's 'Eie' | 4 |
| 3 | Charter of William de Newburgh | 9 |
| 4 | Medieval Swansea | 20 |
| 5 | Reconstruction of Swansea in the Fourteenth Century | 21 |
| 6 | Old St. Mary's | 26 |
| 7 | Cross Keys Inn: Site of the Hospital of St. David | 28 |
| 8 | Chapel of St. John | 33 |
| 9 | Mining in Germany | 43 |
| 10 | Forging of Iron in Germany | 48 |
| 11 | The Seventeenth Century Market House | 54 |
| 12 | Coastwise Traffic in Coal in the Sixteenth Century | 57 |
| 13 | An Elizabethan Merchant Ship | 58 |
| 14 | Coastwise Traffic in Coal, 1603-40 | 64 |
| 15 | Entrance to Fabian's Bay Harbour | 68 |
| 16 | The Place House | 88 |
| 17 | Craftsmen: Blacksmith, Barber, Baker, Wheelwright, Shoemaker | 93-5 |
| 18 | A Tudor Beggar | 98 |
| 19 | Street Scene in an Elizabethan Town | 109 |
| 20 | A Tudor Schoolroom | 111 |
| 21 | Recreations | 114 |
| 22 | Sir Matthew Cradock's Tomb | 133 |
| 23 | An Alderman | 136 |
| 24 | The Seventeenth Century Town Hall | 141 |
| 25 | The Despoiling of the Monasteries | 164 |
| 26 | Sketch of St. Mary's Church | 167 |
| 27 | Colonel Philip Jones | 191 |
| 28 | Oliver Cromwell | 208 |
| 29 | Bishop Hugh Gore's Residence | 220 |
| 30 | Major-General Rowland Dawkin | 231 |

# Introduction

This volume attempts to deal with the history of Swansea from its beginnings as a Viking settlement in the early eleventh century to the Restoration of 1660. The Scandinavian settlers were traders as well as warriors, and their business acumen enabled Swansea to develop during its infancy into a port and commercial centre of considerable importance.

But a new chapter in the history of the town opened with the incursion of the Normans into Gower, since these invaders were to prove the great architects of urban development. A castle was built at Swansea, on a spur overlooking the river Tawe, and this fortress became the military and administrative centre of the seignory of Gower. The presence of a market, where all trading transactions had to be conducted, meant also that the town developed into the business centre of the lordship as well.

Successive lords, royal as well as baronial, granted charters to the citizens and, in response to the privileges contained in them, a framework of municipal government gradually evolved. By the end of the Middle Ages the day-to-day running of the borough was vested in a principal officer known as the portreeve, a small executive council of twelve aldermen, and a body of burgesses sitting in common hall. However, despite the considerable measure of independence and self-government conferred by the charters, Swansea during the medieval period was never able to shake itself completely free from the shackles of lordly control and domination. Since the town was the centre of his lordship, the lord, consequently, could hardly be expected to surrender all his rights in his own 'capital'. Through the agency of his steward he continued to exercise a very real voice in the affairs of the borough.

In its role as a frontier town, Swansea was protected by strong stone defences within which the inhabitants, mainly of west-country origin, could feel reasonably secure; though there were occasions when they were to prove too weak to withstand the onslaughts of Welsh princes and chieftains. However, the liberties of the town extended far beyond these encircling walls and embraced an extensive hinterland within well-defined boundaries.

Here, the burgesses possessed valuable rights and privileges, since only they could lease it and only they could pasture their animals over it.

Though the lord and burgesses generally enjoyed a community of interest, there were times when they came into conflict. In the thirteenth century, the great house of de Breos had been oppressive and dictatorial and the burgesses of Swansea, determined to defend their hard-won privileges, were constrained to appeal to a higher authority. There were occasions, also, when the administrators and soldiery in the castle were high-handed and offensive, and redress had to be sought from the sovereign.

Economically, the town prospered during the early Middle Ages and this prosperity stemmed not only from the town's position as the hub of the commercial life of the lordship, but also from the busy activity of the harbour, with ships leaving and entering the haven with their merchandise. The inhabitants of the seignory conducted their buying and selling in the town's weekly market and two annual fairs, while from the port, commodities such as coal and the by-products of agriculture were exported, and imported goods, particularly fish, salt, and wine, were landed at the quay. Though the main pre-occupation of the inhabitants of the lordship was agriculture—and even the townspeople retained a very close connection with the soil—other industries had developed locally which were making a significant contribution to the town's economy. These activities included ship-building, the spinning and weaving of coarse cloth, tanning, and, most significant of all for the future, the mining of bituminous coal on a small scale in pits in close proximity to the river. In the thirteenth century, these developments more than offset Swansea's diminishing importance as a garrison town consequent upon the cessation of the Welsh wars.

The later Middle Ages bore witness to a contraction in economic activity at Swansea as in most of the towns during the period. The cumulative effect of the Black Death and the subsequent plagues in the fourteenth and fifteenth centuries reduced the town's population appreciably. A void was created which, despite the penal laws of Henry IV, was to be filled, not by yet another influx of English immigrants, but largely by Welshmen. It would appear that, long before the passing of the Union legislation in 1536/43, the Welsh were already important members of the little community at the *aber* of the Tawe, being burgesses and holding the prestigious office of portreeve.

The ecclesiastical life of Swansea during the Middle Ages revolved around three institutions: the parish church of St. Mary, the Hospital of St. David, and the Chapel of St. John, the latter two being foundations of a quasi-monastic nature. In 1332 St. Mary's was annexed to the Hospital, and remained appropriated to it until the sixteenth century. Both the Hospital and the Chapel had been richly endowed by wealthy local patrons, but by the fifteenth century they were demonstrating unmistakable symptoms of decay. The Reformation was to lead to the complete disappearance of these monuments of medieval piety.

Economic growth was accelerated during the period 1485–1640, as a result of the operation of a number of favourable factors. Though agriculture still remained an industry of primary importance, other occupations were rapidly acquiring an enhanced status. This was particularly true of coal, and the ever-greater exploitation of the seams in the immediate hinterland of the town underlay much of its growing prosperity during the period.

The economic conditions prevailing at Swansea determined, to an appreciable extent, the nature of the social scene since it was the quickened tempo of the economic pulse that mainly accounted for the steady increase in the town's population and for the presence there of a virile merchant element. On the other hand, the continuing dependence of the townspeople on the land, and the high prestige attaching to land ownership, were reflected in the existence of a powerful group of gentry who maintained houses in the borough and dwelt there in highly congenial circumstances. Below these two dominant groups, there existed a considerable population of shopkeepers, craftsmen, labourers, and a large number of poor men and their families.

These economic and social conditions, in turn, largely shaped the nature and operation of town government. The leading gentry and merchants and, to a lesser extent, the craftsmen sat on that small executive body, the aldermanic council, and occupied the office of portreeve. There was, furthermore, a marked concentration of this office in the hands of the leading gentry and merchant families, who used their position of authority to promote the more profitable aspects of town life. The Acts of Union provided a new dimension to municipal life since the town was able to share, with the other seven boroughs of Glamorgan, in the election of a burgess member for Parliament.

In the field of religion, the changes effected by the Reformation were to be discerned in the disappearance of such familiar landmarks as the Hospital of St. David and the Chapel of St. John, and in changes in the fabric and liturgy of the parish church. Furthermore, towards the close of the sixteenth century, trends indicative of Puritan sympathies emerged. This latter development was not wholly unexpected, since Swansea was one of the areas in Wales which would have been less immune to the infiltration of Puritan ideas from England than most of the country.

With the outbreak of the Civil Wars, the normal trends of development within the town were interrupted. Swansea was royalist in sympathy—though there are indications that there was a considerable minority of disaffected—and its trade suffered to an appreciable extent from the parliamentary blockade organized from Pembroke. Moreover, after the final capture of the town by the Roundheads in 1645, changes were introduced in the personnel of the administration aimed at consolidating Parliament's hold over it.

During the Commonwealth period, further changes were effected in the identity of the town's rulers, while in 1655 a charter was granted to Swansea which made very important changes in the administrative machinery and brought the lord's control, which had been waning in the early decades of the seventeenth century, once more into much greater prominence. This period also witnessed a recovery, even an expansion, of economic activity, while on the religious side the Puritan plant was provided with unprecedented opportunities for coming into full bloom.

At the Restoration, Cromwell's charters of 1655 and 1658 were simply laid aside, and there was a change in the centre of gravity of political power in the town corporation. Leadership and authority within the corporation were transferred from the hands of the parliamentary nominees sitting on the aldermanic council and became vested instead, once again, in the older governing town families and their allies, the new Restoration families. The wheel had almost come full circle.

A NOTE ON QUOTATIONS FROM DOCUMENTS

To facilitate the reading of passages quoted from manuscripts and printed documents, I have modernized the spelling and punctuation. Quotations in Welsh have been translated into English.

Personal names have been reproduced as in the manuscripts, but abbreviations have been extended except where the right ending is uncertain.

Words or letters introduced by the author have been enclosed in brackets.

# Chapter One

## Early Beginnings and the Medieval Town

Swansea's history before the tenth century is shrouded in darkness. The site of the later town fell within the ancient Welsh commote of Gŵyr, but where the homes of the ancient lords of Gŵyr were, it is now impossible to say. They may have been on the site of the old Roman station at Loughor, though there is no evidence to support this conjecture. As for Swansea, it may well have been no more than the 'haunt of sea-gull and plover'. However, perhaps it was not as completely deserted as this, for it has been suggested that there was a bond vill where Swansea now stands.

While the Roman invader does not appear to have appreciated the immediate and wider prospects of the site at the mouth of the river Tawe by establishing a settlement there, even though a few Roman artefacts have been found, a new situation most certainly arose as a result of Norse incursions into Wales from Scandinavian settlements in Ireland. The Norsemen were traders as well as raiders, and they established little trading communities along the south Wales coast. Since it was one of these Norsemen called Swein, who was King of Denmark between 987-1014 and, briefly, King of England also between 1013-14, who probably gave his name to Swansea, they almost certainly established a small community there. Views conflict concerning the nature of this Norse settlement. W. H. Jones, the Swansea antiquary, emphasized the military nature of the settlement. He believed that Swein, when organising his punitive expedition against Britain, had established the headquarters of the Bristol Channel section of his expeditionary force at Swansea, whence he directed his activities against the seaboard of south Wales, the island of Lundy, and the coasts of Somerset and Devon. The expedition had been undertaken by Swein by way of reprisal for the murder by the English King of some of his relatives during the terrible massacre of St Bride's Night in November 1002.

Viking Longship c. A.D. 800

According to this view, two factors of cardinal importance had determined the selection of Swansea as Swein's headquarters. In the first place, the bay of Swansea provided safe anchorage for his ships; ships which, because of the sable raven on their sails, earned for the Danes from the ancient Welsh chroniclers the opprobrious title of 'Black Pagans'. And secondly, the very nature of the expedition made desirable the possession of a harbour enclosed from the open bay. At Swansea, an island, formed by the scouring of the river brought down in times of flood, existed near the expansive mouth of the Tawe and could easily be reached from the bay. This island formed the very type of sheltered harbourage for which the Danes had been seeking. They probably strengthened it by means of a wooden stockade, and it was this island which was the Swein's 'eie' which in later times became Swansea. However, according to Jones, the connection between Swansea and the Danes was a transitory one. The Norse failed to establish a permanent settlement, and the connection between Swansea and the Danes was finally severed by the Normans.

B. G. Charles in his book, *Old Norse Relations with Wales*, threw an entirely different light on the subject. He sought to demonstrate that the settlement was not as transitory as Jones had made it out to be. He maintained that a list of the twelfth- and thirteenth-century inhabitants of the ports of the Bristol Channel, similar to the Dublin Roll, would almost certainly reveal the presence of a strong element of Scandinavian settlers, probably maritime traders. According to Charles it was doubtful whether Swansea, which in the Middle Ages became an important trading centre and ship-building port, could have developed as such but for the acumen and initiative of the Norse traders in the town. Furthermore, he maintained that in all probability their presence was soon tolerated by the Welsh themselves, who must have realized how beneficial the Norse nautical skill and commercial acumen would be to their own trade and prosperity.

Inferring from its Norse name that Swansea was founded by a Norseman named Swein, and that, consequently, its history goes back to the Viking Age, he emphasized that it was primarily a commercial and not a military settlement. Swansea harbour was a

Sketch of Sweyn's 'Eie'

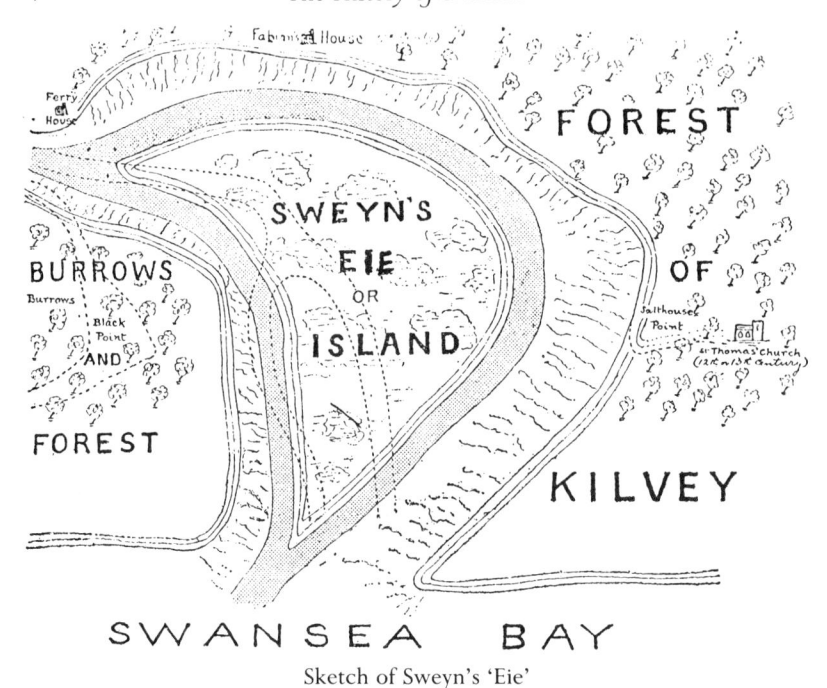

suitable home for the expansion of the commerce of the Norse traders. The Scandinavian traders who had settled at Swansea and other ports in south Wales maintained a very active commercial relationship with Ireland.[1] According to Charles they probably sold Welsh slaves to traders from Norway, Denmark, and Iceland on the Dublin mart in exchange for goods. Wheat, honey and malt were other likely commodities which they may have bartered for wine, furs, hides, whale-oil, butter, and coarse woollen cloth. There was also a flourishing trade in Welsh horses, which were highly prized in Ireland. But it was not only with Dublin and other ports in Ireland that trading took place. It can be surmised that the

[1] The particularly close connection between the south Wales ports and Dublin is demonstrated by the names of the citizens of Dublin at the end of the twelfth century. The population of Dublin at this time was a truly cosmopolitan one but the greater proportion was English; a great number of them hailed from Bristol, Cardiff, Swansea, Haverfordwest and other towns in the Bristol Channel. Godafridus and Ricardus filius Segeri, both hailing from 'Sweinesea' are mentioned in the Dublin roll of names.

Norsemen of the Welsh towns traded with the Continent also, in much the same way as did the Ostmen of Dublin, but not on the same large scale.

It would appear, then, that Jones's argument about the military and transitory nature of the Norse links with Swansea is less than tenable. The connection was primarily commercial, and was of importance to the town because to it Swansea owed the origins of its prosperity and importance in succeeding ages.

THE MEDIEVAL TOWN

As with so many other towns in Wales the history of Swansea begins with the advent of the Normans into Gower. In early Wales there had been no real towns; the Normans were the first to establish corporate towns with their own proper institutions in the country west of the Severn and the Dee.

The paucity of documentary evidence is such that it is extremely difficult to assert with any degree of confidence which Norman first encroached into Gower, though Henry de Beaumont, Earl of Warwick (d. 1119), was undoubtedly the first Norman lord of that area. It is even questionable whether Gower was ever 'attacked' in the true sense of that word by the Normans. History is silent about any battles having been fought in the peninsula at this time. Even though such notices might not have been preserved in writing, it would perhaps be reasonable to assume that an oral tradition would have survived locally. In the absence of such evidence it might be suggested with some justification that the Norman occupation of the old Welsh commote of Gŵyr, which embraced a far wider area than the modern peninsula, partook more of the nature of a peaceful acquisition of authority.

The lordship thus created by de Beaumont extended far beyond the peninsula, since it embraced also the inland region bounded by the rivers Llwchwr, Aman, Twrch, and Tawe. This was an upland region which contrasted very sharply with the fertile lowlands of the peninsula, and these physical features determined the division of the lordship into a Welshry (*Gower Wallicana*) and an Englishry (*Gower Anglicana*). Another physical feature, the great wood which ran between Swansea and Loughor, further divided the Welshry of the interior into two areas known as *Supraboscus* and *Subboscus*.

It has already been established that one reason which had favoured urban development at Swansea was the suitability of the harbour for commercial purposes. With the coming of the Normans a second factor emerges. This was the building of the castle there. The original castle was of the motte and bailey type and consisted of an earth mound or motte surmounted by a wooden tower, with a courtyard or bailey at its base protected by a bank and a wooden palisade. Undoubtedly, this was the structure attacked in 1116 by Gruffydd ap Rhys, the son and heir of Rhys ap Tewdwr, the last king of Deheubarth (south Wales). In the Welsh chronicle, *Brut y Tywysogion*, it is recorded that the Welsh burned the outer castle but failed to carry the tower. The vulnerability of wooden defences to fire, together with continuous Welsh attacks, which resulted in the town being put to the torch at least three times between 1212–1220, led to the castle being rebuilt in stone some time during the thirteenth century.

This was the *caput* or principal castle of the lordship of Gower. Its exalted status meant that not only did it have to occupy a position of particular strength where troops could be garrisoned to keep the surrounding countryside in subjection, but it had also to house the administrative headquarters of the lordship, its courts of justice, its treasury, and the armoury.

The site at Swansea was one which offered distinct strategic advantages. It commanded the most vulnerable land approaches into the peninsula from the east and north, and it also controlled the lowest fording point on the river Tawe. Moreover, it stood near the river mouth—at the *aber* of the Tawe—and thus could be victualled and garrisoned by water. Most important of all, perhaps, in view of Scandinavian incursions, it stood at the most important point for repulsing any seaborne attack.

Having built their castles, marcher lords then further riveted their control over the surrounding countryside by planting boroughs outside the castle walls to which English artisans and tradesmen were attracted by the grants of charters, modelled very largely on the one granted to the mother town of the Welsh boroughs, Hereford. In turn, the privileges conferred on Hereford had been derived originally from Breteuil, one of William Fitz-Osbern's castles in the present Department of the Eure in France. Swansea's first charter is unusual in that it does not appear to have been based on any known charter.

There were in Wales towns which had started their existence within the castle bailey and Swansea may well have been one of these. The castle favoured urban development because of the protection its walls afforded, or seemed to afford. At Swansea, de Beaumont would have been appreciative of the advantages accruing from the existence of an active, progressive population which could act not only as an additional line of defence against the Welsh, but whose commercial activities would also help to swell his revenue and victual his castle. It was in this manner that, in a comparatively short space of time, Swansea acquired two new roles. In addition to being a focal point of commerce, it had now, under the Normans, become both a military and administrative centre. This was to remain its three-fold purpose for nearly the whole of the Middle Ages.

The period stretching from the advent of the Normans to the accession of the Tudors to the throne of England is one of the most formative periods in the long history of the town. Considerable development took place in the sphere of Swansea's government as a result of the granting of a series of charters, while economically it became a flourishing sea-port, as well as the commercial centre and market town of the lordship of Gower. But despite the developments that took place on both the municipal and economic sides, it must always be remembered that during this particular period the town never outgrew its origins as did so many other towns and cities.

Charters were granted to Swansea during this period by William de Newburgh (between 1158-84), King John (1215), Henry III (1234), William de Breos (1306), Edward II (1312) and Edward III (1332). These charters were the result of the operation of certain stimuli. One such stimulus was the fact that the lord, appreciative of the advantages he would derive from the existence of an active and progressive urban population, realized that the best inducements which he could offer to entice traders and craftsmen would be administrative and economic concessions. Another was the early appreciation by the traders who lived there of the advantages that would follow from partially withdrawing the town from control by the feudal lord. They were prepared to pay for the privileges of self-government and self-taxation, for the possession of immunity from tolls and dues which hampered their trading activities, and for the right of excluding the lord's officers from interference in their affairs.

Under the grants embodied in these charters, the burgesses received a considerable measure of independence and self-government but Swansea never succeeded in throwing off completely the control exercised over its affairs by the lord of the seignory. The latter could hardly be expected to surrender all his rights in his own 'capital' and centre of his lordship. Through the agency of his steward, therefore, he continued to exert a very real influence over the affairs of the borough.

The charter granted to the town by William de Newburgh, the grandson of Henry de Beaumont, illustrates the operation of both the stimuli already noted as conducive to the granting of the Swansea charters. The wording of the charter, which was addressed to the burgesses of Swansea, suggests that an embryonic settlement was already in existence. Every burgess was granted a burgage tenement and the burgesses' rights, together with the limits within which they could exercise those rights, were defined. Their rights to land recovered from the waste (assarts) were confirmed, and they were given seven acres of land 'beyond the wood' and above Burlais brook, areas identified now with Cefn Coed and Cwmbwrla. Valuable rights of pasture were also theirs and they were permitted pannage for their swine in the woods about the town. From the same woods they could provide themselves not only with firewood but also with oaks for their houses, fences, and ships, though for every ship built they had to pay the lord 12d. Shipbuilding then was an important occupation of the burgesses, though these ships must have been small and suitable only for coastal navigation. In the same woods wild animals must have abounded and these the burgesses were allowed to hunt, except for

Charter of William de Newburgh

the stag, the hind, the wild boar, and the marten. Wreck of the sea found above low tide was to be shared equally between themselves and the lord. They could erect brew houses and ovens on their burgages, and they were not to plead in any court but the hundred court of the borough. No member of the lord's household could bear witness against them, an indication, possibly, that friction had already arisen between the lord and the townspeople, and no action was to be taken against a burgess without another burgess being present as witness. A delightful peep at social behaviour in a garrison town at weekends is provided by the injunction that any person shedding blood between noon on Saturday and Monday morning should pay a fine of 40s., while during the remainder of the week the fine was to be only 1s. Burgesses could also sell and transfer their burgages on payment of 4*d.* to the lord and, if they failed to find a buyer, they could dispose of the property by any means. They were permitted to leave the town on business, and in their absence hand over their burgages to whomsoever they pleased providing the necessary duties were rendered. In stark contrast was the lot of the unfree tenant, who could neither transmit land nor depart from the place of his birth. Other privileges included valuable fishing rights and, as further protection for their interests, it was enjoined that foreign merchants could buy skins and hides only from burgesses, and these outsiders were also forbidden to cut cloths for retail sale. For all these privileges the burgesses were to pay the Earl and his successors an annual rent of 12*d.*, a sum which appears to have been the standard burgage rent for most of the towns in Wales and the West Country.

Together with the privileges, there were certain obligations which the burgesses had to assume and these provide a valuable glimpse of the military character of life in a garrison town situated in a frontier region. The burgesses were liable to serve in the lord's army, without payment if they could return home the same day, and at the lord's expense if the service was further afield. In recognition of this service they were free to graze their horses along with those belonging to the lord's men-at-arms.

The fact that the burgesses held land and had common and forest rights is a plain enough indication of the strongly agricultural element in the life of the townsmen at this time. The close connection of medieval townsmen with the land needs no stressing. The soil was cultivated within and without the town walls, while animals were pastured on unenclosed forest and common lands. These agricultural pursuits, far from being a mere side-line, were usually quite indispensable to the citizens' well-being.

Though the charter delineated the boundaries within which the burgesses had been granted certain rights and privileges, it did not outline the town boundaries. These are first defined in the *Book of Orders* among various entries for 1584. However, they are more precisely described in the charter which Oliver Cromwell granted to the town in 1655. It was then ordained that the limits should extend, in length and breadth, from the head of Burlais brook to the river Tawe in the north, and from the head of Burlais brook along by the Weig house to the Cockett by David's Well in the west, and from David's Well along David's Ditch to Brynmill and the sea in the south, and thence along the sea shore to the river Tawe in the east.

In the thirteenth century, though the town was the focal point of the economic life of the seignory of Gower, on the administrative side it held a position of inferiority to the castle. This situation led to the oppression of the burgesses by the castle garrison. Indeed, the de Newburgh charter had given earlier indications of discontent on this score. Later on, the rapacity of King John's officers was such that the burgesses and their neighbours in Gower were driven to petition the King for protection and redress. In 1208, John granted charters to the English and Welsh of Gower which, in identical terms, released them from certain of these grievances. The sergeant and officers of the castle were forbidden, while going their rounds, to quarter themselves upon the inhabitants: 'know ye that we have released the Englishmen of Gower from the custom which our servants of the castle of Swansea have had of taking their food (*commendendi*) with the aforesaid Welshmen and we will that here after they be herein neither molested nor aggrieved'. Needless to say, they had to pay heavily for these privileges and it would appear that the relief or quit claim granted by the charters was only vouchsafed at a cost to the men of Gower of fifty marks and two chascuros (hunting horses).

These charters are also of considerable interest in that they indicate the presence in Gower of an English-speaking population. There was, of course, nothing surprising or unusual in this, because it seems to have been a policy generally pursued by the Marcher-lords to establish in their territories communities of English settlers. These tended to congregate around the castles and were as much a part of the foreign settlement as the garrison in the castle. There was a considerable English colonization of Swansea and south Gower, though the paucity of evidence is such that one can only speculate tentatively as to where they came from. However, the linguistic affiliations of the Gower dialect, no less than the ease of sea-communications across the Bristol Channel, would suggest the West Country as the original home of these immigrants. It is even possible that there were English settlers from the West Country in the Vale of Glamorgan and south Gower before the Norman conquest, and that what the conquest did was to encourage them to come over in larger numbers. Typical of the many dialect words peculiar to Gower, but recognizable in their changed form as West Country words by origin, are such words as 'blonkers',[2] 'bett'[3] and 'nestletrip'[4].

In 1215, while the lordship of Gower was still in his possession, King John granted a charter to Swansea. The initiative must have been taken by the burgesses themselves. It is quite possible that John had been approached by them when he visited the town in 1210 and the nature of their requests made clear to him. At that time, however, the burgesses had been unable to find a man of influence who would intercede with the King on their behalf. Fulke de Bréauté, the custodian of Swansea and Gower, had hardly been the man to do so since he was a bluff soldier and a selfish time-server. But, by 1215, conditions had become more propitious as a result of the emergence of an entirely new set of circumstances. Swansea had found a champion in William Mareschal, the Earl of

[2] Sparks.
[3] Prepared turf used for hedging.
[4] The smallest pig in a litter.

Pembroke, who had replaced Fulke as governor of Swansea in 1214, and the King, as a consequence of his struggle with the baronage, was presiding over an empty exchequer and ready to avail himself of any means of replenishing his depleted finances. He signed the charter at Reading on 6 May 1215, with the Earl himself having the satisfaction of witnessing the King appending his signature to the document.

The provisions of this charter may be regarded as supplementary to those originally granted in William de Newburgh's. The earlier one had allowed the burgesses of Swansea to 'carry and sell wherever they wish and can'. By this charter the burgesses were allowed to 'go and come through all our land with their merchandise, buying and selling and trading, well and in peace, freely and quietly and honourably; and that they be quit of toll, passage, pontage, stallage, and lastage, and all other customs, saving in all things the liberties of our city of London'.

One of the main reasons why the burgesses of Swansea had desired this charter was that it would enable them to compete with the merchants of other towns who had been privileged by chartered concessions to buy and sell throughout the land (always excepting London) free from the payment of tolls and dues. On the surface, then, it would appear that the charter was of advantage to Swansea by promoting the expansion of the town's economic life. However, it was one thing to confer privileges; it was quite another to enforce them in other boroughs. Swansea's burgesses were only too soon to discover this to their cost. In 1233 and 1234 Swansea merchants had their ships and cargoes seized at Bristol for non-payment of tolls there and it took the intervention of the Crown to secure their release.

Very little is known about the commercial and trading activities of the Swansea merchants at this time. Trading links with Bristol had certainly been established; and it is more than probable that commercial relations existed with most of the ports of the Bristol Channel, though the nature and extent of this trade have not been established. But that Swansea men traded over a wider area than this is indicated by the letter of protection and safe conduct granted to Peter Edward and other traders of the town in 1283. It appears that they traded in corn and other commodities with the whole of the realm. The Swansea merchants of the thirteenth century were not always allowed uninterrupted enjoyment of their peaceful trading activities. They and their ships were pressed into the King's service during time of war, like those of other maritime towns, and they are found employed in carrying provisions to the King's armies and in fitting out their ships ready for action with the King's fleet.

In the Middle Ages towns had won their privileges from powerful lords, sometimes lay and sometimes ecclesiastical. These lords were inclined to recall such concessions when the immediate needs which had led to the grants had passed. This feature of medieval town history is admirably illustrated at Swansea. There, in the late thirteenth and early fourteenth centuries, the burgesses had to defend themselves against the tyranny of the great house of de Breos. Hitherto, Swansea had been under the control of a succession of Norman earls of strong moral character; men who had been companions and counsellors of the Kings of England. The members of the de Breos family were, however, an entirely different breed and have been described as 'a licentious clan of freebooters who appear to have been so habituated to duplicity and chicanery as to make it impossible for them to be straight-forward and honest in their dealings with their neighbours'.

Because the last William de Breos had been making inroads into their hard-won privileges, the people and tenants of Gower instituted proceedings against him by petition. In 1305, Edward I appointed a commission to inquire into the truth of the allegations they brought. In the terms of reference of the commissioners, however, there was a loophole, of which de Breos fully availed himself. The commissioners had been appointed to hear and terminate all the trespasses and injuries brought against the men and tenants before (as well as after) 'our inhibitions aforesaid made to the said William unless the same William before your coming to the said town of Swansea shall immediately do full justice to the same men and tenants'.

De Breos was fully aware of the penalties which he had incurred as a result of his oppressive practices, but at the same time he realised that disaster could be averted by conferring upon the men of Swansea and Gower a restitution of their freedom and rights. Consequently, in 1306, he granted two charters, one to the burgesses of Swansea and the other to the tenants of the Englishry of Gower.

The charter to Swansea was granted to the burgesses inhabiting an entire burgage or any portion of a burgage and recited, with hypocritical magnanimity, that de Breos would bear them no ill-will for the actions they had brought against him in the king's court. They should have oak for the repair and building of ships—but only for four large ones or an unlimited number of small ones such as would not carry more than twenty casks of wine. Their pasture rights should extend from 'Burlakys[5] Brook to Hakkydeweye[6] and Lyu[7] and as far as the Ditch of St David'[8]. In addition they might take pit-coal from 'Byllywasta' (Gelliwastad, a hill to the north-west of Morriston). They were to have free use of the highways, and they should not be imprisoned for minor offences, nor fined except by a jury of their equals; in their hundred court they might expect speedy judgements. They could select, every Michaelmas, two burgesses as candidates for the office of town provost or portreeve, and the lord's High Steward should appoint one of them to occupy the office. The portreeve so appointed should participate with the lord's bailiffs in the fixing of fines and penalties, and the lord's officers were to be curbed generally within the 'liberties' or borough boundaries. No inhabitant of the borough could be indicted by a Welshman, or by any member of the lord's household, for any offence committed within the borough. Aids granted to the lord should be assessed and levied only by the burgesses. The burgesses should continue to pay the lord 'prisage of wine' on every thirty casks imported in foreign bottoms. No burgesses, except those of Loughor, might trade freely in Swansea, unless they had been privileged by charter to do so. If the lord created any new burgess (except one who was already a burgess of Loughor) he should pay his scot and lot as other burgesses did. In future there

[5] Burlais brook.
[6] This has been identified with the old road running from Carmarthen to Swansea.
[7] River Llan.
[8] Brynmill stream.

was not to be taken from the burgesses an impost of more than twenty marks in money, or the equivalent in goods, and forced loans were to be repaid within forty days. The burgesses of Swansea should henceforth be free of toll upon their ale-brewings, but non-burgesses residing in the town should pay, as hitherto, eighteen pence or twenty-eight flagons. Triers and tasters of ale were to be dispensed with. The burgesses were to have the meadows of Crow-Wood and Portmeade, and henceforth also they should not be called upon for military service outside Gower. But, in Gower, they were to serve as laid down 'in their original charter'. They should no longer have to maintain those who had taken sanctuary in the church, nor be held responsible for their escape. The lord's chancery in Gower should be available for the issue of writs, and he should do justice to those against whom he had trespassed. The lord was 'not to sell justice, nor deny it to any man'. The ferry of Swansea should be available to all burgesses at all times on payment of a sheaf of corn at harvest time or, in lieu of that, the payment of their fare. The lord's officers were not to take fees from any prisoners except in cases of felony, and not then, even, unless they were detained overnight in the prison. Furthermore, no bailiff was to hold a hundred court without the special commission of the lord, nor should any of the bailiffs in future be styled 'Sheriff'. If any of the lord's officers committed any offence within the town liberty, he should answer for it in the hundred court unless the lord, within a month of the offence, gave satisfaction to the aggrieved parties. For every violation of this charter de Breos and his successors were to forfeit to the King five hundred pounds of silver, and to the burgesses five hundred marks of silver.

This charter certainly helps to cast shafts of light into dark corners. From it one can discern the ways in which de Breos had been oppressive in his relations with the burgesses. It is probably fair to assume that the things which he promised not to do in the future were precisely what he had been doing in the past. In which case it is quite apparent that the burgesses had been mulcted of considerable sums of money by de Breos and his officers. Taxes of over twenty marks, which must have been levied by de Breos, were heavy and are an indication that Swansea in the early fourteenth century was already a prosperous urban community. It becomes apparent also that there had been a denial of justice, and that the burgesses had been impeded in their free use of the highways and waterways. They had also been compelled by de Breos to proceed on military expeditions beyond the limits of Gower.

It can also be seen how the necessary qualification for burgess-ship had been relaxed. The charter of William de Newburgh had established the principle 'to every burgess a burgage' and had contained a clear inference that the inheriting of a burgage implied also the inheritance of a burgess-ship. In this new charter a 'portion' of a burgage constituted the essential qualification. The fact that the older rule had been relaxed suggests a changing conception of the meaning of burgess-ship.

The charter also reflects the development in town government which had taken place since de Newburgh's time. The burgesses were now to elect two of their number yearly for the office of 'Provost', though the final selection of the portreeve was to lie in the hands of the lord's steward. It may be that the office was first instituted by this charter. It is more likely, however, that the charter merely formalized procedure and gave legal recognition to an already existing practice.

The pasture rights of the burgesses were defined in much the same way as in de Newburgh's charter. No mention is made, however, of the seven-acre plots that had been attached to each burgage in the earlier grant. Rather were the burgesses given the meadows of Crow-Wood and Portmeade. It has been suggested that the seven-acre plots of de Newburgh's charter were, in all probability, represented by these meadows. If this is the case then the two charters agree well together.

The charter also provides a glimpse into the town's economic life and the structure of its population. The burgesses built ships and for this purpose they could use the lord's woods, though it is significant that this right could only be exercised within certain limits. The number of great ships that could be built was now restricted to four, though the burgesses could build as many small ships, able to carry twenty hogsheds of wine or less, as they wished providing they paid the lord 12*d*. for each vessel. Furthermore, timber could not be sold or given to non-burgesses, and the gathering of deadwood for fuel was placed under the supervision of the lord's forester. It is quite apparent, therefore, that considerable inroads had been made by the burgesses into the natural resources of the area during the previous one hundred years and that the intensive exploitation of the forests which had hemmed in the town on the landward side was causing concern.

That foreign vessels, laden with wine, visited the port becomes evident from the following extract: 'Also, prisage of wine shall be paid unto us, to wit, for thirty hogsheads carried in one ship from ports beyond the seas as hath hitherto accustomed to be given'. The ships must have been small, as four hogsheads may be taken as equivalent to one 'tun' of wine. Coastal navigation was rendered necessary by the frailty of the craft and by the need to take shelter in some friendly port or roadstead during storms and at night. It is impossible to estimate the extent of Swansea's sea-trade at this period but, under the circumstances, it could not have been great and, in all probability, was largely in the hands of foreign merchants.

Mention is also made of the right granted to the burgesses to dig pit-coal at Gelliwastad, for their own use only, and not to sell to any stranger to take outside the limits of the borough. It can be assumed that coal was already being exported from Swansea but the trade was so profitable that the lord wished to keep control in his own hands. The undertakings in the vicinity of Swansea must have been on a very small scale; there was no great demand and the outcrops alone would have been worked. The coal mined was probably used to burn lime and possibly to warm some family hearths. It may also have been used in the smithies.

The English county of Gower, as well as the borough of Swansea, obtained a charter from de Breos in 1306. From its terms it appears that the inhabitants of Gower frequented the fairs held at Swansea. Two of these were held annually in the town: one in the summer on Assumption Day (15 August) and the other in the autumn on the Feast of St. Martin (11 November). In addition, there was a weekly market. The holding of the fairs and markets is a reflection of the central position occupied by the town in the economic life of the lordship.

At least three strata of the population can be recognized: the administrators and soldiers of the lord marcher living within the castle precincts; the burgesses possessing specific rights and privileges for which they had paid dearly; and thirdly, the non-burgesses. The population was mainly of Norman or English extraction, the Welsh being rigorously excluded. The exclusion of the native population was also a feature of the other boroughs in Wales at this time and it is hardly surprising, therefore, that the Welsh should not have been well disposed towards them. This prejudice stemmed, for the most part, from the fact that the town, together with its castle, was symbolic of conquest and the imposition of an alien regime, and the presence within Wales of a privileged burgess element. It was not unexpected, therefore, that in the twelfth and thirteenth centuries, Swansea was repeatedly sacked and burnt by the vengeful Welsh and these attacks must have inhibited the town's development, both as a borough and a port.

The town which thus received a charter from the hand of de Breos probably simply consisted of a cluster of wooden houses huddled around the castle and afforded further protection by an encircling stone wall, interspersed with towers, and a deep broad outer ditch. It is possible that the walls had only recently been built since Swansea received royal grants of murage in 1317 and 1338 which empowered the burgesses to levy tolls on goods entering the town and to spend the money so raised on the walls, either for their repair or construction. In the north, the wall ran along Morris Lane (now King's Lane) and King's Street with the gate at the junction. The defences from this point proceeded south along the line of Orchard Street and the former Waterloo and Church Streets with the gate in this western section of the defences situated probably at the end of College Street. Moving south, the Wassail gate stood at the junction of Church Street and Frog Street, and the wall then ran almost to the river bank following the course of Rutland Street and Victoria Road. At the end of Wind Street stood the South gate and from this point, following a line near Wind Street, the defences

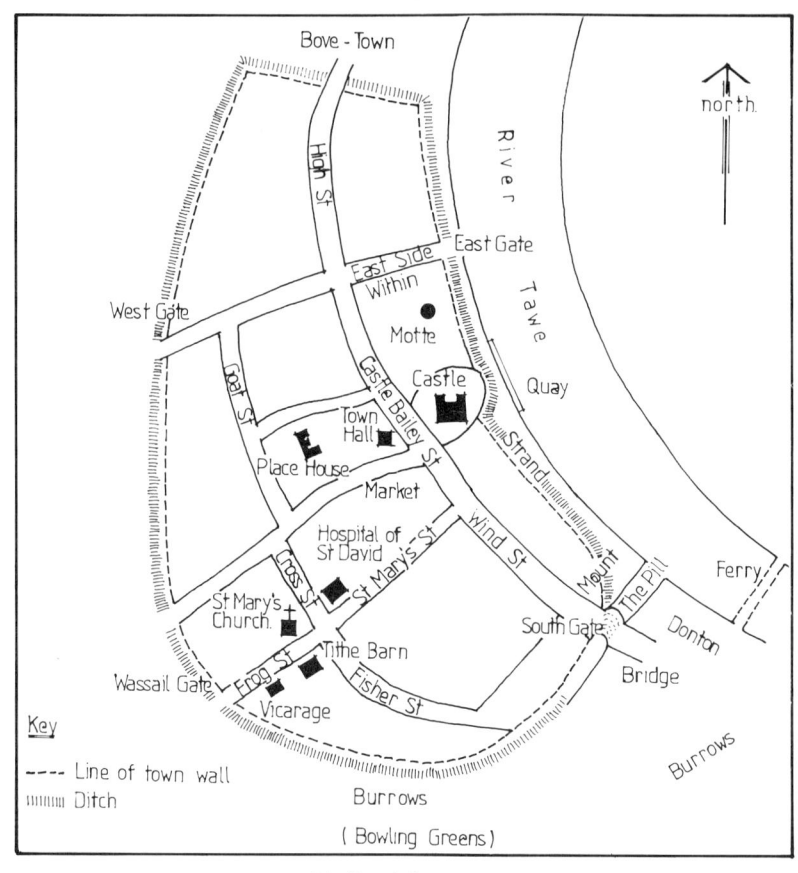

*Medieval Swansea*

swung to the north-west to join the wall of the castle bailey at Castle Street. From the north-east corner of the castle bailey the wall ran north along the Strand to link up with the North gate. The most likely position of the gate in the defences on the east would have been at the end of Welcome Street. Within these defences the town would appear to have been L-shaped with the castle occupying a central position. By the close of the century two suburbs had developed. One, extending beyond the North gate, was known as *Bovetown*, while the one to the south was called *Donton*. Two essential features of the town at this stage in its development also

## Early Beginnings and the Medieval Town

lay beyond the walls. These were the quay and the ferry, and while the quay was to be found at the rear of the castle, the ferry was located near the South gate and was probably of the rope and windlass type.

Frustratingly little is known about the commercial and trading activities of Swansea merchants in the fourteenth and fifteenth centuries. However, this hiatus may partly be filled by postulating that the town's maritime trade would have followed lines comparable with those of Carmarthen or Milford and what documentary evidence has been unearthed would appear to sustain this suggestion. Seaborne trade would have existed with Ireland, Bristol, the Severn ports, ports in south-west England, Jersey and Guernsey, and the Biscayan ports of La Rochelle, Bordeaux and Bayonne. In 1447, a Swansea ship is discovered as far afield even as Iceland and doubtless this vessel would have brought dried cod back to Swansea. From Ireland came fish and Irish cloths; from Bristol and south-west England, cloth and pottery; from Chepstow the iron of the Forest of Dean; from the Channel Islands cloth and wine, and from south-west France wine and salt. In exchange, Swansea would have exported corn and such agricultural by-products as butter, cheese, hides and wool, together with coal and

Reconstruction of Swansea in the Fourteenth Century

lime. It is even possible that Swansea merchants participated in the carrying trade between Ireland and Bristol.

Swansea, like all the ports of Glamorgan and Monmouth, was rarely troubled by the visits of royal customs officials during this period. In 1353 the staple of wool for Wales was fixed at Carmarthen (Cardiff was a wool staple for the brief period 1327-32) and its officials used to visit Swansea occasionally for the weighing of wool. But, in the main, being within the lands of a marcher lord, it apparently lay beyond the reach of royal customs officials. The town may have taken advantage of this to attract to the port merchants who thus avoided royal taxation. Indeed, it may have sheltered a nest of pirates who preyed upon the shipping frequenting the Bristol Channel. In 1483 there occurred an episode which involved Sir Matthew Cradock of Swansea. Under the protecting colours of 'a ship of war of the realm' he had pillaged a ship, the *la Julyan*, while she was lying at anchor off Ilfracombe. He had taken from her gold, harness, wines, cords, mangonels, habiliments and other stuff to the value of fifty marks and had put the owners and the ship to ransom at fifty pounds. At the time there had been no hostilities of any description to justify Cradock's piracy.

In the fourteenth and fifteenth centuries there were many factors at work which would have militated against the economic expansion, or even survival, of the town. Some of these were local in significance while others were of a more general nature. In a local context, the town had certainly suffered from the tyranny of lords like the de Breos. More broadly based, however, was the grave economic depression of these centuries; a depression very largely brought about by the plagues of the period. As a result of these epidemics it has been estimated that about a third or even a half of the population may have perished, and this catastrophic reduction in the labour force resulted in an agricultural and a trade depression. Land went out of cultivation and towns decayed since it was very natural that urban areas, centres of trade and commerce, should have been hit first and fiercest by the onslaughts of the pestilence. There are pointers which indicate very strongly that such had been the fate of Swansea. It may be something more than a coincidence that the series of Swansea charters granted since the twelfth century come to an abrupt end in 1332 and are not renewed again in the Medieval period. This, taken in conjunction with the fact that various buildings in the town were in a state of great decay, a decay that was still evident as late as the early years of the sixteenth century, argues for a decline in prosperity: 'and many beautiful houses... fallen down and decayed, and at this time remain unre-edified, lying as desolate and void ground, and many of them adjoining nigh unto the high streets replenished with much odour, filth and uncleanness, with the pits, cellars, and vaults lying open and uncovered, to the great peril and danger of all the inhabitants and other the King's subjects passing by the same'. As a result of the fall in the town's population, something of a vacuum would have been created and this void would, in all probability, have been filled not by recruitment from England but rather by Welsh villeins and dispossessed freeholders. The increasing numbers of Welshmen to be found in Swansea in the fifteenth century[9] seem to indicate that this is precisely what happened. Owain Glyndŵr's swift and bloodless capture of the town suggests perhaps not only that it was in a state of decay but also that this Welsh element may well have been a substantial one. Again portreeves' accounts for the years 1367, 1400 and 1449 have survived and while the lord's income from rents, the farming of corn mills, tolls, dues from the hundred court and the levy on home brewed beer amounted to £76.7s.10¾d in 1367, by 1449 it had fallen to £39.9s.8d. a reduction of almost 50%. This situation may well have reflected the town's increasing independence of the lord; on the other hand it might be a barometer of the decline which had taken place. Possibly it reflected the operation of both factors. More positive evidence that the town had been affected by the Black Death and the subsequent plagues is provided by a petition sent—probably in 1403—by John Fayrwode, warden of the Hospital

[9] The following are some of the Welsh names of people who resided in the town in the fifteenth century: David ap John, Johanne ap Ievan ap Thomas, Ievan Melyn, Griffith ap Ievan ap Ievan Voya, Ricardo ap Hopkyn Cradoc, David ap Hopkyn, Walter Herbert, David Melyn, Gruffuth Robert, Ievan Gwyn, Iankyn Taylour, Ricardo ap Eynon, Howell ap Philippe Lloyd, David ap Herry and his wife Gwenlyan, Matthew Cradoc, David Cradoc.

of St. David, to the Pope. From this petition it appears that it had been found necessary to appropriate the parish churches, first of Llangiwg, and then of Oystermouth, to the hospice because of the diminution of the revenues of the Hospital 'through pestilences and other evils'.

Little is known about the machinery of government in the borough or of its operation at this time. The charters have established that there was such an officer as the portreeve, annually selected by the lord's steward from two candidates presented to him every Michaelmas (29 September) by the general burgess body. This officer came to preside over a small executive council of twelve aldermen; and this council, judging by the sixteenth century records, seems to have evolved during the later Middle Ages. Furthermore, the enforcement of the rights and privileges granted to the burgesses by their charters would have necessitated the appointment of certain borough officials, such as bailiffs, foresters, catchpolls and toll-collectors, who have already made their appearance. From the findings of an inquest held at Hereford on 15 December 1369, something is learnt about the courts held in the borough, because there is mention of a court held every fortnight (this was the hundred court presided over by the lord's steward), another called *pleas of pie powder* and an English county court held every month. But information of this nature does not contribute greatly to what is known of the administrative set-up and the operation of this municipal machinery. The scarcity of evidence is such that this aspect of the town's history in this period will probably always remain unclear.

The constitution of the burgess body, and the methods whereby it was recruited, are matters of the utmost importance. The freemen had never been co-extensive with the body of inhabitants. In William de Newburgh's charter (1158-84) the principle of 'to every burgess, a burgage', had been established; burgess-ship was to be dependent on the possession of a specific piece of land known as a 'burgage', and the charter contained a clear inference that the inheriting of a burgage implied also the inheritance of a burgess-ship. By the time of de Breos's charter (1306), the freedom was definitely associated with the possession of part of a burgage. At some point between the fourteenth and the sixteenth centuries the possession of even a portion of a burgage ceased to be an essential qualification, and by the opening of the 'modern' period four distinct avenues to the freedom were recognised. The sons and sons-in-law of burgesses naturally tended to be included within the exclusive circle, and it was equally natural that the apprentice to a burgess, who normally lived with him and his family,[10] should also be recruited. Lastly, there was always the possibility that the corporation might wish, for special reasons, to admit a carefully selected number of outsiders; in this way the rights by birth, marriage, apprenticeship, and gift came into existence.

Despite its remoteness from the seat of government and from the main current of central affairs, the town was still engulfed in the eddies, so to speak, of central politics. Swansea men and ships played a part on a wider stage than Gower. During this period the borough was more than simply a *caput* of the lordship, and the hub of its economic life. In the wars which successive English sovereigns fought in France, Ireland, Scotland and Wales, men and ships from Swansea played a far from inglorious part.

In Normandy, William de Breos the Elder fought with distinction on John's side against Philip of France, and when King John assembled an army to deal with the disturbances in Ireland in 1210, Swansea ships were used to transport to Pembroke—whence the main expeditionary force had already been sent—the forces which he had recruited in Glamorgan and Gower. The last William de Breos fought with valour in the Scottish wars of Edward I and Edward II, and doubtless men-at-arms and archers from the town served under his banners. And in the Welsh wars of Edward I Swansea men again drew the broad sword and bent the bow of yew for their King, while the town's ships and mariners assisted in the provisioning of his army.

RELIGIOUS LIFE

The devotional side of life at Swansea during the Middle Ages centred on three institutions: the Church of St. Mary, the Hospital of St. David, and the Chapel of St. John the Baptist.

[10] Infra, p. 105.

The early history of the Church of St. Mary is clothed in obscurity. It has been claimed that there was a church at Swansea before the twelfth century, but the evidence is of such a dubious nature that little or no reliance should be placed on it.

However, it is more than probable that a church existed at Swansea in the twelfth century. The Norman invader and conqueror, having built his castle and planted his borough, invariably established a church as well and at old St. Mary's architectural evidence was found to sustain this argument. Most significant in this context was the allowance of 76s.1d. in alms made in 1193 by Henry I to a cleric named Robert, who was either a deacon or a rural dean living in Swansea. Though it has not been possible to establish whether he merely resided in the town, or ministered there, the likelihood is that he officiated in the parish church. It is only in 1291 that the first conclusive evidence of the existence of a church at Swansea appears.

Unfortunately, little is known about this twelfth century church or what it was like in the later Middle Ages, despite the fact that it

Old St. Mary's

survived until 1739. It was possibly quite large by Welsh standards, and it certainly contained a rood loft and chantries. Some time in the fourteenth and fifteenth centuries there would appear to have been extensive rebuilding—traditionally associated with Henry de Gower—if the chancel windows and the Herbert chapel of old St. Mary's are anything to go by. With regard to vestments and furnishings, the church appears to have been amply endowed.

In its early days the church at Swansea was closely linked with the priory of Llangenydd, which Henry de Beaumont, its patron, the first Norman lord of Gower, had granted before his death in 1119 to the monastery of St. Taurin at Evreux in France, a connection which was to last until the middle decades of the fifteenth century. The affiliation with Llangenydd arose through the gift of William de Breos, who conferred on the monks the advowson of St. Mary's at Swansea.

In 1188, Archbishop Baldwin, accompanied by Gerald of Wales, embarked upon his celebrated tour of Wales to whip up support for the Third Crusade. He passed through Swansea and spent a night at the castle there. On the following day he celebrated mass, and it is possible that it was in the Church of St. Mary that those in the town who had been persuaded to take up the Cross, and fight against the infidel Turk, assembled to dedicate themselves for that purpose.

In 1291, Pope Nicholas IV granted to Edward I, for a period of six years, the tithes of all ecclesiastical benefices in England and Wales toward defraying the expenses of an expedition to the Holy Land. The value of the church at Swansea was then computed and fixed at £10.

From the charter which William de Breos had granted to Swansea in 1306 it is evident that St. Mary's Church enjoyed rights of sanctuary because the charter stipulated that the burgesses of the town and their servants were to be free from maintaining those who had fled to the church for that purpose; nor were they to be held responsible for the escape of such persons. Since the times were turbulent, and the general tenor of life unruly, this right of sanctuary is likely to have been freely made use of by wrongdoers.

In 1332 the Church of St. Mary was annexed to the Hospital of St. David, and its wardens became the rectors of the parish church, though they employed others to minister there as vicars. The Hospital had only recently been founded by Bishop Henry de Gower, and in that act of piety and true charity he had been

Cross Keys Inn: Site of the Hospital of St. David

liberally aided by the great folk of the district, and by none more than the Lady Alina, the eldest daughter and co-heir of the last William de Breos, and wife of the Lord John de Mowbray. Bishop Henry had endowed the Hospital with property and lands in Gower and Swansea, and initially these consisted of thirteen burgages or half burgages in Swansea, together with a scattered group of properties, amounting altogether to about 330 acres. The bishop's intention was that these endowments should sustain a warden and six chaplains who were to celebrate divine service daily and for ever, and should also support the blind, decrepit, and infirm priests and laymen of the diocese. The collation to the Hospital was reserved to the bishop and his successors, and in the event of the see being vacant, to the cathedral chapter.

It was to amplify the Hospital's endowments that Henry de Gower appropriated to it the church of St. Mary which had been granted to him by the Abbey of St. Taurin. Already, by 1331, a perpetual vicar with cure of the parishioners had been established at St. Mary's. Only one-third of the tithe was settled on him, two-thirds being reserved for the warden of the Hospital, which made that appointment an attractive one. Clearly, therefore, the incumbent of St. Mary's was not to enjoy a fat living. It was possibly for this reason that the vicars of St. Mary's in the later Middle Ages are found engaged in the practice, which was very widespread, of exchanging livings in the hope, doubtless, of securing better preferment. In 1400, the vicar of Swansea, Henry Vachan, exchanged livings with Thomas Cotyngham, who was the incumbent of Brawdy in Pembroke. Within a year Cotyngham was on the move again, exchanging parishes with Thomas Gosselyn, rector of Stanley in Somerset.

With the passage of time the Hospital established by Henry de Gower in 1332, in close proximity to the parish church,[11] had its possessions further augmented by grants from pious lay donors, an additional grant of lands from the founder bishop and, finally, by the appropriation to it of two more churches in the neighbourhood, those at Oystermouth and Llangiwg.

---

[11] Infra, p. 80.

The first warden was John de Acum. He and his chaplains were doubtless earnest in their faith and duty, for within two years they founded a chantry for the souls of the Earl of Hereford and his relatives.

In the fourteenth century certain developments occurred which made the financial position of the Hospital very precarious. Plagues and the 'changes of the times' diminished its revenues. Consequently, in order to preserve it, two courses of action were embarked upon. The first was to appropriate the churches of Llangiwg and Oystermouth, and the second to reduce the number of chaplains from six to four. It was only by trimming its sails in these ways that it was able to weather the economic crises which pressed so heavily on the church in England and Wales during the fourteenth and fifteenth centuries.

The appropriation of Llangiwg and Oystermouth to the Hospital did not see the institution at either of these churches of a perpetual vicarage. Instead, the wardens caused the cure of the parishioners to be exercised by 'fit' priests, removable at the will of the warden. The parishioners could hardly have benefited generally from such an arrangement, as stipendiary priests of this kind were much more unsatisfactory than properly endowed vicars since they were usually recruited from more ignorant and less deserving clergy.

Further financial aid was rendered to the Hospital in 1402 by the Pope when he granted, for seven years, remission of sins to those who visited and gave alms for the conservation and sustentation of the chapel of the Hospital of St. David. At the beginning of the fifteenth century, therefore, the Hospital must have become a centre of pilgrimage.

In 1403, not only were the six chaplains restored but the cure of Llangiwg and Oystermouth was to be exercised by two of them who were to celebrate masses and divine service there. Furthermore, they were to be in continual residence at these churches unless recalled by the warden of the Hospital, in which case they were to be replaced. This change was no doubt occasioned by dissatisfaction with the arrangement for removable stipendiary priests when the two churches were first appropriated.

The injunction in the foundation charter of the Hospital that the

## Early Beginnings and the Medieval Town

warden should be appointed by the bishop or, in the event of the see being vacant, by the cathedral chapter, does not appear to have been always observed because on 24 July 1361, the King's clerk, Richard de Thorn, was appointed to that office, while in 1389 John Fayrewode was appointed warden, the King regarding it as being in his gift by reason of the temporalities of the bishopric of St. David's being in his hands through voidance. There was nothing unusual in this practice of royal appointments to benefices, since it was a very convenient method of rewarding the King's servants for services rendered to the Crown. In September 1402, Fayrewode was granted a licence by the Pope to enable him to leave the Hospital for the space of seven years to study Civil Law at a university and, for his maintenance there, he was permitted to enjoy the 'fruits' of the hospice. This dispensation was necessary because one of the rules of the Hospital had enjoined that the warden should take an oath to reside personally within it or within the parish in which it stood.

It appears that the warden could hold a plurality of livings which would contribute to making the office even more inviting. When, in 1357, the archdeaconry of Carmarthen became void through the decease of Griffin de Caunteton, the warden of the Hospital at Swansea, David Martin, was the cleric chosen to replace him.

In general, the Order of St. John of Jerusalem found its earlier and chief donors in Wales among the Norman lords of the Marches rather than among the Welsh magnates. In due course, however, the avowed objects of the organisation could not fail to win the sympathy of the Welsh and, in the latter half of the twelfth century, Welsh rulers came to be included among the benefactors of the Order, possibly as a result of the appeal made by Baldwin and Gerald in 1188. This appeal proved irresistible, and it is no coincidence that many Hospitaller houses lie close to the line of the great preaching tour. The substantial possessions which the Order obtained at Swansea were no doubt partly due to the fact that Baldwin and Gerald passed through the town and even spent a night there. Another powerful factor which made men open their purses to the Hospitallers in the twelfth and thirteenth centuries was the unstable condition of the country, for there is nothing like insecurity for shaking men's nerves and loosening their purse strings.

The channelling in this manner of the charitable instincts of substantial men of property resulted in the Order, during these two centuries, acquiring considerable possessions at Swansea. There was the gift of a burgage from Henry de Newburgh and a donation of a further burgage and twelve acres of land from Einion and Goronwy, sons of Llywarch. More important, possibly, than these was the gift by Robert, son of Walter, of the land of St. John's on the northern outskirts of the town, known later as St. John's fee. The endowment is described initially as one-third of the fee of Brictric, one acre of meadow and thirty acres of land, on which the chapel of St. John was later to be built. John de Penrice (c.1180) gave the House and Hospital of St. John the Baptist.

In the thirteenth century the possessions of the Order at Swansea were further increased. The Chapel of St. John the Baptist had by now become the chief centre of Hospitaller interests in Gower, and its estates were extended by a grant of land in Cwmbwrla by a certain Robert Bured and the manor of Millwood by John de Breos (probably during the years 1220-9).

The little Chapel of St. John must have proved a boon to the townspeople when the Pope, Innocent III, during John's reign, placed the country under an interdict. St. Mary's Church was closed and its sacraments withdrawn. But at Swansea the inhabitants, though denied the ministrations of their parish priest, would have found the Chapel of St. John the Baptist free and exempt from these prohibitions, and here divine service could still be conducted and masses celebrated.

The chapel of the Hospitallers also enjoyed rights of sanctuary. St. Mary's had possessed this privilege as well. But while the sanctuary at the parish church was available to evil-doers and felons from within the town, at St. John's it existed for the benefit of those who came from beyond the boundaries of the borough.

By the middle of the thirteenth century donations were ceasing to flow in the same generous stream as formerly, with the result that the Hospital had to put out to farm the estates which earlier it had itself administered so that the income could be employed to

Chapel of St. John

maintain its work on an unrestricted scale. The letting out to farm of the Chapel of St. John secured a return of £5.6s.8d. per annum.

In 1540, an act for the dissolution of the Order of St. John in England, Wales and Ireland received royal assent. The Slebech possessions in Gower and Kidwelly were purchased from the Crown by the Herberts and Mansels and other families in the neighbourhood. The Chapel of St. John soon disappeared; the dissolution of the Hospitallers' commandery at Slebech found its existence as a second chapel in a town of small population superfluous.

This concludes the survey of the history of Swansea in the centuries preceding the accession of the Tudors. Attention has been devoted to the factors which had contributed towards the establishment, growth and development of the borough, and how it gradually achieved a degree of independence from its feudal overlords, irrespective of whether these were barons or the Kings of England. There were moments when the burgesses had to struggle hard to maintain their dearly-won rights against these powerful men. Though the main function of the town during the Middle Ages was as *caput* of the seignory or lordship of Gower, gradually the importance of the borough as the hub of its economic life, and a thriving port, became of increasing significance. Despite Swansea's growing importance during this period, many factors had militated against this development, and not least among these was the devastating impact of the Black Death which probably decimated the town population. Attention has inevitably and deservedly been focused on the burgesses, and the manner of their recruitment, and revealing glimpses have been provided of the role played by the town on a wider stage than Gower. The devotional life of the inhabitants of Swansea revolved around three institutions: the Church of St. Mary, the Hospital of St. David and the Chapel of St. John the Baptist. It was the piety of substantial men of property locally which ensured that these centres of religious life should be well endowed with landed estates in the vicinity of the town.

However, though an outline of the picture is possible, many of the details remain to be written in, and regrettably these are hardly likely to come to light because of the paucity of material. Estimates of population size at various times during the Middle Ages, and a closer analysis of the composition of this population, would have been of considerable value. All that can be postulated is that the majority was of Norman or English extraction with a sprinkling of Welsh, particularly in the fifteenth century. Little again is known about the borough machinery and its operation though charters and inquisitions have enabled a little information to be gleaned. But despite these undoubted deficiencies, sufficient is known for it to be demonstrated that during the Medieval period secure foundations were laid for the building of an imposing edifice during subsequent centuries.

# Chapter Two

## The Economic Pulse c.1485—c. 1640

The period 1485-1640 was one of rapid economic advance at Swansea, stemming from the operation of several stimuli. A prime consideration was the fact that the economic life of Swansea had been established on a firm basis during the Middle Ages despite the vicissitudes of the times. More important was the encouragement given to Welsh maritime activity by the Tudors who, having an eye for the broad outlines of the economic expansion of their kingdom, fostered the development of native trade and industry. Still more significant was the influence of general economic factors, notably the increasing demand for coal. Finally, there was the considerable attention paid to the port and trading facilities by the town council, drawn predominantly from the leading gentry, merchants and craftsmen of the borough.

The Tudors encouraged Welsh maritime activity in a variety of ways. They improved the defences of the Welsh coast and appointed vice-admirals to certain regions with subordinate officials empowered to deal with maritime causes. Henry VII's Navigation Acts encouraged native shipping, and were intended to give British ships a greater share in the carrying trade between this country and the Continent. The Acts of Union, 1536/43, by conferring on the Welsh equality with the English, enabled the former to share in the economic expansion which was so characteristic a feature of the sixteenth century. This legislation, by extending the laws of England to Wales, also resulted in the establishment of a uniform system of customs regulations, though it took some years for the commercial and port regulations to become uniform throughout all the ports of south Wales. Again, under Elizabeth, strong measures were taken by the government to suppress piracy off the Welsh coast and careful surveys were made of all the ports, creeks and landing places in Wales. But a very important measure by which Tudor statesmen endeavoured to stimulate Welsh maritime activity, and bring the influence of national economic policy to bear upon the everyday activities of Wales, was the re-organisation of the machinery for the collection of customs revenue. About mid-sixteenth century the Welsh ports were grouped under three head or legal ports, Cardiff, Milford and Chester. Swansea came under the head port of Cardiff whose limits were the Worms Head in the west and Chepstow in the east. The town had its own customs house, situated in the market, for which an annual rent of 40s. was paid in 1573. The royal officials at the port included two financial officers, the customer (who collected customs and recorded shipments) and the controller (who checked records and was joint holder of the cocket seal). Then there was the searcher (who checked cargoes and prevented smuggling) and the surveyor (who co-operated with the searcher and supervised the minor port officials of the Crown). From about 1559 'parchment books' were dispatched from London each year to the responsible customs officials of the head ports in Wales: one set for the 'by way of merchandise' or foreign trade entries, and another for the 'port to port' or coasting trade entries. The head port of Cardiff received three separate series of books for Chepstow, Cardiff, and Swansea and Neath. It is from these elaborate record books that the subsequent trade developments of the port can partially be analysed though, unfortunately, the records are spasmodic and intermittent in character, with long gaps of several years' duration all too frequent.

At times, the officers of the customs were blatantly dishonest and corrupt in the performance of their duties. In 1616, Mathewe Price, Edward Jordan and Hopkin Davy were accused of accepting bribes, concealing forfeitures and seizures of merchandise to the value of £500, and allowing ships to be laden without paying custom. Price was collector of customs and subsidies at Cardiff; Jordan was controller in Swansea and Davy was his deputy. Davy in his defence stated that apart from salt, no great quantity of any merchandise was imported, while coal formed the only export. Moreover, the farmers of the new impositions on coal had appointed a deputy who resided in the town 'so that the defendant could not have defrauded even if he had so wished'. Naturally enough, customs officials were not rated highly in the popularity stakes and were frequently molested while at work. In 1575, John Myddletone, while on duty in the customs house at Swansea as deputy to John Leeke, the customer of the port of Cardiff, was, without any provocation being offered, attacked by four men, two of whom were brothers. He was wounded in the head with a dagger 'by reason of which wound he, this defendant, had xxii bones taken out of his said head whereof long time after he languished and lay at the point of death'. On another occasion, Leeke, in his capacity as customer, had been compelled to stand aside as vessels were loaded with leather, bell-metal, and other prohibited merchandise while other ships had been loaded and unloaded without payment of toll.

More important in their effects on the economic life of the town than royal policy were the workings of contemporary economic forces. The vigour of economic life at Swansea at this time can be discerned not only in the expansion of those forms of economic activity that already existed in the town and its hinterland, such as coal mining, but also in the bustling activity of the fairs and markets and the spectacle of ships busily plying their trade in and out of the harbour.

## Coal Mining

The foundation on which Swansea's growing economic prosperity was based between 1485-1640 was undoubtedly a nascent coal industry. Coal was exported in ever increasing quantities, a clear indication that the coal resources of the area were being more intensively exploited. However, judged by modern standards, the industry was still on a very small scale. In this period the outcrops alone were being worked.

Several factors accounted for the rapid development of the industry at Swansea and indeed the whole country at this time. An obvious one is to be found in the proximity of the coal outcrops to the sea, since this simple geological factor went a long way towards solving the transport problem. Adam Smith, the renowned eighteenth-century economist, in his *Wealth of Nations*, remarked that transport by water was the principal nourishment to commerce. For coal, water transport was a necessity, since it is a fuel that is both bulky and heavy, and the fact that at Swansea the coal mines were located in the immediate hinterland of the town, and thus within easy reach of the port, must have provided a boost to the expansion of that industry.

Again, the changes in the ownership of mineral property as a result of the Reformation in the sixteenth century, were another cause of the expansion at Swansea and elsewhere. If capital was to be found to meet the increased expenses of deeper mining, without which no great expansion in the industry could take place, attractive mineral concessions had to be offered in the form of long leases and low royalties. Before the dissolution of the monasteries, though the monks were prepared to lease mineral rights to laymen, sufficiently favourable terms were not to be obtained. A considerable portion of all the lands in which coal had already been mined, or in which it was destined to be mined in the future, belonged to the church. In Glamorgan, areas of at least two of the manors of Gower and Margam, where coal was mined for the growing trade with Cornwall and Devon, and with the Channel Islands and France, belonged to the church. In the immediate hinterland of Swansea, coal was worked in the sixteenth century on lands which formerly had belonged to Neath Abbey and the Order of St. John of Jerusalem. That coal was being worked on lands in Gower, which had formerly been in the possession of Neath Abbey, appears from the depositions of witnesses taken at Neath in December 1577 concerning the coal mines to be found on these lands. The deposition of Philip Williams of Pontardulais is of particular interest: 'Philip Williams of Llandeilo Tal-y-bont in the said county, gentleman, of the age of xl years or thereabouts, sworn upon the Holy Evangelist, and examined, deposeth and saieth that there are three several mines of coals within the manor and dominion in the said commission mentioned, whereof one mine do lie within the said manor at a place there called Tir y Brenin alias Tir yr Abad within the parish of Llandeilo Tal-y-bont aforesaid, one other mine doth lie at a place within the said manor called The Grange, and the third mine lieth at a place within the said manor called Gower-in-Cross within the parish of Oystermouth (as he thinketh in his conscience); and also he saieth that the same mines do lie in plain clay and slimy ground, and that the charges in finding of every of the same mines will amount to the sum of twenty pounds; and also the yearly maintaining of every of the same mines xli for that the same must be maintained and upholden with timber; and further he saieth that the said mines are worth xxs yearly above all charges and reprises'.

Evidence for the working of coal on the manor of Millwood which, before the Reformation, had belonged to the Order of St. John, can be gleaned from a survey of that manor made in 1641. The survey reveals that Sir Thomas Mansel, into whose hands the manor had come at the Reformation, had leased the coal mines there to a Richard Seys and a Roger Vaughan.

The transfer of mineral property at the time of the Reformation from ecclesiastical to lay hands, and the proximity of the coal outcrops to the port, had certainly provided a launching pad for the great expansion of the industry in the sixteenth and seventeenth centuries. However, these considerations do not provide an adequate explanation for the explosion that took place. A more important reason is to be found in the growing shortage of fuel. This shortage, particularly of wood, was common to many parts of the island and led inevitably to an increasing demand for coal as a substitute for it both in the home and in industry.

At Swansea a shortage of fuel 'owing to the excess and disorderly cutting of furze upon the commons' was certainly a source of concern to the bakers and others in the town, who were quick to register their protest with the town council. In the light of this complaint a by-law was introduced forbidding any person dwelling within the town or its liberties (bakers excepted) from cutting more than 60 cartloads of furze annually. Furthermore, the common attorneys were not to sell any furze from the commons to anyone dwelling outside the town liberties without first securing the consent of the portreeve and burgesses.

It is reasonable to assume, therefore, that coal was being used in increasing quantities for domestic purposes in the town during this period. Certainly it was being used to provide some form of heating in St. Mary's Church and the churchwardens in 1604 record 2*d.* as having been paid for 'one burden of coals'. In 1621 4d. was paid 'for coals and fire and a band and for rosin'. Craftsmen, presumably blacksmiths, were also using coal and the Churchwardens' Accounts for 1611 refer to a penny having been paid 'for coal to make fire for the soldering of the gutter'.

This diminution of the fuel resources of Swansea, other than coal, can be accounted for by the naturally limited nature of the supply—alarming inroads had already been made into the timber supplies in the vicinity of the town by the time of the de Breos charter in 1306—and by the increased population of the borough during this period. Doubtless the growing demand for wood in other industries which existed in or near the port at this time, such as house-building, ship-building, and agriculture, had a significant effect on this problem as well.

It was not, however, the local demand for coal that proved the main stimulus to the industry. Far more important was the need for coal in England, the Channel Islands and France. The main demand in these areas also arose as a result of the diminution of the timber supplies, and to the rapid expansion of both industry and agriculture. Coal exported from Swansea to the three western counties of Somerset, Devon and Cornwall was used 'as well for burning of lime as also for firing'. In France, industrial expansion led to a raid on the forests to obtain fuel. The consequent reduction of the timber resources would have had repercussions both on the home and on industry. In each case coal would have come to be used in greater quantities. It is certain that coal was being used in such industries as brewing and distilling, evaporating brine, and in the manufacture of glass, bricks, pottery, alum, soap, and paper; industries, incidentally, which had grown in importance in England as well as in France during the sixteenth and seventeenth centuries. In agriculture, coal was used in the burning of lime, which was extensively employed as a fertiliser. But coal output in France was insufficient to meet the demand. By the end of the seventeenth century it did not amount to more than 50,000 or 75,000 tons per annum, a smaller quantity than was mined in the single manor of Whickam near the Tyne on the eve of the Civil War. Consequently, other sources of supply had to be sought and one such was found in Glamorgan, particularly at Swansea and Neath.

The coal industry at Swansea and its immediate hinterland appears to have been the product of local initiative. Before the sixteenth century the law relating to the ownership of mineral wealth was not clearly defined. However, during the sixteenth and seventeenth centuries, the rights of the landowners to all metals except gold and silver were made absolute. Some of the landowners themselves were actively engaged in exploiting the coal resources on their estates as a means of supplementing their incomes, as becomes evident from the will and inventory of one Roger Morgan, dated 1652. Morgan was possessed of considerable estates in Pontardulais, Llangyfelach, and Llansamlet and in his will he bequeathed to his son, William Roger, 'the sum of forty pounds of lawful money of England to be received from coals, which I now have at the coal place and at the coal pits'. From his inventory it appears also that he had left, unbequeathed, coal to the value of ten pounds. But, on the whole, stemming possibly from the concept that direct involvement in business did not become a gentleman, landowners preferred leasing their mineral rights to the burgesses, who were those most actively engaged in coal mining enterprises. The awareness of the landowners of the financial possibilities of exploiting the coal found on their lands is demonstrated in the terms granted by them in the leases. They were for lengthy periods and the royalties exacted were small. The landowners realised that under no other conditions would the coal be mined. On 8 October 1526, Henry, Earl of Worcester, had let on lease to Sir Matthew Cradock 'all and all manner mines of coals now found or that hereafter can be found and also all the coals of the said mines within the said Lordship of Gower and Kilvey or the members of the same'. Cradock was granted this right for 80 years at the annual rent of £11. In 1629, William Herbert, Earl of Pembroke, leased to William Herbert of Swansea, all coal found in the lordships and manors of Landimore and Weobley. He was to dispose of the coals for 21 years at a royalty of 6d. for every wey[1] so obtained. Again, from Cromwell's survey of the Seignory of Gower in 1650 it

---

[1] Unit of weight varying from two to three cwts.

appears that the Earl of Worcester had leased to one John Williams 'a coalwork in Morwa Llyw . . . and is to pay for every wey that shall be wrought iiiis at Annunciation[2] & Michaelmas'.[3] In addition to these royalties, Worcester also derived a lucrative source of revenue from 'sea-leaves', since he claimed payment of 4*d*. on every wey of coal that was transported over the bar of Swansea from the lordship of Kilvey.

Disputes concerning coal mining were very common in the sixteenth and seventeenth centuries and the burgesses of Swansea, in their mining ventures, were occasionally embroiled in them. One such dispute appears from the affidavit of an action brought by Roger and Richard Seys at Cardiff Great Sessions. It seems that these plaintiffs were working coal at a place called Pen Llwyn Robert, and a confirmation of their right to do so had been secured in February 1640/41 from the Council of Wales and the Marches sitting at Ludlow. Despite this supportive action by the Council, Richard Seys, when he visited the premises, found Robert Gethin, Harrie the Cook and William John Ienkine, all from the parishes of Swansea and St. John, actively engaged in carrying away coal. With the aid of his servant, John Thomas, Seys had unloaded the horses and endeavoured to drive them into a pound. Before his purpose could be accomplished, however, the horses had been forcibly rescued by the defendants assisted by Jane, the wife of Thomas Mansel, John Marker, her servant, Gwenllian Hamon, Marsley Hopkine and others. In the fracas that ensued John Thomas had been severely hurt.

The coal-mining population of Great Britain was, in a very real sense, the creation of the century and a half following the accession of Elizabeth. Before the sixteenth century it is not possible to regard coal miners as a class like the craftsmen in the towns. Except in the Tyne valley, where a few score hewers and keelmen had already found regular employment, most of the men who dug coal were manorial tenants, who did so as a by-employment and depended for their main living upon farming. From the de Breos charter of 1306, glimpses have been caught of the burgesses of Swansea working

[2] 25 March.
[3] 29 September.

Mining in Germany

coal at Gelliwastad, a hill outside Morriston. But whether they worked the coal themselves, or employed others to do so for them—men for whom the mining of coal would have been a sideline—does not appear. What is certain, however, is that by the end of the sixteenth century, coal mining had become so important at Swansea that the coal was being cut by miners regularly employed in this work and who, moreover, had begun to labour in the mines at a very early age. In 1593 it is recorded that Ieuan the collier paid the town corporation three shillings rent for his house. Again, before the end of Elizabeth's reign, certain of the inhabitants of Swansea when called upon to furnish depositions to the Court of Exchequer, described themselves as 'coal workers since the beginning of (their) labour'. Entries such as these indicate plainly that by the end of the sixteenth century coal mining at Swansea had ceased to be a by-employment.

The wages of the miners were low. As early as 1400 the annual earnings of the three hewers at Kilvey colliery only averaged £3.16s.0d. per man. Furthermore, they could be paid in a variety of ways. At Clutton in Somerset, in 1610, hewers were paid by the week. In Gower, however, the method of payment in 1400 was so much 'a last'[4] of coal.

Though no account of the manner in which coal was mined in the Swansea area is available, it seems very probable that the mining methods employed there would have been much the same as those used in Pembrokeshire, which have been graphically described by George Owen, the celebrated Elizabethan antiquary and historian of the shire. He declares that 'the digging of this coal is of ancient time used in Pembrokeshire but not in such exact and skilful sort as now it is for in former time they used no engines for lifting up of the coals out of the pit but made their entrance slope, so as the people carried the coals upon their backs along stairs which they called land ways where as now they sink their pits down right four square about vi or vii foot square, and with a windlass turned by four men, they draw up the coals a barrel full at once by a rope'. Then, having dealt with the way the coal was found, he continues: 'the coal being found the workmen follow the vein every way until

[4] About 16 tons.

it end or be letted by water or rock; the vein for the most part will not be passing v or vi foot deep, so that the coal is carried stooping; for they commonly leave a foot of coal in the bottom undigged to serve for a strong foundation except they find the rock under foot, which they call the doonstone which if they find then they dig clean all the coal . . . and overhead they are driven to timber their work to keep the earth from falling which is chargeable but in some grounds they have a rock above and then they save much labour and cost in sparing of timber'.

After indicating the procedures adopted to tackle the problem of flooding underground, he proceeds: 'they now most commonly sink down right xii xvi or xx fathom before they come to the coal whereas in old time four fathom was counted a great labour: when they find it, they work sundry holes one for every digger some two some three or four as the number of diggers are: each man working by candle light and sitting while he worketh, then have they bearers which are boys that bear the coals in fit baskets on their backs going always stooping by reason of the lowness of the pit each bearer carieth this basket vi fathom where, upon a bench of stone he layeth it, where meeteth him another boy with an empty basket, which he giveth him and taketh that which is full of coals and carieth it as far, where another meeteth him & so till they come under the door where it is lifted up. In one pit there will be sixteen persons, whereof there will be three pickaxes digging, seven bearers, one filler, four winders, two riddlers'.

According to Owen, the summer was the worst season for working coal because of 'sudden damps that happen, which often times causeth the workmen to swoon and will not suffer the candles to burn'. The hours of work were excessively long, from 6 a.m. to 6 p.m. with an hour's break at noon. During this welcome respite they ate their meagre allowance which was a halfpenny's worth of bread to every man and 4*d.* in drink among a dozen.

It appears that in the sixteenth century the miners entered their occupations condemned in advance, almost, to occupy a low position in the social pecking order. This was because only too often they were recruited, at the best, from husbandmen or labourers who were unable to make a living on their holdings; often from the wandering unemployed; and, at the worst, from among prisoners of war or criminals. Such a state of affairs may have existed in and around Swansea, though what documentary evidence there is, seems to suggest that some, at least, of the colliers had managed to attain a more respectable social standing than this. They can be seen renting houses from the town corporation, and from the Church Wardens' Accounts it becomes apparent that miners and their wives were occupying pews in the parish church.

Paucity of information precludes any very definite assertions as to how the miners were recruited, though it has been possible to conclude that some were drawn from areas lying outside the borough. However, before they could be admitted as residents they had to find sureties, usually in the sum of forty pounds, that they would not become burdensome on the town on account of their poverty. On 20 November 1609, Robert Rogers undertook to discharge the corporation of any charges that might arise from Evan ab Owen, collier, or any of his family taking up residence there. In 1621, because of their inability to find the necessary security, 'Michael the collier and his wife' had to leave the town. At this time there was movement of families into Swansea from contiguous areas like Llangiwg, Llangadog, Llangyfelach, Pontardulais, Loughor, Kilvey, Llanelli, Neath, Briton Ferry, Ystradgynlais and Defynnog. The expansion of coal mining operations in the Swansea region, and the consequent increased opportunities for employment, may well have been determining factors underlying this immigration.

IRON

Coal was not the only extractive industry at Swansea, though undoubtedly it was by far the most important. The Exchequer Port Books also indicate that the iron resources of the area were beginning to be exploited. During the first forty years of the seventeenth century iron was being exported along familiar sea lanes to ports such as Southampton, Bristol, Minehead, Fowey and Weymouth in the south of England and the West Country, and also to France. The volume of the trade between 1600 and 1640 becomes evident from the accompanying table:[5]

| Date | Amount | Destination |
| --- | --- | --- |
| Mich. 1602-Mich. 1603 | 3t. | Northampton |
| Xmas 1608-Xmas 1609 | 10t. | Fowey and Bristol |
| Xmas 1612-Xmas 1613 | 1t. | France |
| Xmas 1620-Xmas 1621 | 88t. | Bristol and Weymouth |
| Xmas 1621-Xmas 1622 | 60t. | — |
| Xmas 1627-Xmas 1628 | 60t. | Bristol and Minehead |
| Xmas 1628-Xmas 1629 | ½t. | France |
| Xmas 1629-Xmas 1630 | 126t. 15 cwts. | Bristol and Barnstaple |

SHIPBUILDING

As a flourishing sea-port town, it was to be expected that Swansea should be a centre for shipbuilding. The industry was not new, but stretched far back into the Middle Ages. By the early fourteenth century the demands of the industry on the timber resources in the locality were heavy, and in the de Breos charter of 1306 a limit of four was placed on the number of large ships which could be constructed at any one time. The ships built were probably very small and suitable only for coastwise traffic, fishing, and the carriage of coal down the river Tawe to the port. Glimpses are caught of barks,[6] pinnaces[7] and dows[8] being built at the new quay and on the strand. By the mid-seventeenth century, this practice was a source of such annoyance to the corporation that it ordained that 'no Bark, Boat, or Vessel', except such as were already on the stocks, should be built there and that all timber and planks on the quay and strand should be immediately removed on pain of forfeiture of 10s. to 'y$^e$ use of y$^e$ Lord of y$^e$ Town'.

---

[5] These are the only figures available for iron exports during the period 1600-40. This does not imply that they represent the total export trade in that commodity because not only is the Port Book evidence incomplete—there are only 29 books available in all for the period—but seven of the extant books are imperfect. Particularly is the Port Book evidence unsatisfactory for the decade 1630-40 since four of the six books available are imperfect. This, to a very large degree, accounts for the failure to provide figures for the decade.
[6] A three masted, square rigged vessel.
[7] A warship's double banked (usually eight-oared) boat.
[8] A large flat bottomed sailing barge.

Forging of Iron in Germany

At first sight this would appear to have been a withdrawal by the corporation of facilities for ship building which had been enjoyed for centuries by the burgesses. This was a privilege which they had exercised without constraint while claiming from non-burgesses a fee for similar rights. In May 1624, the common attorneys received 4s. from one Richard Pickart for 'building of his bark upon the strand' while in April 1635 2s. was similarly received from a Bridgewater man for building his trow.

However, this order was doubtless directed against the practice of obstructing the corporation quay and strand with shipbuilding impedimenta, which would have endangered life and limb when ships were being loaded and unloaded, while still permitting vessels to be constructed elsewhere. A graving dock had also been provided by the corporation and in 1642/3 a Guernsey man paid 1s. for the use of this facility.

Not all the materials necessary for the industry were available locally and what the shipbuilders at Swansea lacked had to be imported. Tar, pitch and oakum, all essential to the industry, were imported from France (La Rochelle) and the Channel Islands, and in 1600 one hundred yards of canvas were imported from Normandy.

GLOVE MAKING

Another quite important industry at Swansea was the making of gloves which could have been made of either leather or wool. The industry had existed in the town since the Middle Ages, and the importance that it had assumed in its economy during that period is indicated by the presence in St. Mary's Church of a Glovers' chapel. The industry continued to flourish in the borough in the sixteenth and seventeenth centuries, and the oldest extant corporation books record the apprenticing to glovers of poor children. It was a contractual relationship and the parties involved could be released by mutual agreement. In August 1608, it is recorded in the Book of Orders 'that whereas one Richard William, son to William David Morgan of Loughor, was bound 'prentice to one Leyson Johns of Swansea, glover, for vii years, whereof the said Richard served vi years and viii months and then fell in some controversy, know y$^e$ therefore that the foresaid parties have released one another of all bargains and promises before us whose names are under written'. It was obviously a pity that a dispute should have arisen at all since the apprenticeship had only four months to run. During the period under review it is quite possible, though there is no supporting evidence for this, that the industry may have expanded because of an ever-increasing local demand emanating mainly from the growing population of the town and the neighbourhood. Certainly, gloves do not figure at all as an item of export, possibly because an assured market for them existed in the three fairs now being held annually in the town.

FARMING

Despite the growing importance of industrial ventures in and around Swansea, agriculture, and particularly animal husbandry—though mixed farming would have been practised in the Gower peninsula—was still of primary importance to the town and its neighbourhood. The burgesses had their own tenements and possessed, moreover, valuable rights of common and pasture. Several reasons account for the growing prosperity of agriculture around the borough at this time. Among the most important of these was the rapid growth of towns, particularly of Bristol and London. Another factor was the gradual increase in the population of Swansea itself and its hinterland, and finally there was the development of the port. In other parts of the country in this period, one of the factors which had militated against agricultural advance had been the absence of good means of communication, which had made it difficult for farmers to market their produce. The farmers of the Swansea area, however, saw in the town itself a near and assured market and in the port a means of transporting, coastwise or overseas, any surplus produce which they possessed. As a result of the operation of these factors, the commercialisation of agriculture in the area was becoming more apparent.

A clear indication of this increasingly capitalistic approach to agriculture, and of the cardinal importance of cattle and sheep rearing at Swansea, is to be found in the overstocking of the commons by the inhabitants of the town and its liberties. This was

## The Economic Pulse

a very general practice in Wales and elsewhere at this time, and it appears to have assumed serious proportions in the counties of Merioneth, Montgomery, Radnor and Brecon. The problem greatly exercised the Council in Wales and the Marches and in January 1574 it was ordained that, 'whereas great complaint has been made to the Council divers years past by inhabitants of the counties of Merioneth, Montgomery, Radnor and Brecknock, and lastly by some of the Justices of the Peace of Montgomery and Radnor that wastes, commons and mountains are and for many years past have been surcharged and overlaid by the taking to keep in summer time of the cattle of strangers and foreigners who have no rights of common there, so that those with right of common lose the benefit of the winter succour. And by this the breed of cattle there, especially of horses and mares, is in manner utterly decayed; and many cattle are stolen and carried off'.

The order went on to direct that letters should be sent to the sheriffs of these counties instructing them to establish juries of six to make inquiry into the matter and, on the basis of the information so received, to punish the offenders.

The corporation of Swansea reacted to this abuse of rights of common by introducing a by-law in 1603 which enjoined that, 'whereas the commons of ancient times granted unto ye burgesses and inhabitants of this town are by covetousness & greediness of some of the wealthier sort of the inhabitants of the town and franchises & also by foreigners surcharged ... now for reformation thereof the foresaid portreeve, aldermen, common attorneys and burgesses do agree and order as a by-law as followeth: that no manner of person either dwelling within the town or franchise shall overcharge the said common with sheep or cattle'.

From this by-law it becomes clear also that some of the inhabitants were abusing their right of pasture by maintaining on the commons not only their own beasts but those of strangers as well. The result was that the drain on pasture in summer was so great that the cattle could not be supported in winter.

The action taken by the corporation could not have achieved its declared purpose because in 1617 another ordinance was introduced which focused attention more sharply on the nub of the problem, which was the grazing on the commons of animals belonging to outsiders: 'and now in respect the said commons is overcharged by certain of the inhabitants of the said town with bullocks or yearlings bred in other places so that the poor of the said town is thereby wronged/we the portreeve aldermen & others of the said town whose names are subscribed, do agree upon & order that no manner of inhabitant or free man of this town whatsoever shall turn any manner of bullocks or yearlings whatsoever into or upon the commons aforesaid within the time before limited[9] but such as shall be bred and reared within the liberties of the said town'. In 1622, to ease still further the drain on the commons, the corporation laid down that the owners of pigs or swine found grazing on the burrows should pay 1$d$. for each animal and in 1632 this order was extended to include geese.

The surcharging of the commons was a matter of concern to the authorities since there was a real danger that, as a result of this practice, many of the smaller farmers and freeholders might be deprived of their rights to the commons. These rights were already being eroded because of enclosures. There was now the distinct possibility that they might lose them in another way: by the wealthier sort of inhabitant grazing so many animals that there would be no room for the poorer people to pasture theirs.

The increasing importance attached to property in this period is reflected in the prevailing land hunger of the inhabitants. In 1594, the Earl of Worcester had commenced proceedings in the Court of Chancery against his tenants in the lordship of Gower. It appears that these tenants, with the connivance of corrupt or negligent stewards, had been encroaching on the wastes and carving out freehold tenements for themselves. They had also refused to pay such feudal dues as mises[10] and aids.[11] Having lost about 327 acres of common and waste around Swansea in this fashion, the lord of the seignory understandably started legal action to recover them. In their defence, the tenants had declared that their predecessors had held the land in question in fee. The verdict of the court in 1596

[9] This period was 1 May—1 August.
[10] Payment to a new lord to secure privileges.
[11] A feudal tax levied on the occasion of the ransoming of the lord's body, the knighting of his eldest son and the marriage of his eldest daughter.

was that mises and aids should be paid, the tenants paying £200 for mises and 200 marks for aids—100 marks on the occasion of the knighting of the earl's eldest son, and 100 marks on the occasion of the marriage of his eldest daughter. Swansea's contribution towards the payment of these sums was assessed at £17.15s.7d. for aids and £26.13s.4d. for mises.[12] With regard to the encroachments, it was decided that this was a matter best determined at common law.

CLOTH

Closely associated with animal husbandry was the cloth industry and by the later Middle Ages, judged by the considerable number of fulling mills—*pandai*—to be found in the vicinity of the town, cloth production was assuming some importance in the local economy. The industry would have been conducted along domestic lines, the spinning and weaving being performed in the home by the farmer and his wife and children. The cloth they produced was very coarse in texture, but its manufacture would have contributed to the economic self-sufficiency of the district. In the charter which Henry, second Earl of Worcester, granted to Swansea in 1532, his steward was empowered to exclude, up to a distance of seven miles from the borough, all artificers who practised the skills of 'cutting and carving' unless they resided within the town in which case they were presumably themselves burgesses. It was in this manner that the lord attempted to protect their monopoly position with regard to the cloth and leather trades. Most of the cloth produced would have been disposed of locally in the fairs and markets, though a little was sold further afield since Welsh friezes figure as items of export both in the coastwise and overseas traffic of the town.

[12] The divisions of the seignory of Gower with their ratings in August 1632 were:

|  | Mises | Aids |
| --- | --- | --- |
| Welshry | £60 | £40 |
| Customary Tenants | £60 | £40 |
| Englishry | £60 | £40 |
| Swansea Villa | £26.13s.4d. | £17.15s.7d. |
| Kilvey | £20 | £13.6s.8d. |
| Loughor Burgus | £6.13s.4d. | £4.8s.10d. |

## LEATHER

Not as important as the cloth industry, but certainly of considerable significance in a pastoral economy, was the leather industry and in Swansea, in the sixteenth and seventeenth centuries, there would appear to have been more apprentices in the leather trade than in any other. Tanning, in particular, demanded skills of a high order and the leather workers in the borough tended to be fairly prosperous members of the community.

## FAIRS AND MARKETS

The fairs and markets held at Swansea since the Middle Ages continued to be the *foci* of the economic life of the agricultural population of the neighbourhood. It became abundantly clear from the charter which de Breos granted to the inhabitants of Gower that they had been frequenting the fairs held at Swansea, and it is reasonable to assume that they would have continued to do so in

The Seventeenth Century Market House

## The Economic Pulse

increasing numbers in the sixteenth and seventeenth centuries. In this period, also, with the steady growth of a commercial economy, the products of the peninsula would have been marketed in Swansea in increasing quantities. Certainly it is the role of the town as a trading centre that most impressed the eminent antiquary, John Leland. In his celebrated *Itinerary*, in which he describes what he had seen during his travels around Henry VIII's kingdom between 1534-43, he described Swansea as a 'market town and chief place of Gower Land'.

A market was held weekly at Swansea on Saturdays. It was held in the open, without any form of covering—a factor which would have occasioned acute discomfort to those frequenting it when weather conditions were adverse—but it was not until March 1646 that it was resolved by the town council that a market house should be provided. In May 1651, in order to defray the expense of providing this amenity, it was ordered by the corporation that £60 should be rated upon all the inhabitants with the exception of 'such poor people as have no subsistence besides their daily labour'.

In the old open-air market, standings had been 'set and let' by the common attorneys to the highest bidder. It is rather surprising, therefore, that no mention is made in their accounts of any moneys having been received as rents for these stalls. The only explanation that can be advanced for this is that these receipts were regarded as a perquisite of the office of portreeve.

The regulating of the business life of the market was the responsibility of the council and the earliest Swansea records contain much evidence of their activity in these matters. An important aspect of their work was the standardisation of weights and measures so that market transactions could be fairly conducted. In 1569, the council determined that the peck should be 'xvi quarts just by the brass quart', and the water measure 'to be xviii gallons'. In 1637, £7.9s.0d. was paid by the corporation for weights and measures which it had purchased in London from a John Martin. These items, together with an accompanying letter, were delivered in a basket and a long box and presumably would have come by road.

During this period three fairs were also kept annually at Swansea, on 1 August, 25 March and 8 October. In the fourteenth century, only two had been held in the town, on 15 August and 11 November. The increase in the number of fairs from two to three by the sixteenth century is indicative not only of an increasing population but also of a thriving economic activity. The inhabitants of Gower would have thronged to them in considerable numbers since they were exempt from the payment of tolls and customs.

The fairs were held on church property, presumably in the church yard, as becomes evident from the Churchwardens' Accounts which recount payments having been received from each fair. In 1599 the following receipts are recorded for standings:

'Item at the first fair    iis. x$d$.
Item at the second fair    iii$d$.
Item at the last fair at Michaelmas    iiis. vii$d$.'

The amounts received varied from year to year, presumably in accordance with the number erected. It would appear that 1602 was a better year since 4s.10$d$. was received from the first fair, 17$d$. from the second and 6s.3$d$. from the third.

The right of holding markets and fairs was a valuable privilege to the burgesses since it not only enabled them to attract to the town, under certain conditions, both sellers and buyers from outside their area, but it also saved the inhabitants the trouble and expense of taking their wares or their custom to another centre.

TRADE

Perhaps the clearest indication of the growing importance of Swansea economically is to be found in a study of its trade, particularly the export trade in coal. The coastal trade of the town during the latter half of the sixteenth century, while continuing very largely to flourish on medieval lines, was brought under the influence of forces which both extended its geographical scope and gradually effected important changes in its character. The commodity chiefly exported coastwise was coal. A large proportion of it was shipped to the West of England ports although Swansea ships do not appear to have been employed at all. The vessels used were those of the ports for which the coal was destined. Foreign shipping was excluded as well. Ships from Fowey, Falmouth, and

Looe in south Cornwall; Plymouth (with Stonehouse and Saltash), Dartmouth and Salcombe in south Devon; Barnstaple, Northam (Bideford), Ilfracombe, Clovelly, Lynmouth and Minehead in north Devon; Gloucester and Bristol are all found exporting (or transporting) coal from the town. It is reasonable to assume that they discharged their cargoes at their home ports and were not engaged in the carrying trade to the Channel Islands or France. Few Cornish or Devon vessels brought return cargoes into Swansea. The normal procedure was to arrive in ballast, a practice which was to create serious problems for the town corporation.[13]

Transportation costs remained the most vital consideration in determining which markets the coal of each region would command. It was inevitable, therefore, that the bulk of the coal exported coastwise from Swansea and Neath should be marketed in Cornwall, Devon and Somerset since only a short stretch of water

[13] Infra, p. 68.

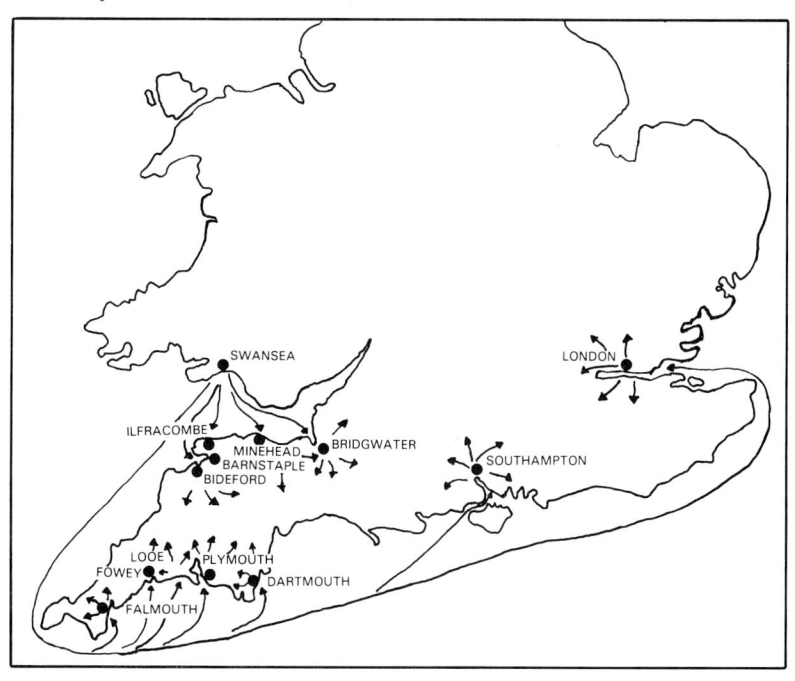

Coastwise Traffic in Coal in the Sixteenth Century

An Elizabethan Merchant Ship

separated the two shores. It took less than a week for a west-coast trow to make her 50 mile voyage from Swansea to Bridgwater. The round trip took from eight days to two weeks according to the testimony of Thomas James, a Somerset husbandman, who had occasionally served as purser aboard such a vessel during the reign of Charles II. Occasionally, shipments of coal were made to Southampton, London and Ireland during the period 1550-1603, although they may, of course, have been greater than the meagre statistics show.

Pembrokeshire should have been in a position to compete on something like equal terms with Swansea. However, the nature of the coal (anthracite) mined there militated against its general use in English homes. The smallness of the blocks of anthracite made it unsuitable to burn in the open fire-places of English houses. Even the biggest pieces, for which the name 'stone-coal' is generally reserved, could not be easily kindled or kept burning in the hearth without supplies of dried branches and soft coal. Indeed, the inhabitants of Pembrokeshire occasionally imported by sea small quantities of bituminous coal, mined in the district behind Swansea bay, to aid them in making their own fires.

The tonnage of the vessels employed in this coasting trade was small, varying from 10 to 30 tons. The customs officers appear to have discouraged the construction of large colliers for the south Wales coal trade because the master of a large vessel, which could easily be sailed across the open sea, was likely to defraud them by slipping over to France with a coal cargo entered in their books to pay coastwise duty only. The customers stationed at Swansea brought an action in 1636 against the shipowners of Bridgwater on the ground that the owners had adapted their colliers for 'foreign transportation'. Several seamen from Swansea testified that 'the trows or vessels of Bridgwater are of far greater burden than they were eleven years since . . . and . . . have been fitted with close decks, masts, sails and tacklings, fit for sail beyond seas'. For the defendants, William Meyricke, a ship's master of Bridgwater, protested 'that he would not hazard his life in any of the trows for foreign parts'. However, when in 1577 a survey of the shipping in Welsh ports was made, a total of six topmen (between 40-100 tons) was recorded for Swansea, the largest number for any port included in the survey apart from Milford which had a similar number. As for the other ports, Beaumaris had four, Cardiff two, Carmarthen four, Conway three and Denbigh two.

Just as the main item for export coastwise during Elizabeth's reign was coal, a similar situation prevailed for the foreign trade. The description of the mineral as 'smith coal' suggests that the bituminous coals of the Llanelli syncline, and of the south crop of the Lower Coal Measures, alone were being exported at this time. The direction of this export traffic in coal is clearly defined. It was taken to Jersey and Guernsey, Normandy, Brittany and south-west France. The volume of traffic to the Channel Islands increased significantly toward the close of the century and the ships participating in the trade also tended to get larger. Practically all the coal was transhipped in the vessels of the two islands though there are the isolated, and obviously exceptional cases, in 1580, of a Swansea ship taking 16 weys of smith coal to Jersey, a Granville vessel taking 7 weys, and a Torbay ship conveying 6 weys. The Channel Island boats usually arrived at Swansea in ballast, and only a few ever brought inward cargoes such as salt, wool-cards and oakum. Moreover, while the Jersey ships remained steadfast in their loyalty to Swansea, Guernsey boats seemed to prefer the neighbouring ports of Burry and Neath. The extent of the trade becomes clear from the accompanying table:

To Jersey

| Date | Amount | No. of shipments |
|---|---|---|
| 1580 | 49 w. | 6 |
| 1587 | 97 w. | 13 |
| 1588 | 96 w. | 11 |
| 1595 | 107 w. | 4 |
| 1600 | 191 w. | 11 |

To Guernsey

| Date | Amount | No. of shipments |
|---|---|---|
| 1588 | 20 w. | 3 |
| 1595 | 52 w. | 2 |
| 1603 | 33 w. | 2 |

The trade to Normandy (Granville, Pero and Langervill) may be regarded as an extension of that to the Channel Islands and, although fairly regular, was much inferior in volume. It was entirely an export trade in coal to the ports of the bay of St. Malo and maintained by Norman ships only.

Finally, there was an active trade in coal to several ports in Brittany at this time and the transport was entirely in the hands of Breton merchantmen. The extent of the Breton trade can be judged from the following table:

| Date | Amount | No. of shipments |
|---|---|---|
| 1594-5 | 288 w. | 10 |
| 1600-1 | 89 w. | 17 |
| 1602-3 | 138 w. | 12 |

The boats involved were, as a rule, small (15-30 tons) but, in the year 1594-5, two boats, one of 80 tons and another of 70 tons came from Brest, while a Lannion vessel, the *Eglantine*, was also of 80 tons. An interesting feature of the Breton trade was that several of the ships brought inward cargoes of bay salt, Rochelle wine, crescloth, oakum and canvas.

There was a steady increase in the amount of coal exported from Swansea, on both the coastal and foreign sides, until 1599. From then until 1602 the amount exported fell rapidly. After 1602 the trade recovered and the upward trend was resumed. However, it is important to remember that these export figures provide an inadequate picture of the total development within the extractive industry of the area. Against the export trade must be set the increasing local demand for coal, both on account of personal consumption, and that used either in agriculture or industry. George Owen comments on the increased use of coal which had occurred within his own memory among the inhabitants of south Wales, and although he placed coal eighth on his list of exports, he declared that it 'may be numbered as one of the chief commodities of this country'.

It has been argued that the fall in coal exports from Swansea after 1599 was due to the exhaustion of the readily available coal seams and, consequently, before exports could regain their earlier levels, further development and exploitation had to take place. Since there appears to be no evidence to support the contention that coal seams were worked out, perhaps a more satisfactory explanation may be found in the new export duties which became effective in that year. From early times a small customs duty of 2*d*. or 4*d*. per chaldron had been imposed on all coal exported. In Elizabeth's reign it was decided to levy an additional tax of 5*s*. per Newcastle chaldron (then about 2 tons). By imposing this new duty, it would evidently be possible to satisfy the popular demand that protection be afforded the subject and, at the same time, add something which eventually might grow considerably to the Queen's revenue.

The new tax was levied on coal exported from all English and Welsh ports and its unpopularity resulted in howls of protest from west-coast traders and colliery owners—who, incidentally, unlike the Newcastle merchants, had not been consulted by the Crown—and from consumers in Ireland, the Channel Islands and the Isle of Man. Corroborative evidence of the adverse consequences of the new impositions may be adduced from an examination of the coal exported from Cardiff, Neath and Carmarthen in the same period. A similar decline in the volume of exports is revealed. When, in 1620, James I introduced even heavier duties on coal exports, the traffic in the commodity from Swansea and the west Wales ports plummeted in that decade.

Though their own involvement in the coal trade was not particularly prominent in this period, ships from Swansea and Mumbles did participate in the export and import trade of the town to some extent. It is clear from the available records that they voyaged to the Channel Islands, Rochelle and the Bay of Biscay ports. Their outgoing cargo was in all cases coal, though occasionally other items were added. In 1580, in *Le Dragon de Swansey* (burden 30 tons), one ton of lead and one pack of bridgwaters, together with 16 weys of coal, were transported to Jersey, while in 1587 seven pieces of frieze, together with 16 weys of coal, were shipped in the *Jonas of Swansea* (burden 40 tons) to Rochelle. The ships returned laden with salt, wine, tar, pitch, iron, cloth and oakum. These were vessels manned by Swansea seamen and trading for Swansea merchants. The salt obtained from the Bay of Biscay was sold not only in Swansea but also at Carmarthen and other Welsh ports and, in the absence of modern methods of refrigeration, would have been used on an extensive scale to preserve meat and as a flavouring for butter and cheese. This period possibly marks the real beginning of the growth of native shipping and commerce.

Apart from lead, bridgwaters and friezes, other Swansea exports included commodities such as barley, women's hose, butter and calf-skins, the latter despite statutory regulations prohibiting the sale of leather abroad. On the import side, in addition to the commodities already enumerated, items such as tobacco (so socially unacceptable today), brass, iron, prunes, apples and pears were brought into the town. In February 1601, 1000lbs. of prunes were imported by a Breton ship in a mixed cargo of wine and pitch, while in March 1603, 1600lbs. of tobacco were imported in the

*Samson* of Rotterdam, a large ship of 400 tons burden. The apples and pears were, in all probability, imported from the Gloucestershire area and from Somerset and Devon. George Owen has described how the apple men of the Forest of Dean came every year to Pembrokeshire with their barks laden with apples to sell at their pleasure. At Swansea the common attorneys' accounts record moneys being received from the masters of ships from Bridgwater and Dartmouth for 'landing' apples. In one instance, eight shillings was received and on another, one. Occasionally, commodities such as cheese, raisins, currants, figs, hops, onions, pepper and bedticks were also imported.

Unfortunately, the port books for the seventeenth, like those for the sixteenth century, do not provide anything like a complete and satisfactory record of the commercial activities of the town and hinterland. Furthermore, such expansion as took place in the volume of trade, occurred despite the operation of factors which militated against it. These unfavourable circumstances included the closure of markets, the need to convoy shipping, and the increasing use of taxation on coal cargoes as a valuable source of revenue for the Crown.

In the seventeenth century coal continued to remain the chief commodity for export from Swansea on both the coastal and foreign sides, though the bulk of the fuel was shipped to France and the Channel Islands. On the coastal side there were considerable fluctuations in the amount of coal exported. The following table will serve to illustrate this as well as being indicative of the extent of the trade. The wey in this table may be regarded as being equivalent to about four tons.

| | |
|---|---|
| Michaelmas 1605—Michaelmas 1606 | 472 w. |
| Xmas 1606—Xmas 1607 | 730 w. |
| Xmas 1607—Xmas 1608 | No figures available |
| Michaelmas 1608—Michaelmas 1609 | 465 w. |
| Xmas 1609—Xmas 1612 | No figures available |
| Xmas 1612—Xmas 1613 | 674 w. |
| Xmas 1613—Xmas 1620 | No figures available |
| Xmas 1620—Xmas 1621 | 651 w. |

| | |
|---|---|
| Xmas 1621—Xmas 1622 | 797½ w. |
| Xmas 1622—Xmas 1627 | No figures available |
| Xmas 1627—Xmas 1628 | 458 w. |
| Xmas 1628—Xmas 1629 | No figures available |
| Xmas 1629—Xmas 1630 | 530 w. |
| Xmas 1630—Xmas 1639 | No figures available |
| Xmas 1639—Xmas 1640 | 2,268 w. |

Comparable figures for Neath, Llanelli and Burry reveal the same irregularity of pattern although the volume of trade in coal was considerably lower than from Swansea.

The direction of the coastal trade in coal from Swansea is clearly defined. The sixteenth-century pattern of distribution was very largely maintained, though one significant difference was the increase in the trade to the south coast. Shipments were taken to the ports of the Bristol Channel, to the west of England ports, to ports on the south coast and, finally, the occasional cargo was taken as far east as Dover, London and Yarmouth.

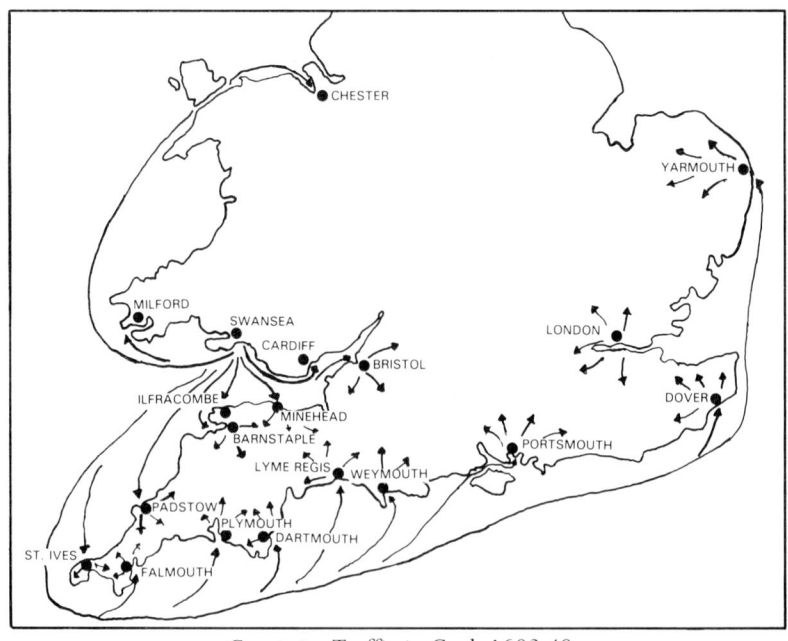

Coastwise Traffic in Coal, 1603-40

This trade, as in the sixteenth century, was very largely carried in the shipping of the ports to which the coal was consigned, though, occasionally, a London ship is found carrying coal to St. Ives, and vessels from Chepstow and Westbury carrying iron to Bristol. Sometimes these colliers carried such additional cargoes as cloth, frieze, iron, leather, laths, nails, brass and butter.

But the Port Books demonstrate that some, at least, of this trade was carried in Swansea and Mumbles shipping. They can be seen conveying coal to Plymouth, Absome, Weymouth, Falmouth, Teignmouth, Watchet and Barnstaple; iron to Bristol and Weymouth; and agricultural by-products such as the skins of goats, calves and sheep, leather, wool, cloth, friezes and butter to Plymouth and to that great entrepôt of trade, Bristol.

The overseas traffic of Swansea throughout the first four decades of the seventeenth century remained tied to the demands of France, the Channel Islands and Ireland. The town's exports in coal increased steadily until 1620 but after this date they fell rapidly, reaching their nadir in 1627-8 when only 134 weys were sold overseas. Recovery followed until 1634 but then contraction set in again. This decay is attributable to the introduction by the early Stuart Kings, James I and Charles I, of new and heavier impositions on coal which discriminated more especially against foreign merchants. In 1620 the duty on exports was increased by 1s.8d. per Newcastle chaldron if the carrier was English but by 3s.4d. if it was foreign. Charles I's need for extra cash led to an additional levy of 4s. per Newcastle chaldron in 1634. To this policy of taxing coal exports may be attributed the lukewarm support rendered by the town to the King during the Civil Wars. These wars had arisen partly from the resistance of the commercial middle classes, whose position within society had been strengthened by the rise of coal mining and industries dependent upon it, to attempts made by the Crown to encroach upon that power by exercising its prerogative.

Considering that on the eve of the Civil Wars coal stood burdened with a tax larger than the value of the fuel itself, 13s.2d. per chaldron for foreign merchants and 11s.6d. for English, it is a remarkable testimony to the need for coal abroad that the foreigner should have continued to buy it in Britain at all. Though it is undeniable that these taxes had an adverse effect on the export of coal to foreign parts, nevertheless, they stimulated considerably the coastal trade. It has been computed that while in 1640 overseas shipments from Swansea had amounted to about 2,000 tons, the coastwise shipments accounted for nearly 9,000 tons.

In 1607, Swansea overseas traffic was made up of 50 shipments to France, 17 to Jersey and 9 to Guernsey. The shipping employed was mainly alien, only 8 per cent of the coal being exported in Swansea vessels. Swansea shipping always exported to France and returned laden with salt and wine. The pattern altered in the second decade when the Channel Island traffic declined and the French trade underwent expansion. In 1613, out of a total number of 96 outshipments, 85 went to France, 2 to Guernsey and 9 to Jersey, Swansea and Mumbles shipping accounting for 8 per cent of the shipments. In the third decade Ireland replaced the Channel Islands as the second main importer of coal from Swansea. Out of a total of 75 outshipments in 1629, 62 went to France, 10 to Ireland, 2 to Jersey and one to Guernsey. Swansea shipping in this year played a slightly more active part in the export trade, accounting for 12 per cent of the shipments. Of the 9 shipments carried in Swansea ships, 6 went to France, 2 to Ireland and one to Jersey. The new pattern of the third decade of increased shipments to France, dwindling exports to the Channel Islands and the replacement of the latter by Ireland as the second largest importer was emphasised in 1630. In this year, out of a total number of 103 outshipments, 87 went to France, 10 to Ireland, 3 to Jersey and 3 to Guernsey, Swansea and Mumbles shipping accounting for 8 per cent of the shipping employed. Unfortunately, for the fourth decade, the Port Book material is most unsatisfactory. Of the four port books available, three have been classified as unfit for production. If a trend can be adduced from the evidence of one port book, it would appear that the pattern of the third decade was not wholly repeated. Though shipments to France still remained at a very high level, the Channel Islands were restored to second position in the import league table. In 1634, out of a total of 95 outshipments, 73 went to France, 8 to Ireland, 12 to Jersey and one to Guernsey. Swansea shipping accounted for 12 per cent of the shipments.

Swansea was by far the chief exporter of coal from south Wales. It has been estimated that the annual tonnage exported from local ports was as follows:

| Port | 1551-60 | 1591-1600 | 1631-40 |
|---|---|---|---|
| Swansea | 1800 | 3000 | 12,000 |
| Neath | 600 | 1000 | |
| Llanelli and Burry | 300 | 400 | 2,000 |

This examination of the export coal trade of Swansea, on both the coastal and foreign sides, leads us to draw two conclusions: first, that it was seasonal in character, the greatest traffic falling in the summer months; and secondly, that it was a calling trade conducted for the most part by non-Welsh merchants.

But coal was not the only commodity exported overseas from the town. Wheat, barley, friezes, coverlets, leather and iron were also exported usually as an additional cargo. The main commodity imported was salt. Other goods included canvas, crescloth, oakum, lockrum, wine, sack, buckram, fish, soap, barley, wheat, rye, figs, vinegar and raisins.

THE HARBOUR

Finally, the economic development of Swansea must have benefited considerably from the attention which the corporation devoted to the more profitable aspects of town life, and particularly to the port and its trade. To encourage foreign merchants to visit the town, it was laid down in a by-law passed in 1553 that if a Swansea merchant defaulted in his payment to a foreign trader, then his goods should be distrained and sold so that the stranger might be fully recompensed. In the commercial world it was obviously imperative that the reputation of the town and its merchants for honesty and fair dealing should be preserved.

The corporation was gravely concerned with the problem of maintaining an accessible approach to the harbour so frequented by foreign merchants. In the sixteenth and seventeenth centuries, and

Entrance to Fabian's Bay Harbour

for long afterwards, there was a very real danger of the river being rendered unnavigable not only by silting and drifting of sand, and by the scourings of the river brought down in time of flood, but also by the thoughtlessness or unscrupulousness of individual traders. These, as they entered the haven, would attempt surreptitiously to dispose of their ballast into the river and, but for the vigilance of the corporation, the harbour could very soon have ceased to exist. As early as 1555, and frequently after that date, regulations, enforced by stringent penalties, were framed to combat the practice. In 1583, an ordinance was introduced that every ship, before proceeding up to the coal place, should discharge its ballast upon the quay. The ballast which the ships still carried to enable them 'to bear their masts' was to be either cast ashore at the lading place or brought down again to the quay.

The discharge of ballast upon the quay, rather than its indiscriminate casting into the bay, placed a real temptation in the way of the burgesses to help themselves to the useful building materials left there. At Swansea, hard dressing stones were obtainable only with difficulty and at great expense since the native stone was of a quickly perishable character, the Pennard stone of Town Hill and Kilvey being soft, friable and flakey. Consequently, on 3 March 1585, a by-law was introduced which stipulated that pilferers were to pay 6*d*. for every cartload, and 3*s*.6*d*. for every ton of stone taken away. Furthermore, in order to ensure that the ballast would not be intercepted before reaching the quay, the regulation provided a penalty for those who 'shall buy any stones that a stranger means to cast there'. The fines collected in this manner were to be shared equally between the corporation and the lord of the town.

Enforcement of regulations relating to the harbour and river was the responsibility of officers known as the layer-keepers, whose duties were, in the eighteenth century, defined in the following terms: 'To serve for the year ensuing, or until he is lawfully discharged. To take care of the navigation of the Bar and River, and to see that the mooring posts etc. are kept in order. To see that no Ballast or other offensive matter be thrown into the River, and that all nuisances or whatsoever might be prejudicial or inconvenient to the ships should be removed. To present all matters and things falling within the duties of his Office justly and without favour or affection'.

The first appointment of layer-keepers, as revealed in the town records, was made in October 1583, the two burgesses then chosen being Rees ab Bowen and John Smyth. There were invariably two selected (three in 1589), since if there had been one layer-keeper only, illness or some other factor could have left the office vacant and it was far too vital a situation for that to be permitted. The office was held on an annual tenure, though re-appointment for another year was possible. The normal procedure was for the appointment to be made at the autumn meeting of the leet court, though 1597 witnessed the unusual spectacle of one Thomas David being appointed and sworn in at a meeting of the Common Hall. From about 1610 onwards, it was found expedient to retain one of the keepers in office so that the newly-appointed officer could benefit from his accumulated experience. The layer-keepers appear to have been vigilant in the performance of their duties, and the accounts of the common attorneys indicate that quite a rich harvest in fines was gathered from defaulters. In 1618/9, one shilling was received 'through Patrick's hand for throwing out the ballast which the Cornish men threw out'. Robert Porter of Watchet paid 2s.6d. in 1624 for heaving ballast into the river, while in 1629 3s.3d. was received from 'a barque of Watchet for throwing of ballast out on the bar'.

QUAYS AND DOCKS

The building of quays and docks in the late sixteenth and early seventeenth century both reflected and stimulated the economic development of the town. The corporation contributed extensively to the provision of these facilities, for it not only provided most of the quays at its own expense but it must also have encouraged the construction of docks by its readiness to lease to individuals, at low rentals, sections of the river bank to be utilized for that purpose. With coal exports becoming an ever more important feature of economic activity in Swansea these developments had become imperative.

During the later Middle Ages a quay had been provided at Swansea, since the town was already a thriving commercial community. The significant increase in the volume of shipping frequenting the haven from the sixteenth century onwards would have necessitated the expansion of the port facilities, and during Elizabeth's reign two additional quays were provided. The first reference to a new quay is to be found in an ordinance of 1583 when it is ordered that 'every owner, master mariner or company of any ship, bark, pinnace, lighter, creer or any other boat or vessel arriving at the said town shall before they go up to the coal or lading place discharge and cast ashore upon the perroge by the pill near the passing pole now called the new quay place'.

The description of the quay as being by 'the pill near the passing pole' has enabled its location to be established. The 'pill' is the recognizable landmark; it was at the outlet of the little creek which ran a considerable distance along the burrows and discharged into the river on the upper side of the old 'mount', which stood at a spot still marked by Mount Street. At this time the 'pill' (which is the word used in the Bristol Channel for a river or creek) was so wide that it had to be crossed by a substantial bridge which conveyed the road from the town to the ferry; a bridge whose maintenance and repair was a continuous source of expense to the burgesses. Below the pill were the burrows; above it the town wall. Also below the pill, in all probability, was the 'passing pole', the actual limit of the haven, above which the layer-keepers exercised their jurisdiction. It was above this pill that the town built its new quay upon the site which had been previously known as the 'perroge' or 'perch'.

The reference to the 'passing pole' suggests an ancient observance at this point on the river. A similar pole on the river Severn at Gloucester had been called the 'hoecepol', a word which meant a place for the levying of tolls. It is not improbable that from very early times, reaching out across the river at Swansea, had been a pole at which dues were collected on ships entering the haven.

In the 1583 order, it had also been laid down that any fines imposed for any breach of its regulations should be devoted to the construction of the new quay. By 1585, in the ordinance forbidding the pilfering of stones by the burgesses, the fines had once again reverted to the lord and the common coffer. This strongly suggests that by the latter date the quay had been completed.

By 1597, another quay was needed and so, on 18 August, the portreeve, William John Harry, 'did set one William Morgan, mason, to lay the ground wall of the quay and did work upon it until Michaelmas after'.

However, the building of quays was not solely the responsibility of the corporation as a body, since in 1615-16 yet another quay was begun at his own expense by the then portreeve, Walter Thomas; a remarkable testimony to his enthusiasm for promoting the advancement of the town. His ambitions were enshrined in these words: 'the new quay, lying right over & against the store house late of Robert Phillips, it was begun to be made & builded by me Walter Thomas Portreeve for the time being of the said town of Swansea & by the consent & assent of the aldermen & burgesses of the said town the charge of what was builded now at the beginning in this my year came to seven pounds and two shillings and I hope that he which shall succeed me in my office will be a means that this good work being begun shall be set forwards & finished'.

Though it is certainly true that this further quay was begun by Walter Thomas from his own pocket, it was completed at the expense of the corporation who also assumed responsibility for keeping it in a good state of repair thereafter. Continuous as were the charges for maintenance on the borough, donations were occasionally received from individuals toward this end. In 1618, a John Davids gave 18s.7d., and in the same year Rees Lison contributed 20s. Not infrequently there were fines imposed for damage done to the quay, as in 1618 when 3s. was received of 'a Breton for breaking of the quay'. A few years later, in 1620, Bretons were again at fault in this respect and atoned for their carelessness by paying 18d. 'for wrong done unto the quay'.

Together with quays, docks were also constructed during this period and these were the product of private initiative. The common attorneys' accounts indicate that a dock had been built as early as 1624, probably the first on the river and certainly the first referred to in the corporation papers. The entry is among the receipts for the year and runs: 'received of Edmund Rich for making of the dock by the quay, xs'. This suggests that Edmund Rich or Richard was the pioneer of dock construction at Swansea, who provided the amenity at his own expense and paid the corporation for the privilege of doing so. This was probably the only dock in the haven until 1631. However, by the following year, another dock had made its appearance since it is recorded by the common attorneys that £1 had been received from 'Mr Thomas Mansell for the coal place, dockage and plankage, at the end of the little burrows'. This would point to the dock having been provided a little lower down the river, because the Little Burrows were situated considerably to seaward of the quay. The next year, 1633, the common attorneys acknowledge receipt of 5s. which 'William Thomas Richards left in John Williams's hands to be d[elivere]d the common attorneys for part of moneys which he received for plankage from the dock under Roger Ienkin's garden', and this entry points to another dock, a third, having been constructed, possibly a little further up river than the corporation quay. But the spate of dock building was not over yet because from the disbursements of the common attorneys in 1636-7 it becomes evident that yet another had been provided at St. John's, later to be known as the 'higher dock'. The entry reads: 'paid for a plank for the Dock of St. Johns, 2s.8d.'. This was a dock built on land for which an annual rent of £1 was paid to the corporation, and in 1642 a certain Thomas Harry paid this rent to the town 'for the higher dock'.

PIRACY

Commercial expansion at Swansea may well have been assisted by the absence of that extensive piratical activity which had made Milford Haven and Cardiff so notorious. Though, in the late fifteenth century, Sir Matthew Cradock had been involved in an episode which smacked strongly of piracy, in the Tudor and early Stuart age the port had not become a retreat for those who sailed under the skull and crossbones. Although the available evidence makes it difficult to tell why this was so, it does appear that the policy of the corporation toward the port possibly played an important part. It is certain that town officials enforced very strictly on all merchants entering the port the obligation of communal trading. By-laws of 1553, 1555 and 1569 provided that all cargoes brought into the haven must be open to purchase by the general body of burgesses in the first place, and only when they had made their choice was the residue available to private individuals. These, and other similar regulations aiming at a careful supervision of all commercial activities, would have tended greatly to complicate the activity of the pirates dependent as they were on some degree of secrecy and the co-operation of a limited number of influential supporters. However, despite the vigilance of the corporation, Swansea tars are found occasionally engaged in activities of a piratical or quasi-piratical nature.

Swansea men appear at times as sailors on board pirate ships, though never on those operating in the locality. A pirate with quite a considerable reputation was Hugh Griffith, one of the three sons of the squire of Cefnamwlch in Caernarfonshire. Hugh's favourite haunt was the Breton coast. Two members of the crew of his ship, the *Pendragon*, had certainly been recruited at Swansea. These were the master of the ship and a lieutenant. In 1575, a Henry Francklyn of the town was said to have 'rigged forth in warlike manner a ship called the *Margett*, but at a time when it was advisable for legitimate merchant ships to be armed, there may have been nothing exceptional in this act. Yet another member of the same family, William Francklyn, appears in 1576 as a customer of the notorious pirate Callice in Cardiff. The famous captain Richard Grenville wrote to Sir Edward Stradling in 1575 asking him to assist in the recovery of certain goods belonging to some 'poor neighbours' of his which had been taken by a pirate who had later been himself captured with his prize off Mumbles. Apparently the goods on board the ship had been taken ashore and had fallen into the hands of local people: 'My request to you is that, according to justice and equity, their goods may be again by your help the rather restored to them again, so as they have not more cause to complain on your neighbours than on the pirates'. The details given are too vague to substantiate any definite charge against the men of Swansea although some suspicion remains. Again, Callice was said to have paid at least one visit to 'Oystermouth Road'. On that occasion a certain John Hopkin Llewelyn Richard had bought from him a chest of sugar, while Walter ap Howell of Swansea had supplied the pirate with a cable and an anchor.

In 1581, there were occurrences of a very interesting nature. Toward the end of that year a ship called the *Primrose* of London, which only a short time previously had put into Swansea to lade coal after a voyage to Ireland, appeared again in Mumbles Road, allegedly not putting into Swansea or Neath because of the harbour bars. This had made the local officials suspicious because it was thought that she had been engaged in piracy and did not wish to be too closely scrutinized. The county piracy commissioners, Sir Edward Mansel of Margam, Sir Edward Stradling of St. Donat's and William Mathew were summoned, and the master, Philip Smithe of Bristol, the purser and the gunner of the *Primrose* were examined. The customer of Swansea, Henry Watkines, declared later that they were discharged with clear characters, after which they with 'other of their company came daily to Swansea town and there made merry in sundry places of the town and behaved themselves very civilly and honestly'. The story which the master of the vessel, Philip Smithe, told was that they had set out from Southampton to lade coal at Swansea and Neath which they were to bring to France. On their way along the Devonshire coast they had encountered a well-known pirate, Stephen Haynes, in Tor Bay, and William Munke the purser and Richard Allyn the gunner, had bought from him a quantity of goods, brazilwood (a valuable red dyewood), cotton (then something of a luxury), Brazil pepper, monkeys and parrots. These had evidently come from a French ship which had been trading in Portuguese Brazil and had, if Smithe's story is to be believed, been captured by Haynes, who had then disposed of the goods at one of the many prize-marts along the south coast. It is not impossible that the *Primrose* herself was the pirate, but the chances are that Smithe was telling at least part of the truth.

The piracy commissioners seem to have accepted the story that the *Primrose* was not herself a pirate ship, and to have passed her and her recently-stolen goods without even charging customs duties. They did not do so without consideration. Sir Edward Mansel was said to have been given a monkey, Sir William Herbert of Swansea another, while the customer, Henry Watkines, got two parrots. The latter maintained that his parrots were given to him when he had William Munke and others 'to dinner and supper with him at his house being in the Christmas holidays', and that he had little joy from them since they died within a fortnight.

Once she had been cleared—or the local officials squared—the *Primrose* was free to trade, and she now proceeded to Neath where arrangements had already been made to supply her with coal. There the question of paying for her lading arose, as Munke and his company complained of being short of ready money. Eventually they persuaded John White, the Neath merchant from whom they were buying the coal, and his associate Hopkyns ap Price, to accept some of their goods as payment. White got 4 tons of Brazilwood for £26.13s.4d., two or three hundredweights of cotton, a broken anchor and two small broken cannon. In return he supplied a consignment of coal of 43 weys at 10s. a wey, and later another smaller load which left him with a balance to pay in cash. White and the men of the *Primrose* parted apparently well pleased with each other.

The French merchant, however, from whom the goods had been stolen, one Adrian Le Seigneure of Rouen, had evidently a good intelligence service in England and Wales. In some way, he traced part of the goods to the *Primrose*, and thence to Swansea and Neath, and succeeded in getting John White, Henry Watkines, and Philip Smithe brought to London to answer for their faults in the High Court of Admiralty. There, before a Welsh judge, Dr. David Lewis, they made the depositions from which the events related above have been reconstructed. The result of the case is not known. It is probable, however, that John White had to pay over to the French merchant the value of the commodities he had bought.

In 1626, another incident, which certainly bordered on piracy, took place at Swansea. It seems that a ship, the *Fortune* of Hamburg of 150 tons, laden with merchandise, had been driven by cross winds into the harbour. The master and some of the mariners had gone ashore and stayed for some part of the day in the town intending in the evening, when the tide was favourable, to depart for Bristol. For this purpose they had already hired a pilot and obtained leave from the bailiffs and aldermen. During their absence the ship was seized and carried away to sea by eighteen persons from the adjoining parishes. From a petition sent to the Council on 7 July 1626, it appears that one of these men was Robert Daniel of Swansea. He states that he and his friends had seized a ship 'riding at the Mumbles' for the King's use and had brought her into Barnstaple. The cargo comprised oranges and lemons. He further stated that the crew were 'variable in their relation as to the place to which she belongs, some affirming Rotterdam and others Hamburg'. He concluded by praying for directions.

The owners had also begun proceedings in the Admiralty Court, and there an order had been made for the restitution of the ship and goods. Sheltering, however, behind a former order made by the Council with regard to the ship, the 'malefactors' had opposed its execution. The owners had then sought legal remedy from the Council and, after having given due consideration to the premises, the Council ordered that the master and owners of the ship should be left at liberty to prosecute for relief touching the vessel and damages by them sustained, at the common law.

Economically, then, the town had made great strides in the period 1485-1640. Local agriculture was being commercialised and the coal and iron resources of the town's hinterland increasingly exploited. All this was reflected in the expansion of the town's trade, both coastwise and overseas, and in the provision of quays and docks on the river. It remains now to examine how this affected the population of the borough, the distribution of wealth among the various social classes and the use to which the townspeople put their increased resources.

# Chapter Three

## THE SOCIAL SCENE

Professor G.M. Trevelyan defined social history 'as the history of a people with the politics left out'. He demonstrated how difficult it was to disentangle the social web from the political and economic background; political events to a very large extent grow out of the social scene, while the social scene itself represents a response to economic conditions. To Trevelyan, then, social history provided the essential linchpin between economic and political history, as well as having its own positive value and peculiar concern in presenting a picture of the everyday activities of our ancestors. He shows that the generalizations which are the stock-in-trade of the social historian must necessarily be based on a small number of particular instances, which are assumed to be typical, but which cannot be the whole of the complicated truth. In this account of social conditions prevailing at Swansea between the accession of Henry VII and the restoration of Charles II, a rough sketch of the town will be presented, and an attempt will be made to estimate the size of the population and account for any changes within it. The distribution of wealth will be examined, and an analysis undertaken of the social and occupational structure. Attention will also be focused on dwellings, poor-law administration, public health, and education. Finally, the recreations of the townspeople, together with the general tenor of life within the borough, will be discussed. An account of the daily routine of a cross-section of the population would have been invaluable as well as being of great intrinsic interest. Unfortunately, the paucity of material effectively precludes such an attempt. Compared with the sum total of what could be known, so little evidence has been preserved.

The town, during this period, can be delineated in broad outline from a survey of Gower made by Oliver Cromwell in 1650 since the names of the streets, together with their various tenements, have been preserved in this document. The streets included 'Goat Street'

(21 tenements), 'East Side Within the Gate' (8 tenements), 'Castle Bayly' (17 tenements), 'West Side of the Market' (5 tenements), 'Wind Street, the East Side' (21 tenements), 'Wind Street, West Side' (18 tenements), 'Fisher Street' (12 tenements), 'Frog Street' (6 tenements), 'Cross Street' (11 tenements), 'Goat Street' (17 tenements), and 'Mary Street' (26 tenements). These various streets had lain within an encompassing stone wall but, since much of the intra-mural area had never been available for building, suburbs had developed outside the town walls, probably along the roads of approach, forming what is now generally known as 'ribbon development'. Though there were within the walled area considerable stretches of open ground, development was not possible since some of it belonged to the castle, some to such religious institutions as the parish church of St. Mary and the Hospital of the Blessed David, and a great deal comprised in burgage tenements. Two small suburbs had developed before the close of the Middle Ages known as *Bovetown* and *Donton*.[1] The streets in the extra-mural area were now known as 'Above the Gate' (17 tenements), 'Without the Gate' (7 tenements) and 'East Side' (12 tenements). The surviving material precludes definite assertions as to how many suburban dwellers there were. A very rough estimate can be made, however, by comparing the number of burgage tenements within and without the walls. There would appear to have been 162 tenements inside and 36 outside. This would provide a ratio of 9 to 2. Assessed by this method roughly 22 per cent of the total population would have been suburban.

Beyond the built-up areas lay the meadows, commons and waste which belonged to the town. The meadows, which had been considerably diminished as a result of the economic trends of the later Middle Ages, comprised Portmeade and Crow-Wood, while the commons embraced Cefn Coed (covering 700 acres, though 200 acres were enclosed in the last decade of the sixteenth century) and the Burrows (extending for about a mile in length). The wastes, on the other hand, included the Little Burrows and Poppet Hill. The enjoyment of this borough property was strictly limited to the

[1] Supra, p. 20.

burgesses; only they could lease it and only they could pasture their animals over it.

The size and changes of population in any given unit constitute one of the most important problems, if not indeed the most important problem, confronting the social historian. Unfortunately, it is not possible to provide a precise estimate of the population at any time within this period because the first official government census was not introduced until 1801. Consequently, reference has to be made to such sources as chantry and episcopal returns and parish records. The difficulty is compounded by the unreliability of contemporary estimates which are often wild conjectures and distortions.

On 14 February 1545/6, twenty-four commissions were drawn up for the survey of all chantries and similar institutions in England and Wales. The commissioners were to inquire into certain articles and make a return of the certificates to the Court of Augmentations. According to the third article they were to inquire which and how many of the chantries, hospitals, colleges, free chapels, etc. had been 'parish Churches & how far distant they and every of them been from the Parish Church within which any of them standeth and be set'. To this article, the commissioners made reply that the Hospital of St. David was 'distant from the said parish church of Swansea xx$^{ty}$ yards yet the said Master or Warden or parson is instituted and always inducted as warden or parson as well into the said hospital or Wardenage as also into ii Chapels there unto Annexed & the parsonage of Swansea parcel of the same possessions which parsonage is endowed with a vicar that hath cure of soul to the number of vi$^c$ houseling People'.[2] Adopting a multiplier of 1.5 this would provide a population figure for Swansea of roughly 900-1,000. Comparable estimates for other towns in south Wales are: Cardiff, 750 houseling people (1125), Neath, 400 (600), Cowbridge, 300 (450), Tenby 900 (1,350), Kidwelly, 540 (810) and Carmarthen, 1500 (2,250). The figure for Swansea's population provided by the chantry commissioners

---

[2] Houseling people were those people old enough to take holy communion, i.e. everyone over the age of twelve.

The Social Scene                                    81

cannot be regarded as anything better than a rough guide. It seems, perhaps, a little lower than might have been expected but does not appear to be wildly out of proportion to other south Wales towns.

An estimate of the population made in 1563 was probably even more of an approximation and less reliable than that of the chantry commissioners. The bishops were in that year directed by the Privy Council to answer certain interrogatories, the precise nature of which is learnt from the returns for the diocese of Bangor where they are set forth at length. Six questions were asked, one of which had a direct bearing on population. This was the fifth interrogatory which related to the number of householders within every parish, or within any such member of any parish that had such churches or chapels of ease. The task of ascertaining the number of householders was an undertaking which the Elizabethan bishops found rather difficult, owing to the limited time allowed and the difficulties of inter-communication. The returns for St. David's were consequently submitted without the answers to question five: 'The fifth article, that is how many householders are within every parish, etc, is not possible to be answered unto at this time for that it requireth both a longer time and also painful inquisitions and diligent consultations with the parson, vicar or curate of every parish, which cannot be done so shortly as I am required to answer, as I doubt not but that your honours doth well consider and weigh'.

However, the bishop, like his learned brother of Bangor, was again called upon to furnish the desired information, and the estimate of the population of Swansea in 1563 is based on the supplementary returns for St. David's. The assessment is based on the number of *familiae*. In the parish of Swansea the number of householders was given as 180. Adopting a multiplier of 4.68, this provides a population figure of 842. Carmarthen, a shire and corporate town, and undoubtedly the largest town in Wales at this time, had 328 households giving an estimated population of 1535; Laugharne, a village, had 90 households (421); Kidwelly, a corporate town, 101 (472); and Llanelli, another village, merely 12 (56). Little comfort can be derived from the figure for Swansea, as it is based on sheer guess work. Thus, it is extremely unlikely that the population of the town which in 1546 stood at about 900-1,000 should have fallen by 1563 to 842. Furthermore, the fact that the venerable bishop, when called upon a second time to furnish the required figures, could do so without loss of time is a clear indication that he was basing his estimate on a very rough and ready calculation. The 1563 figures applicable to the Gower area, however, demonstrate that the environs of Swansea, a crescent-shaped belt from Oystermouth and Mumbles in the south-west, to Llansamlet in the north-east, were the most densely populated part of the region. A secondary nucleus of population existed around the Burry estuary, with Loughor registering 60 households (280), and Llanrhidian parish 162 (758). These two concentrations of population arose in direct response to their natural advantages. These were the marketing of the products of the adjacent agricultural lands, the development of the export trade from Swansea and the Burry ports, the working of coal, and finally, the ferry traffic across the Tawe and Loughor rivers.

The parish registers of the first half of the seventeenth century offer a better basis for assessing the town's population. The method of computation used is that of Rickman who was responsible for the first four censuses. His figures, based on an examination of the parish registers of the land, assumed that the population stood to the average of baptisms, burials and marriages at certain earlier times in the same proportion as in his base year. For the purposes of these calculations, 1781 has been taken as the base year; and statistics for births, deaths and marriages for the year have been provided by T.H. Marshall. For the average birth rate per 1,000 he gives 37.7, 28.6 per 1000 for deaths, and 17.2 for marriages. Since it is well established that not all births, deaths and marriages were recorded in the parish registers, Marshall applied, when arriving at these figures, multipliers of 1.243, 1.2, and 2, respectively, to the recorded baptism, burial and marriage figures. Applying this technique to Swansea, it is found that in 1631, when the parish registers first become available, the number of baptisms was 56, burials 36 and marriages 7. Adopting the multipliers used by Marshall, figures of 69.608 for births, 43.2 for deaths and 14 for marriages have been returned though it is quite possible that for the seventeenth century these are rather low. In order to ensure greater accuracy for the year 1639, the number of baptisms, burials and marriages for three years around this date were counted and the average taken, a method impossible to adopt in calculating the population in 1631 since the information for 1632-7 is missing from the register. This method gave a baptism figure of 64, a burial figure of 57 and a marriage figure of 10. Applying Marshall's multipliers again, figures of 79.552 for births, 68.4 for deaths and 20 for marriages have been arrived at. On the basis of these data a population figure of 1,390 for Swansea has been calculated for 1631 and 1,887 for 1639. Taking the average of these two figures, it would appear that the population of the town in the 1630s stood at about 1,600 which would make Swansea still a mere village by modern standards.

| Year | According to Births | According to Deaths | According to Marriages | Average |
|---|---|---|---|---|
| 1631 | 1,846 | 1,510 | 814 | 1,390 |
| 1639 | 2,110 | 2,391 | 1,162 | 1,887 |

The unsatisfactory nature of the evidence makes any positive statements about population trends dangerous. But there does appear to have been a marked increase in Swansea's population during the period c.1540-1640. It may well have risen from about 900 to about 1,600.

This increase in population can be explained not only on the grounds of natural increase but also on the basis of immigration; an immigration which was probably brought about by the expansion of the coal industry. Most of these immigrants, naturally enough, came from the valleys lying inland of the town but there were others who came from much further afield. Whole families were moving into the borough from Kilvey, Loughor, Llangyfelach, Pontardulais, Llanelli, Ystradgynlais, Neath, Llangiwg, Llangadog, Defynnog, Briton Ferry, Cardiff and Bristol. They were, however, required to find sureties of £40 that they would not become a financial burden on the town.

There are positive indications that there must have been a substantial, possibly even a preponderant, Welsh element in Swansea during this period. It has already been suggested[3] that during the later Middle Ages the Welsh were moving into the town to fill the vacuum consequent upon the Black Death and the economic malaise of the fourteenth and fifteenth centuries. The 'extent' of the town compiled in 1400, records at least six burgage holders with Welsh names, while five of the twelve portreeves holding office between 1437-1449 could similarly be identified as being Welsh. The Acts of Union, 1536-43, by providing the Welsh with full denizen rights, must have provided a great stimulus to this development. Certainly, the subsidy assessment of 1543 indicates that roughly half of the 111 tax-payers were unmistakably Welsh. They had become important members of the little community nestling at the *aber* of the Tawe, and they are frequently to be seen holding municipal office. In 1573, a Welshman with the very distinctive name of Ryse ap John ap Iēnn was portreeve, while in 1594 George Herbert occupied this very prestigious office. Among the aldermen who appended their signatures to an order of 1573 appear John David Vaughan and Mathew Owen. At a court leet held in 1583 the following Welshmen were appointed officers: Ienkin ap Inon and Thomas Vechan as common attorneys; Rees ab Bowen as one of the keepers of the layer; Dav(id) fab David as one of the constables; Owen Philipps as one of the raters of the poor; and David Bowen Phillipp, Rees ab Owen and Thomas Owen as three of the six 'which is on their oath to point the poor of the town'. Finally, the presence of a dominant Welsh element in this urban community is indicated in the request made by the parishioners in 1592/3 for the divine and funeral services to be conducted in the Welsh tongue.

It is unquestionably true that by the sixteenth century the Welsh, numerically, constituted the largest element in the town population, a situation far removed from that of a bygone age when their forerunners had regarded urban settlements as bastions of English influence, privilege and dominance and whose destruction they had frequently sought by means of fire and the sword.

[3] Supra, p. 23.

So far as the distribution of wealth among the town's population is concerned, an important source of evidence is the assessment made in 1601 toward the payment of mizes and aids to the lord. In this document 137 names are listed. Since in 1563, in the returns of Bishop Richard Davies to the Privy Council, the number of *familiae* (householders) in the parish of Swansea was stated to be 180, it would appear that at least 43 families had been so poor that they had not been included in the assessment. There may have been many more than this. It has already been demonstrated that the bishop's return was no more than a rough estimate.[4] Furthermore, his figure had referred to the number of householders, whereas there is definite evidence that some, at least, of these had other families living with them.[5] A further possibility of error arises from the fact that there was a time lag of almost forty years between Davies's returns and the assessment during which there would have been an increase in the town's population. However, since the gap is a relatively short one, and because the corporation was beginning to limit entry into the town, the increase in population might not have been so great as markedly to affect our calculations. On the other hand it is not certain whether there was any evasion of the assessment, and to what degree it was merely conventional. Bearing all these factors in mind, it is difficult to avoid the conclusion that the figure of 43 is, in all probability, too low and that an appreciably larger number of very poor families lived in the town.

The assessment shows, as might be expected, that the gentry figured prominently among those who contributed most. The highest assessment of all was that of Sir William Herbert, who was portreeve in 1580. Next came Robert Rogers, Owen Phillipp, John Moris, Owen ap Penry and Ienkin Francklen. These were among the wealthier members of the community who, to a very large extent, controlled the corporate life of the town, since they were all aldermen and as such sat on that small executive council which had evolved during the later Middle Ages to regulate the conduct of affairs within the borough. A further analysis of the assessment has provided the following indication of the spread of wealth:

[4] Supra, pp. 81-2.
[5] Infra, pp. 102-3.

| Assessment | No. in group |
|---|---|
| Over £1 | 11 |
| Over 10s. to £1 | 7 |
| Over 5s. to 10s. | 12 |
| Over 2s. to 5s. | 36 |
| 0s. to 2s. | 71 |

To the above table those who were too poor to be assessed have to be added. This group, as has already been shown, comprised at least 43 families, or just under a quarter of the total population, and it may well have been considerably larger. Taking all the groups together, and estimating the poor families at the minimum of 43, the following percentage ratios have been arrived at:

| Assessment | Percentage Ratio |
|---|---|
| Over £1 | 6 |
| Over 10s. to £1 | 4 |
| Over 5s. to 10s. | 7 |
| Over 2s. to 5s. | 20 |
| 0s. to 2s. | 39 |
| Too poor to be assessed | 24 |

From this table it appears that at least 24 per cent of the population were too poor to pay any direct taxation, while another 39 per cent only just came within the net. The first group may legitimately be regarded as the 'poor', and the second as living dangerously near the margin of poverty, precariously dependent upon employment as wage earners, small craftsmen, or shopkeepers. To this category belonged Leison David, a yeoman, who died in 1608 and whose personal estate was valued at £2.7s.0d. The group assessed at over 2s. to 5s. can be regarded as constituting the lower middle class and they comprised 20 per cent of the population. Typical of these was Edward Bennett, a dyer, who died in 1606, and whose personal estate was valued at £27.5s.10d. Those assessed at over 5s. to 10s. can be classified as the upper middle class and they accounted for about 7 per cent of the population. To this group belonged John William Morgan, who died in 1601, and left property valued at £80.6s.8d. Those assessed at over 10s. were very comfortably off and they comprised the top 10 per cent of the population. To this section of the community belonged John Moris, a gentleman, who died in 1608 and whose worldly possessions were valued at the very considerable sum of £322.2s.1d.

However, not unexpectedly, a social classification of this kind does not always work out with mathematical exactitude. Thus, Thomas Bidder, a yeoman, who was assessed at 14s. and accordingly might have been expected to belong to the same section of the community as John Moris, was valued for probate purposes in 1608 at only £47.3s.6d. Again, John Butler who was assessed at 5s. and who should consequently have been found in the same social group as Edward Bennett, was valued for probate purposes in 1628 at only £4.16s.0d. Or again, John Wiet, who was assessed at only 4d. in 1601, turned out at his death to have a relatively large personal estate valued at £17.16s.2d. This disparity between assessment and social classification may be explained on two grounds: first, it is quite possible that the assessment was conventional and secondly, it may be that by the time of their deaths the personal estates of the people concerned had either been impaired, or improved, through circumstances which have not come to light.

A noticeable feature of the social structure at Swansea is the number of people who were quite wealthy and this situation might well have arisen from the fact that the town, during the sixteenth and seventeenth centuries, was a thriving sea-port where a considerable concentration of wealth could be expected. Another significant feature was that fully one-half of the population lived below or very near the poverty line, a dangerously large element in the borough population.

From an analysis of the 1601 assessment and the inventories, of which some 135 have survived, it would appear that there were, broadly speaking, three strata of population within the town. The topmost stratum comprised the gentry and merchants, the middle the tradesmen, craftsmen, small shopkeepers and yeomen, while at the base of the social ladder were the colliers, labourers and the poor. These sources of information have also demonstrated conclusively that the gentry and merchants were, to all intents and purposes, the wealthiest members of the community, though it must be confessed that some of the 'middling' sort, like the occasional shopkeeper, yeoman or mariner, were possessed of greater personal estate. Together with being the most affluent, the gentry and merchants were also the dominant members of this urban community, playing a leading role in the municipal as well as the social and economic life of the town. From the inventories, the wealth of some of these august personages has already been established. John Moris's goods were valued at £322.2s.1d. while William John David Phillipp's were assessed at £180.2s.4d. Others who belonged to this group, and whose valuations for probate purposes have survived, include Phillip Mansell, a gentleman (£180.18s.4d.) and Thomas Hopkin, a merchant (£753.6s.0d.).

As befitted their exalted position, this particular section of town society lived in houses which were larger and better furnished than those of the rest of the community. Sir George Herbert lived in the 'Place House', High Street, a very imposing stone mansion which he had inherited from Sir Matthew Cradock. Sir Matthew had built

The Place House

his residence in close proximity to the castle, and in his will referred to it as 'my New Place in Swansea'. It remained a conspicuous feature of the town's landscape until its demolition in 1840. John Moris occupied a house which contained a hall, parlour, 7 chambers, shop, buttery, kitchen and cellar, while John Henderson's home contained a hall, parlour, kitchen and 3 chambers, one being on the ground floor. The merchants, however, do not appear to have placed such emphasis on domestic grandeur as the gentry, for Thomas Hopkin, an extremely wealthy trader, lived in a residence which simply contained one very large storeroom and one other room. There seems also to have been a significant difference in the disposition of the wealth of gentry and merchants. The merchants appear to have had by far the greater portion of their wealth invested in stock, whereas the wealth of the gentry was far more equitably distributed between stock and household furnishings. This differentiation between the disposition of the wealth of gentry and merchants becomes clear from the following table:

| Name | Total of Inventory | Household furnishings | Stock |
|---|---|---|---|
| John Moris (gentleman) | £322.2s.1d. | £207.0s.1d. | £115.2s.0d. |
| Phillip Mansell (gentleman) | £180.18s.4d. | £73.8s.4d. | £107.10s.0d. |
| John Henderson (gentleman) | £54.13s.4d. | £30.0s.0d. | £24.13s.4d. |
| Thomas Hopkin (merchant) | £753.6s.0d. | £18.0s.0d. | £735.6s.0d. |

Next in the social scale came the tradesmen, craftsmen, small shopkeepers and yeomen, the middle class element who, on the whole, occupied a far more lowly habitat than that of the gentry. In the great majority of the inventories, the rooms are not listed and this may indicate that there was only one room, the hall, and therefore no need to distinguish where the household goods lay. In this type of dwelling, a lath and plaster partition towards one end of the room would have formed a smaller second room known as the parlour and invariably used for sleeping, while an open loft reached by a ladder over the parlour might possibly have been used by the children. Some members of the middle order of society, however, lived in houses far more pretentious than this. Indeed, they vied with the gentry in their degree of domestic comfort. The house of John Symonds, a shoemaker, contained a hall, chamber, loft and shop, while that of Robert Gamon, a mariner, was provided with a hall, parlour, five chambers, buttery and kitchen. Henry Vaughan, a shopkeeper, dwelt in a house which contained a hall, shop and two chambers, while Francis After, another shopkeeper, resided in one equipped with a hall, little hall, kitchen, five chambers, cellars and shop. The chambers were generally used as bedrooms and invariably denoted a second floor. In the dwellings where there were no rooms above, it must be assumed that the medieval arrangement of the lower rooms being open to the rafters still survived, modified here and there by some planking which formed a loft in the roof space.

The furnishings of the best 'middle class' houses at Swansea, however, show no luxuries at all comparable with those of the well-to-do gentleman. The dwelling of Henry Watkins contained feather beds, tables, stools, chests, cupboards, carpets, table napkins and a silver bowl; it was comfortable but nothing like as luxurious as the house of John Moris which, with its glazed windows valued at 50s., contained, besides all the usual furniture and furnishings, such fripperies as silver plates and spoons, drawing table, a large looking-glass, two embroidered chairs, one carved chair, one Spanish bed, a Turkish carpet, custard plate, two flower pots, rugs, five cushions of gilded leather, five curtains of taffeta with a silken fringe, towels and a great quantity of presumably gorgeous apparel. The middle class, as representative of the business interests, were far more practical in their outlook, more down to earth. Their personal estate consisted more of the solid basic furniture, kitchen ware, tools of their trade and stock-in-trade and, with the more substantial among them, cattle and sheep scattered over the fields in the immediate vicinity of the town.

Finally, at the bottom of the social ladder, there were the miners, labourers and poor. These do not figure very prominently in the Swansea inventories as they rarely made a will, having little or nothing to leave. Occasionally, one comes across a collier or labourer who has prospered but such cases are exceptional. Unlike the dwellings of the upper echelons of town society, built in all probability of stone, the poor must have lived in one-roomed cottages made presumably of timber, or of 'half-timber', with clay and rubble between the wooden uprights and crossbeams. Not only were their dwelling houses far meaner than those of the middle and upper classes in the town, their standard of domestic comfort was also immeasurably lower. The gentry, merchants, craftsmen, shopkeepers and yeomen slept on feather beds with feather bolsters and pillows. They had invariably eaten and drunk from silver, brass or pewter dishes and vessels. The more well-to-do among them had trodden on carpets and rugs, some imported from eastern countries. Among the poor, however, these conditions were unknown. They ate and drank from wooden vessels and slept on straw beds, with perhaps a log under their heads for a bolster. William Harrison, the celebrated Elizabethan topographer and chronologist, writing in 1577, declared: 'Our fathers yea and we ourselves have lien full oft upon straw pallets, covered only with a sheet, under coverlets made of dagswain or hop harlots—and a good round log under their heads instead of a bolster—As for servants, if they had any sheet above them, it was well, for seldom had they any under their bodies, to keep them from the pricking straws that ran oft through the canvas of the pallet and razed their hardened hides'.

When the occupational structure of Swansea in this period is examined, one is immediately beset with difficulties. Despite the fact that admissions to the freedom were registered in the leet court, the nature of the employment of the freeman was seldom stated and in the great majority of cases it has not been possible to supply this deficiency by reference to other sources. Again, many of the townspeople had identical names and, consequently, it was not possible to ascertain to which trade each particular person belonged. Furthermore, many of the craftsmen did not enjoy burgess status and as a result did not appear in the records of people admitted to the freedom. Rather did they have the status of 'chensers' (non-burgesses), and paid for the privilege of following their trades within the liberties of the town. Finally, many of the people who were playing quite an important part in the economy of the borough, and whose omission from any list of Swansea occupations would give an entirely false impression of the occupational structure, were rarely to be found among the ranks of the burgesses. They were the yeomen, colliers, iron-workers, sailors and labourers. Unfortunately, although it has been possible to tabulate the town's trades and occupations, it has not been possible to list them in order of importance. However, even in a small town like Swansea, the range of crafts was impressively wide:

| Clothing Trades | Food and Drink Trades | Leather Trades | Textile Trades |
|---|---|---|---|
| Shoemakers | Bakers | Saddlers | Glovers |
| Tailors | Vintners | Curriers | Weavers |
| Buttonmakers | Cutlers | Tanners | Dyers |
| Hatters | Millers | | Feltmakers |
| Tuckers | Victuallers | | |
| Seamstresses | Pewterers | | |
| Lastmakers | Butchers | | |
| Cappers | Fishmongers | | |
| Cobblers | Inn-keepers | | |

| Building Trades | Rural | Distributive | Miscellaneous |
|---|---|---|---|
| Carpenters | Smiths | Merchants | Tinkers |
| Joiners | Hoopers | Mercers | Barbers |
| Tilers | Yeomen | Pedlars | Mariners |
| Paviers | Husbandmen | | Sailors |
| Masons | | | Labourers |
| Glaziers | | | Shipbuilders |
| | | | Colliers |
| | | | Ironworkers |

From this table it appears that the town was still predominantly non-industrial in character. Most of the trades adumbrated, such as the clothing, food and drink, textile and building trades, had no industrial flavour. But while the town may have been predominantly non-industrial in character, trades and occupations with a very strong 'industrial flavour' were playing an increasingly important part in its economy. This industrial flavour was provided by the tanners, colliers, iron-workers and ship builders. Coal mining, in particular, was developing as an 'industry' of great and significant importance in Swansea at this time, as the Exchequer Port Books have conclusively shown. The export trade in coal, both coastwise and overseas, may very largely have accounted for the substantial merchant community in the port and, for the period 1550-1640, it has been possible to establish the presence of 68 traders and there could have been many more than this.

Blacksmith

Barber

Baker

# The Social Scene

Wheelwright

Shoemaker

Another facet of the town's economy which does not emerge very clearly perhaps from the table, but which has been highlighted in the town records, particularly the inventories, is the high degree of dependence upon the surrounding countryside. This is reflected in the holding within the town of three fairs annually, together with a weekly market, the nature of some of the trades that existed there and also, more significantly perhaps, in the number of townspeople who had interests in, and may have depended ultimately upon, the countryside for their livelihood. The inhabitants of Swansea, like their ancestors in the Middle Ages, had little desire to rely on the charitable instincts of others for their food and so they cultivated their own fields, growing wheat, barley, oats, corn and hay, and grazed their animals—cattle, sheep, horses, pigs and geese—on the commons and wastes. As a consequence, within the town there would have been barns, granaries, dairies, cowsheds, stables, gardens and orchards. Swansea, therefore, like other towns in Wales, would have been both noisy and dirty with its streets strewn with animal dung and other filth exuding a most unpleasant odour and a breeding ground for all manner of diseases. The town's close affiliations with the countryside become clear from the following table compiled from the local inventories:

| Date | Name | Occupation | Stock |
| --- | --- | --- | --- |
| 1603 | John Lewis | 'Labourer' | 1 ox, 1 cow, 2 heifers, 2 steers, 1 calf, 1 mare, poultry. |
| 1604 | John David Morgan | Yeoman | 2 oxen, steers, 10 sheep and lambs, poultry, corn, 2 geese, 2 swine. |
| 1605 | John Symonds | 'Shoemaker' | Barley, 22 sheep, 1 calf. |
| 1606 | Edward Bennett | Dyer | 3 kine, 2 horses, 1 mare, 40 sheep and lambs. |
| 1608 | John Moris | Gentleman | 32 kine, 6 oxen, 10 horses and mares, 1 gelding, 1 colt, 5 heifers, 78 sheep, corn, hay. |

| Date | Name | Occupation | Stock |
|------|------|------------|-------|
| 1613 | John Boycott | Collier | 1 cow, 1 heifer, 2 calves, 1 horse. |
| 1614 | Griffith Hopkine | 'Tanner' | 1 horse, 1 cow, corn, hay. |
| 1618 | Morgan Thomas | Tanner | 3 kine, 13 sheep. |
| 1619 | John Wiet | Shoemaker | 1 cow |
| 1620 | Robert Gamon | Mariner | corn, malt, wheat, 4 kine, 1 heifer, 1 horse, 1 mare, 2 colts, 6 swine. |
| 1638 | David Symonds | Weaver | 2 kine, 1 heifer, 8 sheep, barley. |
| 1646 | Thomas Morgan | Baker | 2 mares, 4 kine, 1 cow, 2 heifers, 10 ewes and lambs, 1 yearling beast, barley, oats. |
| 1652 | Richard Jones | 'Tailor' and alderman | 10 kine, 4 oxen, 1 horse, 1 mare, 32 sheep and lambs. |
| 1625 | Phillip Mansell | Gentleman | 15 oxen, 27 kine, 29 steers and heifers, 1 gelding and 1 nag, 6 horses and mares, 5 colts, 60 wethers and ewes, 35 lambs, 7¾ acres wheat, 12 acres barley, 16 acres oats. |
| 1629 | Henry Vaughan | 'Shopkeeper' | corn, 100 sheep, 4 kine, 1 horse, wool, lime, limestones. |

Finally, in this analysis of town population, it can be averred that it was rare for a Swansea family to survive more than three generations. The exceptions stand out quite conspicuously. These were such leading Swansea families as the Herberts, Francklens, Mansels, and Sadlers. On the other hand, notable families such as the Cradocks, Flemings, Daniels, and Morises quickly disappear completely from the records. The disappearance of town families at this time is explicable on two grounds. First, and most important, was the tendency to 'get out' of trade. Once a family had made its fortune in commerce, it was faced with the almost irresistible temptation to invest in land and thereby establish itself as one of the country gentry. Another reason was the very high rate of infant mortality owing largely to the primitive state of medical science, and particularly midwifery, which was so characteristic a feature of every century preceding the nineteenth. Since, however, the Cradocks, Flemings, Daniels and Morises were already gentry stock, and had a stake in the land, their disappearance has to be attributed to the failure of heirs.

With at least half the population of the town living on or below the margin of poverty, it was inevitable that provision of relief for the poor, and the punishment of the sturdy beggar, should be

A Tudor Beggar

problems of the gravest concern for the corporation. The beggars were the characteristic evil of the sixteenth century; a period which saw their numbers swollen by the victims of the economic revolution, the price rise, and the wars so endemic at the time. They were the objects both of fear and pity, and their entry into a town has been immortalized in the following lines of nursery verse:

> Hark, Hark, the dogs do bark, the beggars are come to town,
> Some gave them white bread, some gave them brown,
> And some gave them the horsewhip and drove them out
>    of the town.

The whip, stocks, and the bed of 'short and musty straw' were the lot of the beggar in most towns. This was, in all probability, their fate at Swansea also, though no actual accounts of that have survived.

In 1552, an act, 'for the provision and relief of the poor', was passed 'to the intent that valiant beggars, idle and loitering persons, may be avoided, and the impotent, feeble, and lame provided for, which are poor in very deed', and although it confirmed the acts of 1531 and 1550 as to vagabonds, it was mainly directed to the increase of the charitable fund out of which the poor were to be relieved. Two collectors of alms were to be chosen from the inhabitants of every town or parish annually in Whitsun week, 'which Collectors, the Sunday next after their election . . . when the people is at the church and hath heard God's holy word, shall gently ask and demand of every man and woman what they of their charity will be contented to give weekly towards the relief of the poor'. The contributions so promised were to be entered in a register containing the names of the inhabitants and of the impotent poor of the parish for whom provision had to be made; and the collectors were to make a weekly distribution of alms to the poor so registered. A novel provision brought the authority or wrath of the bishop to bear upon recalcitrant householders since, in the event of the exhortations of the local clergy failing, they were to be summoned by the bishop who would, by 'charitable means', endeavour to make them mend their ways. This legislation was modified in some minor points in 1555. Both these acts, however, were permissive in character and consequently failed to evoke any response from the corporation of Swansea.

In 1563 an act was introduced which made a new departure of considerable importance in the history of the poor law, as it applied for the first time the principle of compulsion to the collection of funds for poor relief. Persons sent for by the bishop and wilfully declining to be moved by his pleas, were to be bound over by him in recognisances to appear before the justices of the peace at their next general sessions, and if they refused to be so bound, they could be committed to prison. If the justices were no more successful than the bishop, they were empowered to assess the contribution which each 'obstinate' person should pay towards the relief of the poor and, in default, to commit him to prison until payment should be made.

Consequent upon this legislation, between 1563-1601, a 'Benevolence for the Poor' was collected at St. Mary's church every Sunday. The two collectors entered the names of the contributors, together with the amount received from each, in a book provided for the purpose, though for the period for which documentary evidence has survived (1563-69) there was very little change in the identity of those who contributed. The actual number of donors on any one Sunday varied from a single individual—this was Sir George Herbert and his sole presence was obviously due to some exceptional circumstance—to twenty-three, with an average of fifteen for the whole period. The amount collected naturally varied from Sunday to Sunday, both according to the actual size of the congregation and the charitable disposition of each member, though the practice at Swansea was to appoint those who were to contribute and occasionally they got behind with their payments. However, on average, it would appear that the poor benefited to the tune of 3s.8d. a week in total. On a typical Sunday, like 5 September 1563, Ris ap John ap Ieuan and John Thomas Sadler collected 3s.7d. in benevolences, the contributors being Sir George Herbert, Robert Phillip, Roger Iankins, John Francklen, William Watkins, David Emlod, John David Vichan, John Fox, John Morgan ap Ris Lloyd, Iankyn Harries, Richard Yeroth, Ris ap John ap Ieuan, Morgan Simond, Thomas Smyth, Austin Cutkliff, Hugh David ap

Ieuan, John Smyth, Thomas Sadler, Ris ap Owen, Harry Watkins and John Thomas Sadler the Younger.

Sir George Herbert, the lord's steward, whose contribution was always a shilling, and the portreeve, the principal borough officer, invariably headed the list of subscribers. The unfortunates who were succoured in this manner varied in number from thirteen to twenty-one between 1563-1569, with a weekly average of sixteen for the period as a whole. It does not appear that the identity of the recipients of the doles changed greatly during these years. They included persons of both sexes, a few who were presumably widows, a poor boy, and a blind woman. On that same Sunday in September 1563 the number that should have received relief was fourteen, though for some reason or other, payment was made only to twelve, the amounts varying from 2*d.* to 6*d.* The indigent then were David Marchaunt, the wife of Owen John, Janet Cranne, John Hopkin, Ell(ai)ne, Hugh Lewis, William Harp(er), Elzabeth Smyth, the wife of Inon Crowther, Catt(eri)n Dee, Edward Rivell, Marget Griff(ydd), Elzabeth Richard and Marget Hopkyn.

However, the town council, on its own initiative, and without the stimulus of national legislation, was attempting to grapple with the problem of poor relief. It did this by limiting entry into the town, regulating the price of corn, providing the needy with such necessities as food, drink and clothing and, finally, administering bequests left for their benefit.

The corporation, in order to stem the inflow of migrant poor, forbade the townspeople to entertain poor inmates, and newcomers had to find bonds that they would not become burdensome to the town by reason of their poverty. In 1569 it was agreed that 'if any of the said burgesses of the said town, or any other householder of the same town, or any householder within the franchises of the same, do at any time hereafter keep, or suffer to be kept, any unlawful games in their houses inordinately, or receive to lodge into their houses any queens, harlots, or vagabonds, or any idle persons, that then such offender or offenders for every such fault & offence shall pay xii*d.*, the one half to the high lord of the said town and the other half to the common coffer of the same with a day of imprisonment'.

This by-law must have proved ineffective for in 1603, as a result of the outcasts of other towns being allowed to enter Swansea, an ordinance was introduced to prevent any stranger from settling in the town without the portreeve and constables being first notified so that they could question the newcomer as to why he had departed from his last place of abode. From this by-law it becomes clear that the laxity of the town officers, together with the greed of those inhabitants with lodgings to let, had led not only to 'sufferance of ungodly living & unlawful keeping of disordered alehouses, playing & other disorders, but also great loss unto the burgesses that are bound to keep victuals & lodging & good rule . . . by reason that lewd people do most frequent such places of liberty & misrule and upon presentments of the offenders . . . the stranger will run away in debt for corn, malt, house rent & leaveth behind either poor wife or children or strumpets with child which, being here born, cannot be expelled'.

Again immigrants had to find sureties that they would not become a financial burden to the town. If they failed to secure these, then they were ordered to depart. The surety demanded was usually in the sum of £40, a quite substantial amount although, occasionally, it was less. In 1621, Thomas Olyver and Edward Morgan undertook to 'save the town from being at any charge with one Antony Barber, his wife nor any children of theirs, between this and the first day of May, in condition of ten pounds before the then portreeve and aldermen and burgesses being then present'. With the sureties fixed as high as this, it is not surprising that many newcomers failed in their quest and had to leave, though it is quite apparent that there were householders in Swansea prepared to accommodate them because of the high rents that could be charged. Among those who departed the town in 1621 were:

| | |
|---|---|
| In David ap Owen's house | Richard Morgan, his son-in-law and his wife. |
| In the vicar's house | Thomas ap Owen, tanner, his daughter and her children. |
| In Richard John's house | John ap Eynon and his wife. |

| | |
|---|---|
| In Thomas William Bevan's house | Anthony Berow and his wife. |
| In William Dene's house | Michael the collier and his wife. |
| In Mr Say's house | The woman of Kilvey and her daughter. |

These were the able-bodied seeking employment and consequently mobile. Cripples, on the other hand, would have experienced difficulties in removing themselves and, as objects of pity, were conveyed out of the town either on horseback or by horse and cart.

Another means by which the corporation endeavoured to assist the poor was by pegging the price of corn through eliminating the unfair practices of forestalling and engrossing. To this end, in 1585, the following by-law was drawn up by the portreeve, aldermen and burgesses sitting in common hall: 'Whereas there is great complaint for the excess price upon corn in the market of this town of Swansea, which was not so at this time of the year so high of a long time, it is agreed that no manner of person, whether he be burgess, chenser, or foreigner shall be as bold as to buy . . . any corn before xi of the clock upon any saturday upon pain of forfeiture of iis for every bushel so bought to be levied out of hand, and from eleven forwards that those that have corn of their own, and will sell hereafter, shall not buy any at all in the said market otherwise than they will depose that it is for their present need, and that none of the town or country shall buy on saturday above ii bushels wheat, one bushel barley, & ii bushels oats at the most upon pain aforesaid'.

Another indication of the care which the council displayed for the welfare of the poor was the buying of clothes and victuals for them. Money for this very laudable objective was forthcoming from the corporation chest, and a study of the common attorneys' accounts serves to reveal the extent of the generosity of the town authority in this respect. Unfortunately, these accounts do not exist for the sixteenth century, but it can be reasonably assumed that these gifts of food and raiment were not phenomena peculiar to the seventeenth century only and that they had been distributed among the destitute from a much earlier period. The following selection of characteristic entries from the accounts will help to illustrate the nature of the benevolences dispensed by the corporation in this fashion:

> Item paid to Rees Lison for meat and drink to a poor man—v*s.* vi*d.*
> Item paid to Mr Walter Thomas for three yards of canvas for to make a shirt to Ienkin Asse—ii*s.* ix*d.*
> Paid for xvii yards and three quarters of gray cloth for the poor—xvii*s.* ix*d.*
> paid for bread—ix*d.*
> paid for a quarter of canvas—iii*d.*

Finally, the town assisted the poor by administering bequests left by benefactors, the corporation acting in the capacity of a public trustee. Money from this source was put to profitable use in three ways: it was loaned at interest to the burgesses; loaned to them without interest being charged; and lastly given as outright gifts to the very poor.

Where bequests were left to be lent at interest among the burgesses, the money so received was to be employed either for the support of 'poor, impotent and fatherless children', or for their placing as apprentices. The bequest of Hugh Atwill, parson of St. Tew in Cornwall, and previously the incumbent of Caverley in Devonshire, was distributed at interest among those burgesses whom it was considered 'fittest to have it', and the money so received used to relieve the needs of poor children. David Griffith Harry, a tanner, Richard Johnes, a weaver, John Daniell and Richard Seys, aldermen, had similarly bequeathed money to be used for a like purpose.

Ienkin Francklin, on the other hand, an alderman who died in 1622, and who had been portreeve on three separate occasions, in 1588, 1599 and 1603, left £50 to be let out at interest, but this money was to be employed to promote the apprenticing of poor children. In 1626, in execution of his will, Edward Thomas, the son of a pauper, was bound apprentice by the portreeve and aldermen to Rowland Rees and his son John Rowland to be taught the trade of a weaver. Other children, under the terms of the will, were bound apprentices to curriers, blacksmiths, shoemakers, glovers, tailors, and tilers, and were expected 'after the manner of apprentices with them to dwell'.

Another type of bequest was that which was distributed among the burgesses without interest being charged. In 1608, John Moris, whose worldly possessions at the time of his death were valued at £322.2s.1d. left £50 to be distributed in this manner. The freemen who were to benefit were those craftsmen and tradesmen of the town who were down at heel.

This benefactor had been sworn a burgess in October 1586. Two years later, however, he was disfranchised for having bought salt from a foreign merchant without having rendered a third part of the purchase to the common attorneys. It would appear that he was re-instated on the same day, being restored to favour on payment of 6s. to the common coffer. On 14 September 1593 he was elected alderman and, in 1598, selected deputy portreeve. When in pursuance of his duties as deputy portreeve he attempted to arrest one Morgan ap Owen for unruly behaviour, he was physically assaulted for his pains. He and his wife Johan were involved in 1601 in a pew dispute with one Edward Morgan, gentleman, and his wife Mary. This quarrel was submitted to arbitration and the judgement was that both parties should be reconciled and jointly occupy the pew in question. John Moris, as befitted a gentleman of means, lived in considerable style in what would appear to have been a fairly substantial and well-appointed house.

Finally, certain legacies were to be divided outright among the poor. Thomas ap Thomas of Cheriton in Glamorgan bequeathed on his death bed five shillings to the poor of Swansea 'which was distributed accordingly (unto the church poor of the said town) by Francis After & Owen Donnell, collectors for the poor with the overseers' consent'.

In 1601 a very famous Poor Law Act was passed which, notwithstanding later changes, determined the main features of poor law administration until the passing of the Poor Law Amendment Act in 1834. But the principles of 1601 were all enshrined in an earlier act of 1598. Parishes became responsible for the care of the poor and a very important distinction was drawn between the able-bodied vagabonds and those who were old and impotent. The former were to be set to work in a house of correction or the gaol, while the latter were to be provided with relief, either by alms or by supplying them with stocks of hemp, wool, and similar material to work on. For this category of poor, parishes could build 'convenient houses of dwelling'. Poor children were to be apprenticed and begging was made illegal. The scheme was to be financed by the imposition of a compulsory rate on householders and it was to be administered by officers, known as overseers, appointed by the justices.

At Swansea the earliest recorded instance of the nomination of overseers and collectors for the poor occurred in a Leet Court held in October 1609. Two overseers and two collectors were then chosen by the portreeve with the consent and assent of the aldermen and burgesses. This seems to indicate that there was a time lag of eight years between the enactment of the legislation and its implementation in the town. There are two possible explanations for this: one is that the system of poor relief already in operation at Swansea was, until then, quite adequate to meet the needs of the poor; or else the town council was lax in its attitude towards the enforcement of the law. Certainly, in January 1630/31, the government's concern at the apparent 'neglect' of poor law legislation relating to vagabonds, the binding of apprentices, and the provision of work and relief in parts of the Kingdom, found expression in the issuing of a Book of Orders by which the Privy Council attempted to secure a far more efficient application of the law. This action had immediate results at Swansea, as is indicated by the following entry in the Common Hall Book in 1631: 'Whereas there came lately from the King's majesty a special command through the whole Kingdom with certain orders & articles to be observed towards the punishing of rogues and wandering persons, as also for maintaining of poor people in every parish at work & for placing of poor children prentices, we the portreeve & aldermen, with consent of one of the justices and overseers of the poor, have within our town on the 7th day of June 1631 placed and set forth these children, whose names are under written, prentices according to the statute in that case provided per me John Williams portreeve'.

There followed a list of poor children who were placed as apprentices with various craftsmen in the town. David Thomas, the son of Thomas Gibb, was apprenticed with David Thomas, a glover, for nine years, while Owen Thomas, the son of Thomas Owen, was placed apprentice with John Daniell for the same length of time. With the apprentice there was invariably given a sum of money to provide him or her with clothes. When Anne William, the daughter of William Toocker, was bound apprentice with Owen Morice for seven years, the corporation gave him 'towards her clothes the sum of ten chillings', and when Phillip Thomas, the son of Thomas David, was placed an apprentice with Thomas John Prichard, a hooper, there was given the master 'towards his clothes the sum of twenty shillings'. In 1634, the Swansea rate toward the relief of poverty amounted to 23s.11½d. weekly.

It can be declared with a reasonable degree of confidence that persistent mass pauperism was unknown at Swansea. The poor law regulations sat lightly on the shoulders of the inhabitants. Where vagrancy and mendicancy showed their heads, they were to a very large extent due to some temporary and extraneous factor, such as the unauthorised landing of destitute Irish fleeing from famine to unwatched creeks on the Pembrokeshire coast. Many of these found their way to Swansea and their appearance must have been rather pitiful because they invariably stirred the civic conscience sufficiently to receive financial assistance from the corporation chest as they passed through the town. It would appear also that these migrants did not move singly around the country but rather in droves. In 1647/8 the portreeve ordered seven shillings to be paid to three women and five children who had come from Ireland, while in 1654/5 two shillings and six pence was paid to ten Irish people 'for their quarters'.

When a study is undertaken of the provision made by the corporation for such essentials as public health and education, it is essential to judge the town council by sixteenth and not by twentieth-century standards, and disabuse our minds entirely of modern conceptions of the nature of local government. Only the minimum of provision was made for such essentials; the corporation was far more concerned with the more profitable aspects of town life such as the port and the market. However, the town authorities were not entirely neglectful of their responsibilities towards the general body of inhabitants, and this is demonstrated by the attempts made to safeguard the purity of the water supply, to clean and pave the streets and, finally, repair the fabric of the school.

The concern of the corporation over the cleanliness of the water supply was fully justified, since wives and servants were in the habit of washing clothes, skins and the entrails of freshly killed animals near or in the town well. Consequently, in 1553, it was enjoined that 'no woman nor servants shall wash any manner of clothes, skins, innards of beasts, or any other filth near to any winch or well in this town where that people use to fetch water to dight their meat'. Furthermore, it was this fear of drinking contaminated water which partly accounted for the wealthier citizens drinking wine in such abundance. It was certainly nicer to the taste; but it was also far safer.

Again, the corporation was naturally concerned about the standard of cleanliness of the streets, the market, where one would expect a great deal of rubbish to accumulate, and streets and lanes converging on it. All came in for some attention. Furthermore, this was an age when water closets were unknown and householders would have disposed of filth by simply throwing it into the streets. The corporation attempted to tackle this vexed problem by employing people to clean them, prohibiting the winnowing of corn on them, and by ensuring that certain sections of the streets, at least, probably the most frequented, were paved. From the Common Attorneys' Accounts something is learnt about the disbursements for achieving the very desirable goal of keeping the streets clean and the following are characteristic of them:

> Item paid to Anes Lovid for making clean the market and lane to wind street viii*d*.
> Item paid to Alse William for making clean the market and lane iiii*d*.

Street Scene in an Elizabethan Town

Paid to Alles Rees for making clean of the way as goeth to the strand ii*d*. a week  16*d*.
paid to Morgan Gibbon for making clean the street by Thomas William Bevan's house  vi*d*.

A further degree of cleanliness was ensured by regulations relating to the winnowing of corn and disposal of waste. In a by-law of 1553 it was ordered that no man, woman or servant should winnow corn in Wind Street, Fisher Street, St. Mary Street, the market place and the 'above town within the north gate' on pain of a fine of 4d. for every such transgression. Corn, having been harvested in fields adjacent to the town, would have been stored in barns within the town walls and then winnowed in these streets, possibly because they had the advantage of being paved. This practice would have alarmed the town council not only because of the health hazard involved since it would have attracted rats in large numbers to areas in the centre of the town—and rodents were among the main carriers of disease and plague—but also it would have constituted a nuisance by impeding movement along these roads when the operation was in progress. Furthermore, the chaff would have proved an annoyance because it would have been carried on the wind into people's homes.

In the same code of by-laws it was further stipulated that 'no man nor woman nor their servants shall not (throw) no dung nor filth of their houses or streets in any place (on) the strand side, except they cast it without the marks that shall be limited to them by the portreeve & aldermen & that no person cast any filth in the gardens in fisher street, except they cast it over the bank to the ca . . . ell nor th(at) no person cast any filth in the town ditch without the sou(th) gate and all this doing in pain of a mercement of iiid a . . . every default doing to be paid incontinent'. By enjoining where filth was to be disposed, the corporation went some way towards combating the spread of disease, because undoubtedly one of the main causes of the frequency and virulency of plagues among urban communities was the accumulation and putrefaction of filth in the streets.

Finally, the corporation attempted to improve the cleanliness of the streets by securing that sections of them, at least, were paved otherwise they would have become deeply rutted under the weight of traffic and these holes would have been filled with water and decaying matter. Entries in the accounts of the borough treasurers, the common attorneys, relate to payments being made to the pavier and his assistant for work done in this respect. The following are representative of entries of this kind:

paid the pavier for to pave against George Smith house   vs.
paid William Thomas for the paving by the corner house going to church   xd.

paid to the pavier for paving of the both lanes by Saint Telinds
xxxxs. xd.
paid the pavier for 65 yards of work done by St. Johns church at id. per yard February 25th.     vs. vid.
paid for 3 days work to a man for to serve him     is. iid.

Together with the informal and very practical education possible to children through the system of apprenticeship, there was also available a more formal education by attendance at school. Regrettably a few tantalising glimpses only are provided by the extant records, and it has not been possible to construct more than a vague outline of the nature of the establishment. It would have been most stimulating and instructive to have ascertained who was educated there and what they were taught. Even if the corporation had not provided the school itself—and there are no records of any payments having been made by the common attorneys to a schoolmaster, in which case the school could have been either a private or an endowed grammar school—the town council had still assumed responsibility for the maintenance of the fabric. Instruction was provided 'in the town house' and, in 1631, 2s.6d.

A Tudor Schoolroom

was spent on nails to repair the stairs. In the same year a further 6d. was paid to 'Thomas John, cooper, for setting up of the bench in the hall & mending the loft & fastenings of the posts of the stairs of the school house'. From this entry it may be inferred that the school consisted of a main room or hall, where the children would have been taught sitting on benches, and a loft reached by a stairway. The loft could have been used either for storage, in which case a ladder only would have sufficed, or as a dormitory, and it is tempting to speculate whether the scholars, all or just a few, were boarders. The school was in existence in Elizabeth's reign and possibly even earlier. In 1584, the master, who evidently occupied a house owned by the church, paid 3s. rent to the churchwardens. The schoolmaster's wages, on the other hand, could have been derived from one of two sources: the endowment of the founder or payment by the pupils.

However, despite the presence of the school, many, possibly most, of the inhabitants of the town, burgesses and the very poor alike, were illiterate and when occasion demanded that they append a signature to a document, they had to resort to the device of simply making their marks. When, in 1624, David ap Owen and John ap Owen became jointly responsible that David Howell of Neath would not become a burden on the town, both made their marks. In 1631, David Thomas, a glover, put his cross to the agreement which bound David Thomas, the son of Thomas Gibb, an apprentice to him for nine years.

Though the corporation was mainly concerned with the business aspects of town life, and made the minimum provision for such essentials as public health and education, smaller amenities, which helped to break the monotony of what must have been for most a humdrum existence, were not entirely neglected. Among the spectator sports, and undoubtedly the most popular entertainment of all, were the brutal practices of bull-baiting and cockfighting. At Swansea, bull-baiting was officially sanctioned by the corporation until as late as 1769. No butcher could kill a bull which had not been baited on pain of a fine graduated according to the size of the animal, and it was a generally held view that baiting the animal before it was slaughtered helped to improve the quality of the meat.

The Social Scene                                    113

Intriguing insights into the preparation of the bull-ring, and the harness used, are provided by the accounts of the common attorneys:

paid to William Thomas, mason, for digging, paving and setting up of the bullring                                    x*d*.
paid to John Letten for making a swivel and the buckle for the collar of the bull                                    x*d*.
paid for a block to set the bull ring and the holing of the block
                                                                iiii*d*.
paid Mr Francklen for a rope for the collar of the bull xviii*d*.
paid to Mr Francklen for a rope towards the bull baiting cont(aining) 9li ½ in weight                                    iii*s*.

Equally horrific was cockfighting. The fighting birds had their beaks filed to a sharp point, and razor sharp spurs were strapped to their legs. Occasionally it was a conflict between a single pair of birds; at other times twenty or more would be pitched into the ring together and allowed to fight until only one remained alive. In so many respects it was a cruel age, and this particular blood sport would have attracted a large following among the town population despite the silence of the town records about it all.

For less violent moods there were games like bowls and tennis, but these would have been leisure activities associated with the more well-to-do elements in town society. At Swansea the bowling greens appear to have been at the Burrows, for a Rosser Vaughan, in his answer to a bill of complaint of one Hopkyn Vaughan, declared that when the alleged assault on the complainant took place, he was walking down St. Mary's street 'minding to go towards the Burrows there adjoining to play at bowls'.

In this Star Chamber case a fleeting glimpse is caught of a Swansea gentleman, Humphrey Lloyd—in whose employ, incidentally, Hopkyn Vaughan was to be found—playing tennis 'in his shirt out of his doublet'. Unlike tennis today, which is played mostly out of doors, at this period the game would appear to have been played indoors by persons who would have belonged to the upper classes.

Games like cards and dice were also very popular and were recreations which were shared by all classes in the community.

Recreations

However, they were frowned upon by Tudor governments because of the craze for gambling associated with them which led to many a gentleman's undoing. They were also condemned by the Welsh bards since they bred 'anger and cursing, debility and killing, and fighting among men'. Significantly, Hopkyn Vaughan, the defendant mentioned in the Star Chamber case, had contended that he had been assaulted while he was engaged in a game of cards in the kitchen of Rosser Vaughan's house at Llansamlet. The popularity of dice was such that many a gentleman's house contained a dice table. Among the goods listed in the inventory of Philip Mansell, a gentleman, whose valuation for probate purposes when he died in 1625 was £107.10s.0d., were a 'pair of playing tables'. These games, together with chess and backgammon, would have helped to while away many a long winter evening.

It had been the practice at Swansea to give each burgess a shilling on 24 May and 5 November and this quaint custom survived until 1737 when, owing to its 'inconvenience', it was abolished by the corporation and replaced, on both dates, by a bonfire and the dispensing of ale and wine in the market place. Drummers, at the town's expense, were also to be present. The total amount to be expended in this way was not to exceed fifty shillings.

Perhaps not the least acceptable feature of corporation life were the feastings and junketings at Michaelmas and Easter, and on the occasions of the perambulation of the borough boundaries. In an age denied the benefits of the ordnance survey map, the perambulation of the boundaries was a prime necessity and was an occasion for high festivity paid for from the corporation chest. Beer, particularly, was quaffed in huge quantities. The expenditure on food and ale in 1620 was as follows:

> It(em) for a barrel of beer which went to meet the town in their p(er)ambulation the Rogation week     xs.
> It(em) for bread     xviiid.
> It(em) paid for the porters to carry the beer     xviiid.

On 25 May 1625 nine shillings were spent on 'bread and cheese and beer to go to the parish the rogation week'.

The corporation also patronised the English travelling companies which occasionally visited the town and used the town hall for the presentation of their art. The entertainment was paid for by the town which also received compensation from the company when windows were broken. The smashing of the hall windows can be accounted for in two ways: either the audience was unruly or the entertainment was knockabout. The following are typical of the entries relating to these players to be found in the accounts:

> 1619 paid to John Scott and Jeames Leaighten     iis. vid.
>    more paid to the rest of their company     xviiid.
> 1622 Received of the stage players towards the hall windows     is.

1624/25 Rece(ived) of the stage players the viiith of January towards the mending of the windows     vi*d*.

From the town records it would appear that the general tenor of life at Swansea was fairly even and uneventful. However, sporadic outbreaks of lawlessness and violence provided stormy, albeit brief, interludes. Though the accession of the Tudors had ushered in more stable times, habits of disorder were still prevalent and died hard. People were only too ready to resort to the blade rather than to the law for the settlement of disputes. The Star Chamber case which follows demonstrates that the streets of Swansea must have echoed at times to the sounds of strife even though depositions made to the court have to be accepted with caution. They cannot be taken at face value because, without exception, they were partisan and often violently sensational.

On 20 July 1581, while going about his work in his shop at Swansea, William Thomas, a saddler, was threatened by a group of men armed with forest bills, swords and daggers among whom he recognised William Harrys, Owen ap Penry, Harry William and John Penry. They attempted to provoke him into coming out into the street by insulting him and his wife. This subterfuge having failed, they ran to his mare which was standing before the shop door and, having removed the 'car[6] or shed upon her ready to be sent to fetch wood', they beat the inoffensive animal with their bills and swords. Pity must have brought the wife forth because they now assaulted and beat her. Despite this outrage the husband still refused to be drawn, and perceiving that by no means could they entice him out of his shop, they left. William Thomas immediately reported the incident to one of the town constables, Howell John Richard, desiring him to apprehend them so that they could be brought before the portreeve and bonds taken from them to keep the peace. The constable promptly arrested two of the wrongdoers, William Harrys and Owen Penry. However, before they could appear before the portreeve, they were freed by the other constable, Owen John Sadler, who declared that he would answer for them. The outcome of this case is not known but the incident

[6] Cart. Garevians called it a 'car' or 'carr'.

serves to illustrate vividly the heights to which passions could rise and how near the surface violence lurked.

The developments which had occurred in the town's economy, together with its social structure, and the relations between the social classes, were bound to exercise a powerful effect on the organisation of municipal life. Social and economic conditions largely shaped the framework and personnel of town government and the changes brought about within it during this period. It is to this aspect of the town's life that attention will now be paid.

# Chapter Four

## MUNICIPAL GOVERNMENT, 1485–1640

*'Whoso desireth to discourse in a proper manner concerning Corporated towns and Communities must take in a great variety of matter, and should be allowed a great deal of time and Preparation.'*
(Madox: *Firma Burgi*: 1726)

Swansea, by virtue of a combination of favourable topographical factors, charters granted by some of its lords, and the resolve and courage of its townspeople, had emerged from the Middle Ages with a corporation possessing valuable property rights and exclusive privileges which the council continued to champion long after every justification for them had vanished. During the period 1485-1640 further developments of great significance took place. Some of these were responses to national legislation like the Acts of Union; others stemmed from the continued economic advance of the town. It is on the nature and significance of these developments that attention will now be focused.

In the late fifteenth century the Somerset family had come into possession of the lordship of Gower. Charles Somerset, the illegitimate son of Henry Beaufort, had, in 1492, married Elizabeth the daughter and heiress of William Herbert, the second Earl of Pembroke, who had died in possession of the lordship in 1491. It was not, however, until 1504 that Somerset adopted *jure uxoris* the title of Baron Herbert of Raglan, Chepstow and Gower. In 1514, as a reward for his valour in battle at Tournay, he had been made Earl of Worcester. It was his eldest son, Henry Somerset, the second earl, who, in 1532, on payment of the sum of three hundred marks, granted a charter to Swansea which was practically a confirmation of the one granted by de Breos in 1306. The town desired this charter, even though it was mainly a confirmation of one granted in the Middle Ages, because it had come under the control of this new noble house which might not recognize the rights and privileges bestowed by an earlier lord. Consequently, in seeking another charter, Swansea was, in effect, once again seeking legal incorporation, a very general characteristic of the history of towns in the sixteenth century. A charter was the hallmark of a self-governing urban community; it was an instrument which defined its precise rights and privileges and made them secure. But this charter is a most significant document in other ways. In the first place, it clearly demonstrated the continued hold of the lord over the town. Many towns, as a result of the decay of feudalism and the disappearance of the class of feudal barons, had emerged from the Middle Ages freed from the control and exactions of their overlords. This was not so with Swansea. Despite the fact that the charters granted to it in the Middle Ages had conferred on it valuable rights and privileges, the lord had never relinquished his hold on the town. It was the centre of his lordship and, consequently, he could hardly be expected to surrender all his rights in his own 'capital'. This control he continued to exercise in the sixteenth century and this charter is confirmation of that fact. By it, Henry, Earl of Worcester, gave authority to his steward to exclude from the town, if it was so desired by the portreeve and burgesses, all those artificers and handicraftsmen who did not reside there. Furthermore, he authorized the appointment of two new minor officers. The charter declared that 'the portreeve of the said town for the time being shall elect and (ap)point two burgesses of the said town to search all such tanned leather as shall come to the said town, or shall be tanned in the said town, so that the said burgesses may see the said tanners have no leather but that shall be good, able, and lawful upon the pain of the forfeiture of the same leather so insufficient, and the tanner also to forfeit for every hide so insufficiently tanned vi*s*. viii*d.* the one half of the said forfeiture to the use of the said Earl, and the other to the use of the common coffer of the said town of Swansea'.

Secondly, the charter seems to indicate that there had been a revival of prosperity in the town following that contraction in economic activity in the late fourteenth and fifteenth centuries which had followed in the wake of the Black Death and the subsequent plagues. Three hundred marks was a very substantial amount of money and the townspeople would have had to be prosperous before they could have afforded to raise such a capital sum.

Within a few years of Worcester's charter came the Acts of Union of 1536/43, which markedly influenced the municipal development of Swansea in the sixteenth century. The consequences of the union policy of Henry VIII and his chief minister, Thomas Cromwell, can be discerned in four directions: first, it made unnecessary the existence of Swansea as a garrison town; second, the doors were thrown wide open to the admission of the Welsh; third, the burgesses were granted the right to participate in the election of members to Parliament; and finally, a new significance was given to the influence of the lord within the borough.

The Acts of Union made irrelevant the existence of Swansea as a fortress town because by this legislation marcher lordships were abolished and, consequently, their former capitals were no longer required. These quasi-kingdoms were merged into the realm and turned into shires. Some were attached to existing shires, both English and Welsh, thereby enlarging their boundaries, while others went to create entirely new ones. In addition, the acts gave the Welsh equality with the English since they were to enjoy the same rights and privileges as those enjoyed by any other citizen of the realm. Consequent upon this legislation, those boroughs which had been founded as mere appendages to castles, and whose primary function remained, with these, to 'rivet the shackles of Norman domination upon a subject people', decayed in the changed conditions. George Owen of Henllys, a late sixteenth-century observer, put the matter very succinctly when he said, in 1598, that 'such of those towns as stood convenient either to serve as a throughfare or a convenient place for a market town or else had some good port or harbour fit for trading by sea, those towns fell to some good trade and so flourished and doth yet uphold themselves in some reasonable wealth, the rest being placed in wild and obscure places inapt for any trade fell into ruin and utter decay'. Some of the Glamorgan boroughs illustrate quite clearly the truth of these generalizations. Cardiff, as late as 1796, was chiefly an agricultural centre for the surrounding districts; Cowbridge had no trade or manufactures; Llantrisant had also decayed, and so had

Kenfig. Aberavon, in the third decade of the sixteenth century, was a 'poor village'. However, it so happened that Swansea was well situated from the standpoint of trade and commerce and as the hub of the economic life of the seignory of Gower. Although Swansea, as a result of the Acts of Union, had lost its importance as a garrison town, a second line of defence against the Welsh—a military function that had been diminishing since the ending of the Welsh wars in the thirteenth century—the fact that it had donned a new mantle as a thriving seaport and agricultural centre was a positive guarantee against any likelihood of decay.

Another effect of the Acts of Union was that the floodgates were thrown wide open for Welshmen to enter the towns. The penal legislation of Henry IV still remained on the statute book but it was entirely superseded. Letters of denizenship were no longer necessary, for Welshmen now obtained full rights of citizenship. Henceforth, they could participate freely in the corporate life of the towns both of Wales and of England and these acted like a magnet. The process had in fact begun during the later Middle Ages when the Welsh had been entering Swansea to fill the vacuum caused by the sharp decline in its original population. By the early sixteenth century they may well have formed the numerically preponderant element in the population. The union legislation would not only have legalized an existing situation but it would also have provided a further considerable fillip to Welsh immigration into the town.

The Acts of Union also enabled Swansea to participate in the election of burgesses to Parliament, so that the town gained at least an indirect representation at Westminster. In the 1536 legislation it was laid down that each shire should be represented by one knight, while each shire town, with the exception of Harlech, the county town of Merioneth, should be represented by one burgess. These members of Parliament were to be paid, the knights receiving 4s. daily and the burgesses 2s. Furthermore, the burgesses' wages were to be levied not only on the shire towns, but also on 'all other ancient boroughs', although these had no voice in the election; an obvious injustice which was remedied in 1543. A system of 'contributory boroughs', entirely peculiar to Wales, thus came into existence, and willingness to contribute to the members' wages no doubt determined what persons were entitled to vote and which boroughs were to participate in the elections. The election of the representatives was 'to be in the manner Form and Order as Knights and Burgesses of the Parliament be elected and chosen in other shires of this Realm'. But while it was easy for the counties to proceed with elections in the same manner as in England, the boroughs were faced with a more difficult task. The county franchise of England had been made uniform by the forty shilling freeholder act of 1430, so that the county constituencies in Wales had a standard franchise which they could adopt. In the English boroughs, on the other hand, a multiplicity of franchises had already appeared before this date, and it is obvious that this point was overlooked in the legislation which conferred on Wales the privilege of parliamentary representation. In the boroughs the franchise became invariably a freeman franchise, the right of election being vested in the burgesses duly admitted through the four avenues of birth, marriage, apprenticeship, and gift. In Glamorgan the borough groupings appear to have been fixed from the very beginning. Here the 'ancient boroughs', which shared with Cardiff, the shire town, in the election of burgesses, were those of Cowbridge, Llantrisant, Kenfig, Aberavon, Neath, Swansea, and Loughor; and in all the right to vote was vested in the duly elected freemen.

Some light on the nature of Swansea's contribution towards the payment of members' wages is shown by a receipt for £3, dated 27 August 1587, received by William Fleming, the portreeve, from Gabriel Lewis, deputy sheriff of Glamorgan, being the sum rated upon the town to defray the expenses of George Lewis, the sitting member at that time, for two sessions. The total amount due from the eight boroughs appears to have been £17.12s.01d. In 1593, 26s.8d. was rated upon Swansea towards the member's allowance and again this sum was paid by the portreeve to the deputy sheriff of the county, on this occasion one Marmaduke Mathew. These notices of payments being made in the late sixteenth century to the representatives of the Glamorgan boroughs are of special interest since the practice was being discontinued in England at this time.

On the other hand, they appear to have ceased where the county was concerned. In a letter written by Henry, Earl of Pembroke, from Wilton to his cousin, Sir Edward Stradling of St. Donat's in Glamorgan, exhorting him to whip-up support among the freeholders there for the election of his brother-in-law, Robert Sidney, as knight of the shire, he declared that Sidney, if successful, would 'demand no charges of the country at all'.

Finally, the Acts of Union gave a new significance to the influence of the lord within the town. The class which desired membership of Parliament, the gentry, had come to regard the manipulation of the boroughs which shared in the return of members as their chosen field of activity, and the constitutional history of the boroughs in the early modern period largely revolves around the methods which they employed to control them. At Swansea there were three ways in which the electorate could be managed: by controlling borough appointments; limiting the number of burgesses; and by the mass creation of non-resident burgesses. In the town, during this period, the operation of the first two methods can be discerned.

All corporate appointments at Swansea were made in the manorial court leet of the lord which was presided over by the steward and portreeve. The fact that the steward was the nominee of the lord enabled the latter to exercise a considerable influence in the court, since the steward was responsible not only for swearing in the new officers and the duly admitted burgesses, but the responsibility for the final selection of the portreeve and, in all probability, of the other borough officers as well, also rested with him. On the face of things it would appear that the steward's role was limited to confirmation of the burgesses' choice. In reality, his influence, especially in the sixteenth century, would have gone much deeper than this, and it is certain that the burgesses would not readily have appointed any officers, or admitted any burgesses, not acceptable to him. The authority of the steward is further strikingly demonstrated in that, at least until 1569—after this date it does not appear that the steward's consent was necessary before a by-law could be put into effect—no regulations introduced by the corporation could be enforced without his permission. There is still extant a petition from the burgesses to the steward, Sir George Herbert, containing a copy of several ordinances which, on 1 October 1548, are said to have been made by the aldermen with the consent of the steward as 'their chief head and governor'. The petitioners beseech him for the sake of 'charity & for God's love' that the laws might be put into force. Again, in 1553, the by-laws introduced in that year, were 'devised by John Fleming, portreeve of the town of Swansea, by the assent and consent of his brethren of the said town, by and through the advice & counsel of the Right Worshipful Sir George Herbert Knight, steward of the said town, for the common weal of the said town and the inhabitants of the same'.

Another method of controlling the electorate at Swansea was by limiting the number of burgesses. The fact that the town was already under the control of a manorial lord who had a constitutional right of interference in its affairs must have greatly facilitated the task of controlling the voters, who were generally quite willing to accept the guidance of the lord or his agent in political matters. The interests of the lord and the burgesses seem to have coincided to a remarkable degree; the lord wished to limit the electorate, for the smaller the body of burgesses the easier it was to control; the burgesses could readily agree with this policy because the material benefits which went with burgess-ship were correspondingly increased. Since Swansea was destined to develop into a considerable industrial centre and to increase steadily in population, the contrast between the narrow exclusiveness of the corporation, on the one hand, and the material growth of the town, on the other, became more and more obvious. At the same time, the actual value of the exclusive privileges to the members of the narrow circle of burgesses increased in proportion to the growth of the town's wealth.

It was by the employment of these two methods that the lord had been able to control the town electorate and, as far as the corporation records reveal, there was not a single instance of the mass creation of honorary and usually non-resident burgesses for election purposes. The classic illustration of this practice in Wales was the Caernarfon constituency, where hundreds of non-resident freemen were regularly admitted on the eve of elections. One of the reasons for this was the appreciation by the burgesses that the fewer they were in number, the greater would be the material benefits which would come their way. The full import of this is only appreciated when it is realized that the enjoyment of privileges was an essential feature of corporate life. It may be as well now to indicate their general character.

Perhaps the most important of the privileges enjoyed by the burgesses was freedom from the payment of tolls. These included quayage, wharfage and market dues, tolls on goods brought into the town by land or sea by non-burgesses and levied upon all manner of commodities. These dues had been imposed since the Middle Ages. The income from this source naturally tended to vary from time to time but, with the growth and increasing prosperity of the town, the tendency was for it to increase. In 1553 the corporation agreed on the new tolls to be imposed on merchandise entering the town, and the document is particularly interesting as an indication of the products sold there. These included wines, iron, fruit, apples, salt, pitch and tar, oakum, honey, herrings, white fish, hakes, linen cloth, woollen cloth, calf skins, corn, timber, beef, mutton, pork, cheese, horses, mares, and haberdashery items.

From this source it also becomes evident that cattle were occasionally driven through the borough, because 8*d*. was charged on 'every score of beasts that goeth through the town'. This undoubtedly is an oblique reference to the activities of the drovers (*porthmyn*) who, having gathered together the store cattle available in Gower, and having had them shod, would then have shipped them across the Bristol Channel in large numbers to the West Country. There the cattle would have been sold in local fairs and at Bristol. Following sale they would have been slaughtered to feed the ever expanding population of that thriving city, by far the largest in western England, with a population of some 12,000 by 1600 and, by virtue of that fact, itself a major consumer of agricultural produce from south Wales.

Finally, among the list of tolls, there was keelage, dues on all vessels entering or leaving the harbour, and the assize of ale, a tax on all public houses within the borough. Since there would have been many of the latter they would undoubtedly have been the source, even inspiration, of many a drunken brawl.

To this category of privileges also belongs the careful insistence on the right of exclusive trading within the borough. The burgesses enjoyed a monopoly on trade as well as a monopoly on goods. In his charter to the town of 1532, confirming an earlier one granted by de Breos, Henry, Earl of Worcester, had undertaken to exclude, at the request of the corporation, all artificers who practised 'cutting and carving', with the exception of smiths and tailors, unless they were inhabitants of the town and thus, presumably, burgesses.

Since, during the Middle Ages, the burgesses had been forced to defend their dearly-won privileges against the tyranny of lords like the de Breoses, it was only natural that they should wish to exclude 'interlopers' or foreigners from the more profitable aspects of town life. In 1569 the corporation introduced an ordinance which tightened still further its hold over the production and sale of goods within its jurisdiction. By this by-law it was stipulated that non-burgesses were not to follow any craft, or open any shop, in the borough unless they had been specifically licensed to do so by the portreeve and aldermen. Failure to comply with this injunction would result in the levying of a fine of 5s. weekly, one half to be paid to the lord and the other half to the town. The practice of fining non-burgesses for infringement of this rule was followed until the close of the seventeenth century; and graduated lists of fines, rated according to the value of the privilege to individual chensers, occasionally appear in the borough records until 1695.

Equally important, at least until the close of the sixteenth century, was the insistence on communal trading. By an ordinance of November 1553 burgesses were not permitted to board a vessel before the portreeve had ascertained what merchandise she carried and until he had entered the custom. The merchant, furthermore, was not to sell his goods to any 'foreigners' but only to burgesses for the space of fifteen days. After the expiration of the fifteen days he could 'carry away his ware at his pleasure'.

In August 1555 there was a further definition of this privilege. The council now stipulated that all merchandise brought by sea, with the exception of such perishable products as wine and salt, should be conveyed immediately to the town house or hall, there to remain until a third part had been disposed of among the burgesses. It was further laid down that commodities bought by a burgess from a foreign merchant had first to be offered for sale to the burgesses. Only after they had been satisfied could these goods be offered for sale generally. The penalty for any breach of these regulations was severe; the guilty party was to be disfranchised.

The penalty to which the burgess was liable for offending against these regulations, that of 'discommoninge' or disfranchisement, was one of much severity for it involved the loss of all the privileges attached to the freedom and reduced the offender to the status of a foreigner, a person from outside the borough. A penalty as draconian as this was necessary because some, at least, of the burgesses resorted to the most dubious practices in order to evade these by-laws. Some attempted to buy surreptitiously from a foreign merchant without delivering a third part of their purchases to the town; others bought through the agency of their wives in the fond hope, presumably, that their actions did not come within the purview of the regulations. They also resorted to the practice of delivering the thirds to the common attorneys at a higher price than that at which these had been originally bought. And finally, there were those among the burgesses who sold their commodities at a profit at Neath without first having offered a third part for sale at Swansea. The corporation officials, however, appear to have been vigilant and quite zealous in the performance of their duties and the illicit activities of the burgesses were usually detected and brought to light.

A burgess who had been disfranchised was not thereafter forever debarred from gaining re-admission to the freedom. He could be restored to favour on payment of a fine. On 24 September 1588, Thomas ap Ievan and John Moris were disfranchised for having bought salt from a foreign merchant without first delivering a third part of their purchase to the common attorneys. However, John Moris, a gentleman of considerable substance and standing within the community, was restored to the freedom on the same day. He atoned for his transgression by paying 6s. to the common coffer. Thomas ap Ievan had to wait considerably longer, and it was not until 14 September 1593 that he finally gained re-admission on payment of 6s.8d. to the town.

Regulations affecting the sale of merchandise brought into the harbour continued to be made at intervals by the corporation. On 15 October 1560 it was agreed by the portreeve, Roger Iankyn, and the aldermen that no burgess was to be allowed to purchase a whole cargo into his own hands. The foreign merchant was himself to retail his wares, subject of course to the former regulation that they should first be offered, under the supervision of the corporate officials, to the burgesses of the town.

The enjoyment of borough property again was strictly confined to the burgesses who alone could obtain leases of it, usually at low rentals. On 20 December 1543 John Thomas, a common attorney of the town, with the consent of the council, leased to a burgess with the very distinctive Welsh name of John ap Ieuan ap Hopkyn, arable and waste lands known as the 'Mawdelens' at Bryn Melyn. The lease was an extremely long one, for a term of 99 years, and the annual rent was 6d. In January 1547 the council leased to another burgess, Richard Yoroth, who was to become portreeve in 1561, 'one parcel of marsh ground being a parcel of our commons set and lying by west St. Ellens now being void containing by estimation six acres'. Again the lease was for 99 years and the annual rent charged was fixed at 3s.4d. William Flemying, a very substantial freeman since he was three times portreeve—in 1586, 1592 and 1601— leased for 21 years from the council in 1592 a fourth part of the meadow of Portmeade, situated in the parish of Llangyfelach and adjacent to the road leading to Loughor. For this very desirable property he paid an annual rent of 20s.

Together with the leasing of corporate lands, the council was also letting town property in its possession as well. Glimpses have been caught of miners and their families residing in dwellings leased from the corporation and in November 1583, Richard Sadler, a merchant who was to occupy the office of portreeve fifteen years later in 1598, leased from the council a cellar 'set and lying by the market place of Swansea under the town house there, adjoining of the one side unto a garden of Sir William Herbert Knight,[1] and the

[1] He was the grandson of Sir George Herbert and eldest son of Mathew Herbert of Swansea.

street called the market place of the other side'. Here is important corroborative evidence that the market was the focal point of the corporate life of the town. It was centrally positioned and adjacent to it was the town hall, where a school was also conducted. Furthermore, in close proximity also was the Place House, the residence of town stewards like Sir Matthew Cradock and Sir George Herbert, and the parish church of St. Mary's. As a trader, Richard Sadler would have needed the cellar for storage purposes. His lease was for 21 years at an annual rent of 11*s*. Other merchandise was stored in or under the town hall as well, since the thirds of all goods imported by sea into Swansea were kept there until the burgesses had made their choice of what they wished to purchase.

Together with the enjoyment of borough property, the burgesses also possessed valuable common and pasture rights. One such common was Cefn Coed, an extensive area of land extending for about a mile in length and half a mile in width and consisting of some 200 acres. Here the burgesses had 'entered common time out of mind without interruption'. The boundaries extended from St. John's in the east to the Cocket in the west, and from the Weke in the north to Pantgwyder in the south.

Such then were the privileges and rights of the burgess body and it is now appropriate that an examination should be made of the machinery by which they were administered. The essential components of the mechanism for town government were the lord, the steward, the court leet, the portreeve, a small executive council, the common hall and the vestry. Diagrammatically it can be expressed as follows:

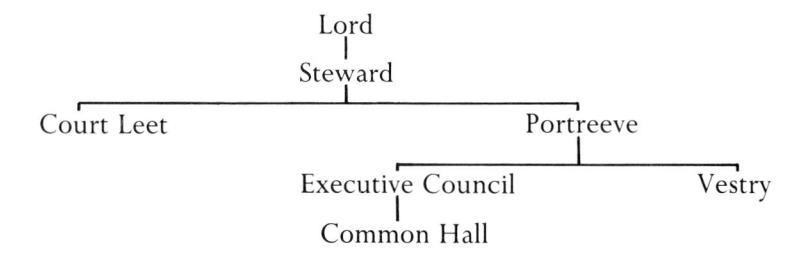

```
                     Lord
                      |
                   Steward
         ┌────────────┴────────────┐
     Court Leet                Portreeve
                         ┌────────┴────────┐
                   Executive Council     Vestry
                         |
                   Common Hall
```

During the Middle Ages the lord had never relinquished control over the town and this hold he wished to maintain for several reasons. In the first place, the town formed the 'capital' of his seignory of Gower. Secondly it was a sphere of influence to him for electoral purposes; and thirdly, and possibly most important of all, it represented a valuable source of income. Indeed, it was for this very reason that the lords of Cemais had never relaxed their hold over the little borough of Newport in Pembrokeshire. At Swansea the lord's income was derived from a variety of sources and must have amounted to a substantial sum in a year. There were rents, fines and heriots,[2] tolls on markets and fairs, assize of ale, mises and aids, and, finally, wrecks of sea and felons' goods. In 1593, of the £7.17s.10d. due from rents to the common coffer there was to be deducted for the lord's share 30s.3d. The lord was also in receipt yearly of a payment known as the burgage shilling for the various tenements lying within the town walls. At a leet court held in 1638 £40 was received by the corporation from the tenants of Portmeade by way of a fine. Of this sum Henry, Earl of Worcester, received £25 as a penalty and heriot. From Oliver Cromwell's survey of the seignory it becomes evident that the portreeve was to pay annually to the lord for tolls of markets and fairs, keelage, and other like duties the sum of 40s. 'which rate he hath time out of mind continued the possession thereof as it is affirmed'. From the same survey it appears that the portreeve was to pay yearly to the lord for assize of ale the sum of £8. Rather than suffer fluctuations in his income from tolls and taxes on ale-houses, the lord had obviously deemed it wiser to settle for a fixed income by farming out both sources of revenue to the corporation.

On certain special occasions, as when he first entered into possession of the lordship, and on the occasion of the knighting of his eldest son and the marriage of his eldest daughter, the lord was in receipt of feudal dues. In 1594, the Earl of Worcester had started proceedings against his tenants in the lordship of Gower for encroachments on the wastes and a wilful refusal to pay mises and aids. A Chancery decree of 1596 had laid down the amount of each

---

[2] Originally the rendering to the lord on the decease of a manorial tenant of the best beast; later it became commuted into a money payment.

to be paid. According to this judgement, £200 were to be paid for mises and 200 marks for aids. Towards the payment of these sums Swansea was assessed at £26.13s.4d. and £17.15s.7d. respectively.[3]

The lord was also entitled to wreck of sea and felons' goods within the liberties of the town. The vigilance of the lord and his steward concerning wrecks is admirably illustrated in the events which followed the driving aground of a French ship at Oxwich during a gale on St. Stephen's Day, 1557. France being at the time very conveniently at war with England, the Mansels and their tenants had lost no time in despoiling the ship of her goods. Sir George Herbert of Swansea, as steward of William Somerset, third Earl of Worcester, and vice-admiral of the Crown, had a lively interest in all wrecks along the Gower coast and, without consulting the Mansels, had proceeded to recover from their tenants all the commodities removed from the ship. The outcome of his action was an affray in the gateway of Oxwich castle when he and Edward Mansel, the son of Sir Rice Mansel, the lord of the manor, came to blows. As a result of this skirmish, Anne Mansel, Edward's aunt, and an innocent party to the whole proceedings, had been struck on the head by a stone thrown by Watkin John ap Watkin, one of Sir George Herbert's servants. From the wound she received, Anne Mansel shortly afterwards died. In his handling of this situation Sir George, who might well have been motivated as much by thoughts of personal gain as by devotion to his responsibilities and duties as an officer of both the Crown and the Worcesters, had considerably exceeded his authority. Sir Rice Mansel brought an action against him in the Court of Star Chamber and Herbert and his men were heavily fined. Furthermore, it was directed that they should be imprisoned in the Fleet until the fines had been paid, the confiscated property restored and reparations made for the damage they had caused. Afterwards, they were to stand trial at common law for their part in the killing of Anne Mansel. The outcome of the trial was that on 19 September 1559 a pardon was granted to Watkin John ap Watkin. This feud between the Herbert and the Mansel families was extremely bitter and caused quite a sensation at the time. Moreover, it survived the

[3] Supra, pp. 52-3.

decease of the two main protagonists by quite a few years. But though the Star Chamber case may well have ended what interest Sir George Herbert had in the fate of the ship, the continued interest of the Worcesters themselves in the wreck was to be strikingly demonstrated, as late even as 1572, in a letter which William Somerset wrote on 24 May in that year to Edward Mansel. In this letter Somerset authorized Mansel to sell the ship for him, and at the best possible price, to one David Ogan.

The lords of Swansea throughout the whole period from 1492-1640 were the succeeding members of the Somerset family: Charles Somerset (?1460-1526), first Earl of Worcester, Henry Somerset (d.1549), second earl, William Somerset (1526-1589), third earl, Edward Somerset (1553-1628), fourth earl, and Henry Somerset (c.1577-1646), fifth earl and first Marquis of Worcester. The history of the Somersets, however, lies outside the purview of this study. Men of some influence in national politics, they never themselves resided in Swansea and delegated their authority to deputies. Nevertheless, they realized the importance of choosing, as stewards, men of strong character and considerable local standing. Three of these stewards, Sir Matthew Cradock, Sir George Herbert, and Sir Thomas Mansel, were men of special eminence and are deserving of brief pen-portraits.

Sir Matthew Cradock was one of the descendants of Einion ap Collwyn and the son of Richard ap Gwilym ap Evan ap Cradock Vreichfras and Jennett Horton of Candleston castle near Newton in Glamorganshire. A daring opportunist, he was a man of considerable business acumen as well as of military and naval skill. In 1526 he had leased from Henry, Earl of Worcester, all the coal found, or to be found, in the lordship of Gower and Kilvey. The lease was for 80 years at an annual rent of £40. His skill in the arts of war on both sea and on land is amply demonstrated by the fact that in 1483, when an abortive attempt was made by Henry Tudor to overthrow Richard III, he was captain of one of Richard's warships, while in 1491 he was among those commissioned by the King to go to the lordships of south Wales to raise an expeditionary force to invade French territory. An ambitious man, he had acquisitive gifts of no mean order and, in and after 1486, office after office had fallen into

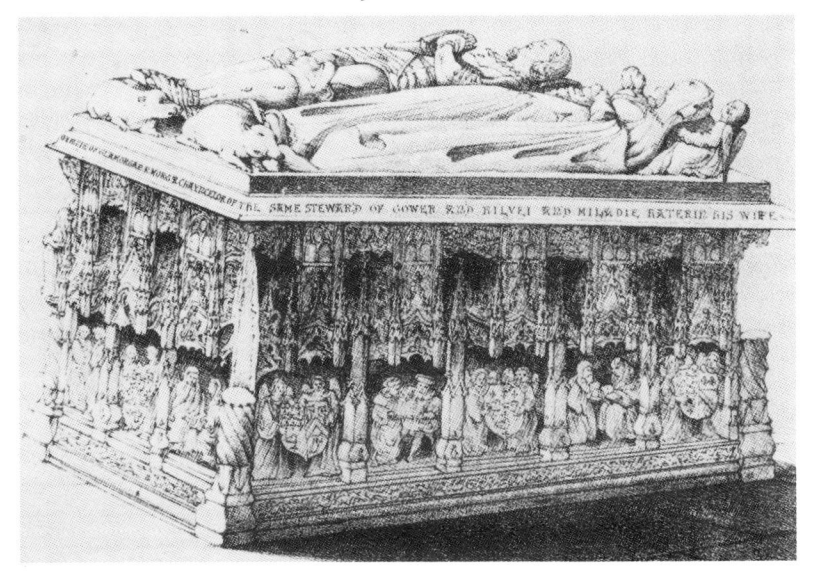

Sir Matthew Cradock's Tomb

his hands, one being the grant for life in that year of the position of constable of Caerphilly and Kenfig. Deputy steward of Gower under Jasper, Duke of Bedford, Henry VII's fraternal uncle, he had in 1506, to all intents and purposes, become steward under Charles Somerset, the first Earl of Worcester. He married twice. His first wife was Alice, the daughter of Philip Mansel of Oxwich castle, and his second was Lady Katherine Gordon, widow of Perkin Warbeck, one of the impostors who posed such a threat to Henry VII's throne. Some time between 1517-19, presumably for his loyal and devoted service to the Crown, he was knighted. He died in 1531 and was buried in St. Mary's church, Swansea, where his magnificent alabaster tomb was the most elaborate monument in the church. The tomb survived until the *blitz* of 1941 when irreparable damage was done to the stonework by the intensity of the flames which devoured the church.

A kinsman of Charles Somerset, Sir George Herbert was the second son of Sir Richard Herbert of Ewias. Possessed of a very strong personality and a fiery temper, he was a man whom it was very dangerous to affront. Descended as he was from the great Herbert clan, he was full of their pride and courage. These aspects of his character are all revealed in his conduct of affairs at Oxwich in 1557.[4] But he could also be cruel and unscrupulous, and these traits can be adduced from the circumstances surrounding the hanging by him of a boy of sixteen on the grounds that he had stolen some sheep from his father, reputedly a man of considerable wealth. The father had denied the felony but Sir George, to respite the hanging, had demanded from him a large sum of money. The father had taken the matter to the Council in Wales and the Marches, and this body had ordered Herbert to delay execution until it had made due examination of the case. Sir George, on receipt of this order, had promptly hanged the boy, and had even threatened the father with the same fate.

However, against these more undesirable aspects of his character must be placed his patronage of the bards, for he entertained in his household some of the leading poets of Glamorgan. He was also cultivated in the sense that he appreciated the visual arts and he was the proud possessor of a portrait of Lucrece painted by a contemporary artist.

Undoubtedly the most important and influential man in Swansea during his lifetime, he played a dominant role in the affairs of the town and, as befitted his exalted social status, his home was a very substantial stone edifice known as the Place House which he had inherited from his maternal grandfather, Sir Matthew Cradock. His landed possessions were considerable and a substantial proportion of these had come into his hands as a result of his acquisition of the lands of the Hospital of St. David on its dissolution in 1550. Typical of so many of the gentry of the time, Sir George was also deeply involved in the business world and he had a personal interest in developing the coal mines around Neath, for he drew a good income from the coal which he supplied as a return cargo to ships engaged in the importation of salt from the Biscayan port of La Rochelle.

By the time of his decease in 1570, he still had not paid, or paid in full, the fine imposed upon him by the Court of Star Chamber for

[4] Supra, p. 131.

his misdeeds at Oxwich, and he had attempted to frustrate the Queen in her attempts to recover the money by making deeds of gift in trust of all his possessions for the benefit of his second wife, Dame Grace Herbert.

Sir Thomas Mansel was the eldest son of Sir Edward Mansel and Jane Somerset, the daughter of Henry, second Earl of Worcester. Well known at court, he was knighted before 1593 and created a baronet on 22 May 1611, being second in precedence of the first batch of baronets created on the institution of that order by King James I. He held high office in the county of Glamorgan since he was sheriff on three separate occasions, 1593-4, 1603-4 and 1622-3, and for many years also he was a justice of the peace. It has not been possible to establish precisely when he became steward of Gower but he was certainly in occupation of that office in 1601, and retained it at least until October 1630 and possibly until his death in December 1631. For the greater part of this period he had as his deputy his brother, Philip Mansel. As a justice it would appear that he was not always too assiduous in the performance of his duties, for in 1626 he had been reprimanded by the Council in the Marches for failing to observe the wishes of that jealous and autocratic body with regard to the licensing of ale houses in Swansea. In 1628, together with Sir John Stradling of St. Donat's, he had been called upon to investigate a charge against two sailors who, it was alleged, had spread a report that the King, Charles I, was dead, poisoned by the hand of the royal favourite, the Duke of Buckingham. The following year he had been involved in a dispute concerning a vessel which had been driven ashore at Oystermouth. As justice, his duties and responsibilities were certainly diverse. He died on 20 December 1631 and was buried at Margam.

Though the stewards were responsible for safeguarding the rights and privileges of the lord, they were occasionally tempted to place their own interests before his, especially when it was to their advantage to do so. At Swansea this situation was all the more surprising since in this period the stewards were mainly recruited from the ranks of the Herberts and Mansels, who had ties of kinship with the Worcesters. In 1594, Edward, fourth Earl of Worcester, had started proceedings in the Court of Chancery against his

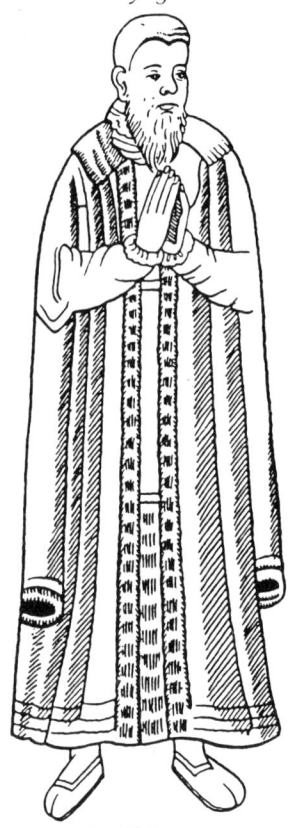

An Alderman

tenants in Gower. In his replication to the answer of Sir William Herbert, the grandson of Sir George Herbert, to the original bill of complaint, the earl stated that the 'said defendant having subtly gotten into his hands a great number of court rolls, surveys, terriers, & other evidence of right belonging to this complainant, thinks now by that means utterly to extinguish & cover all the several abuses wrought by his late ancestors who were indeed the only persons whose corruptions or negligence (being put in special trust as chief stewards of the said seignory of Gower under the ancestors of this complainant) have been the very principal ground and foundations almost of all the whole abuses there offered and executed'.

A very important function of the steward was to preside, with the portreeve, over the court leet. There were two courts leet or tourn courts held annually in the town, one in the spring on 1 May and the other in the autumn on 29 September. It was in these courts leet that the borough officers were elected and burgesses admitted to the freedom. At the October leet were chosen the portreeve, common attorneys, sergeants-at-mace, and subsidiary officials such as the constables and layer-keepers; the Easter leet witnessed the election of the stewards of the burrows and those for the mountain, and their duty was to supervise the common lands. The most important officer to be elected in the leet court was the portreeve and he was chosen in the following manner: 'Item further it is accustomed in the said town that upon every day and feast of St. Michael the Archangel the whole burgesses of the said town shall assemble themselves together and then to elect and choose by their most of voice two of the xii aldermen of the said town to be portreeve of the (town) which two being elected the lord or his steward hath to swear one of the said ii to be portreeve for the year following'. Other officers that were elected, probably in much the same way, were the constables (4), sergeants (2), layer-keepers (2), ale-tasters (2), haywardens (4), guardians of the market (2), overseers of the poor (2), and the officer for 'sealing, searching and registering of leather'. The common attorneys, who were the borough treasurers of that day, were, however, after 1549, elected by the aldermen, significantly described as the 'xii men that be named to make good order in the said town'.

The other business that was transacted in this court was the creation of burgesses. They were admitted through the four avenues of birth, marriage, apprenticeship, and gift, at the Michaelmas session of the court and on admission they had to pay a composition fee which in 1613 was fixed at 20s., a regulation, however, which was not strictly adhered to for more than a few years. It was this court leet which enabled the lord to bring influence to bear on the corporation through his agent the steward. Even though the basis of town government might appear quite democratic at first sight the presence of the steward, in whose hand were vested the powers of final selection, and of swearing in the officers, militated against anything like complete independence of action on the part of the burgesses.

The chief corporate officer for whose final selection the steward was responsible, the portreeve, exercised during his year of office functions of a most important nature. He was the coroner of the liberty; he was responsible for the distribution of bequests among the poor and, in this respect, for keeping a careful system of audit; he collected the rents and other dues payable to the lord; he presided over the leet court, over meetings of the aldermanic body and over the vestry. He imposed fines on those guilty of breaches of municipal regulations. As befitted an important dignitary of the town he was afforded extra-legal protection. This was very necessary since it is evident that he was the target for both verbal and physical abuse. In the code of by-laws drawn up in 1569 the nature of these onslaughts is made abundantly clear, since it is laid down that if any burgess or commoner misused the portreeve 'in words as to call him knave, whore's son, churl, or any other unsuitable or indecent words that then such person or persons so misusing himself to pay xxs of fine, the one half to the high lord of the said town and the other half to the common coffer of the same; and further if any of the said burgesses or commoners of the said town at any time hereafter do violently lay hand, or strike the said portreeve for the time being, that then such every offender to pay xxs apiece fine—and forthwith upon the committing of any such offence he so offending to be discommined and to lose his freedom'. A stranger, for striking the portreeve, had the fine doubled to 40s. and since, as a non-burgess, he could not be disfranchised, he suffered the further penalty of six days' imprisonment.

On one occasion only is the family of the portreeve recorded. It appears that on 1 October 1632 the leet court was held before 'Walter Thomas steward and alderman of this town, and Francis After, portreeve, son unto John After minister and preacher of God's word, and late vicar of this town of Swansea and so forth'. The portreeves were undoubtedly recruited mainly from the ranks of the gentry and the wealthier merchants; but they were also drawn, though to a lesser extent, from among the more prosperous shopkeepers, yeomen, and craftsmen of the town. Among the ranks of the gentry were such people as George Herbert,[5] Sir William Herbert and Ienkyn Francklyn; the merchants had included William Watkins, Walter Thomas, Richard Sadler and Mathew Francklen; Francis After, on the other hand, was a shopkeeper, and John David a yeoman. From among the craftsmen were recruited Rees David, a shoemaker, John Williams, a tanner, and Lewis Jones, who was a mercer. Between 1485-1640 the office was, to a very large extent, concentrated in the hands of a few of the foremost families of the town. As far as can be ascertained, the Flemyngs and Francklens during this period had each occupied the office on no fewer than eight occasions, the Sadlers, and Davids each on five, and the Williamses, in the person of John Williams, on four. Between 1607-1640 the Daniells family had held the office three times, while between 1627-1640 a Jones-Patrick Jones (3), David Jones (1) and Lewis Jones (1)—had between them occupied the office on five occasions. Though it has not been possible to establish ties of kinship between them, it is possible that some such relationship did exist.

The small executive council of twelve aldermen, over which the portreeve presided, had emerged at Swansea during the Middle Ages, though it is not until the sixteenth century that it is first discerned in action. It had evolved as an executive body as appears from the preface to a by-law of 1569, when it is stated that 'the custom and usage of the town of Swansea long before time of memory hath been that the ancient burgesses of the said town, now termed and named aldermen, from time to time have used and had authority to make and erect laws and ordinances for the well government of the public estate and wealth of the said town'. It is obviously impossible to date with mathematical exactitude the emergence of this council, which was the result of historical evolution. The burgess body must have been found rather unwieldy because of its size for the purposes of town government and the advantages of a smaller body, composed probably of the ablest, most influential and affluent from among the burgesses, must have become apparent from an early date. The twelve aldermen did not

[5] Not to be confused with Sir George Herbert.

co-opt themselves. Rather were they chosen from the ranks of the burgesses by what was, ostensibly, popular election. On 18 January 1630 'for as much as there wanted four of our full number of twelve aldermen the day above written we, whose names are subscribed, and the burgesses there then present, by most of voice have, elected and nominated for aldermen David Johns, William Daniell, Francis After, and John Daniell and were called upon the 22 day of January 1630 to the town hall before me the then portreeve and the rest of the aldermen to take their oaths of aldermanship'. Unfortunately, it seems impossible to determine how free these elections really were, but the fact that aldermen held office for life probably led to a good deal of pressure for their own election from the wealthier and more prominent burgesses.

During the sixteenth century, attendance at this council became compulsory, because in the ordinances drawn up in 1553 it was laid down that if, having been duly summoned, the aldermen failed to appear before the portreeve they should forfeit half a pound of wax. From this particular order it is unclear who should summon the aldermen, or who was responsible for collecting the fines incurred for non-attendance. These details, however, become available from a by-law of 1569 where it is apparent that while one of the sergeants was responsible for giving warning of attendance, the portreeve was responsible for the imposition of the penalty. If the portreeve himself should prove neglectful in enforcing this rule, then he was to forfeit 2s.6d. on every occasion he so offended.

Since the function of this council was to act as an executive, it was obviously desirable to maintain the full complement of twelve aldermen, otherwise the pressure of business on those that remained would have become too great. An alderman who had been absent from the town for a year and a day was dismissed from his office. In 1593, one Richard Daniel was to suffer this fate.

An alderman held office for life, though he could be deprived of this status at any time if circumstances warranted such a move. Non-residence in the borough for a year and a day was certainly regarded as justifiable cause for dismissal. But behaviour inimical to the best interests of the corporation could also lead to an alderman's downfall. In 1564, 'for certain considerations', the aldermen removed from their company John Fox and Mathew Morgan. John Fox was a merchant. In a presentment of the church goods of St. Mary's in 1549 before Sir George Herbert, the commissioner appointed by the King to oversee them, he appears as one of the wardens. However, since the accounts did not balance, and had a totally unsatisfactory appearance, the nature of the transgression which led to his undoing may well be found here. The fox had been ensnared.

Aldermen occasionally voluntarily relinquished their office for such reasons as a decline in their fortunes or some impairment of their faculties which affected their efficiency. In 1597, Robert Barrett yielded up his aldermanship on the ground of his imbecility and poverty which, he maintained, incapacitated him from executing 'anything imposed upon him'. Implicit in this statement is the assumption that wealth was an important qualification for this office.

It would appear that the executive council was, in theory at least, subject to the general burgess body, which was evidently responsible for general policy because the actions of the council seem to have required confirmation by them. When in 1573 it was determined that the aldermen should pay for one mace, and the 'commons' for the other, it was expressly stipulated that this

The Seventeenth Century Town Hall

decision had been taken by the portreeve and aldermen 'with the consent and agreement of the common burgesses of the said town'. Again in 1594 it was concluded and agreed by the portreeve and aldermen 'together with the burgesses then & there assembled' that all the ordinances entered into the Common Hall book and the Book of Orders 'tending to the public & common wealth of the said town (& not before disannulled) shall stand & continue in as good & full force & effect as the same were intended at the first making thereof'. And finally, it is learnt that in 1610 Ienkin Pugh and a merchant, Patrick Jones, were disfranchised by William John Hary, portreeve, 'and other the aldermen—together with the consent of Owen John Richard & Hary Vechan, common attorneys of the said town & the rest of the burgesses there present' for not having paid that portion of a tallage rated upon them.

The general burgess body to which the aldermanic council was responsible met in common hall. Since at Swansea there were four avenues to the freedom, the number of burgesses would have varied from time to time. They did not consist of all the male adult inhabitants of the town; rather they represented a small proportion of the whole. Though the number of burgesses at any particular time within this period is not stipulated, by taking a base year, and then collecting the names of as many burgesses as possible for a period of five years before and after this date, it has been possible to arrive at a figure which, it is hoped, will not be wildly disproportionate to their actual number at that time. By adopting this method a figure of 79 burgesses has been arrived at for the base year 1583. Since the population of the town then could hardly have exceeded 1000, the burgesses would have formed at least 8 per cent of the total population. Similarly, for the base year 1634 the names of 115 burgesses have been collected. As the population of the town stood at roughly 1638 the burgesses would have constituted 7 per cent of the population. This provides an entirely different picture from that presented by the town in the nineteenth century. In 1833 there were only 104 burgesses out of a total population of 15,621, giving a percentage ratio of only 0.7. From this it becomes evident that during the intervening centuries the corporation had become increasingly exclusive.

The burgesses—and burgess-ship was a male monopoly—were recruited from the more substantial elements of town society and particularly from the ranks of the craftsmen, shopkeepers, and merchants, with a leavening of gentry like Sir William Herbert, who was portreeve in 1580. On 15 October 1621 six persons were admitted as burgesses and in four cases the occupation is stated. Griffith John was a weaver, Howel Richard a shoemaker, John Bowen a fishmonger, and Thomas William a sailor. There were four admissions to the freedom in the autumn leet in 1628 and the trade is indicated in two instances. John Griffith was a joiner while Owen John was a feltmaker. At other leet court proceedings, tailors, tanners, mercers, dyers, millers, smiths, victuallers, carpenters, tuckers, tinkers, glovers and merchants are witnessed being admitted as burgesses.

Since the corporation had the right to admit burgesses by gift, strangers are occasionally found receiving the freedom of the town. In 1583, two Irishmen were so privileged though they were restricted from the full exercise of the rights of other burgesses. These were obviously traders for it was stipulated that they were not to convey their goods, either by horse or on their own backs, abroad in the countryside for sale, but only to fairs and markets.

As with the aldermen, a burgess who was absent from the town for a year and a day was disfranchised, unless he continued to pay his share of any tallages or taxes rated upon the town. In 1614, four burgesses were deprived of the freedom because they had decided to dwell outside the borough. The corporation pursued this policy because it held that burgesses who were continually absent from the town were not in a position to fulfil their obligations, which were enshrined in the oath which they took when they were first admitted to the freedom. By this oath the freemen promised to be true, to be obedient to the portreeve, to pay any tallages or taxes rated upon them, to maintain the privileges and liberties of the town, to acquaint the portreeve and aldermen of any developments which might endanger those liberties and, finally, to 'do all other things that becometh a true burgess for to do'. Under this last obligation were included the duties of serving in any corporate office and of keeping watch and ward. But of all these duties, the payment of tallages and the occupancy of municipal office were by far the most vital.

The tallage or town rate was assessed by four men: two drawn from among the aldermen by the portreeve, and two from among the burgesses by the common attorneys. They were to rate the inhabitants 'according to their ability'. The four assessors in turn had authority to nominate two collectors. If any person refused to pay these local taxes, then the collectors were to distrain his goods. Any attempt on his part to rescue his goods would result in his being presented at the next court and fined 3s.4d. For a burgess, however, failure to pay might well result in disfranchisement because, in 1610, Ienkin Hugh and Patrick Jones, both burgesses, were deprived of the freedom for having refused to pay the tallage rated upon them. Ienkin Hugh had been assessed at 5s. and Patrick Jones at 10s.

Only burgesses could fill municipal offices and any refusal to do so led to immediate disfranchisement. On 11 May 1611 Walter Johns, having been sworn one of the sergeants-at-mace, and refusing to execute the duties of the office, was removed from the freedom. In 1615 a similar penalty was incurred by David Morgan, a tailor. Having been appointed by the Grand Jury at a leet court to be one of the ale tasters, he had refused to take the oath.

An essential qualification for burgess-ship was marriage, for in 1563 it is expressly and quaintly stipulated in 'an order for freemen' that no man was to be made a burgess 'except he or they be first married in matrimony'. Furthermore, before any man could be made a freeman, he had to be resident in the town for a year and a day, unless he was the son of an apprentice or burgess.

The common hall then consisted of burgesses admitted through the four avenues of birth, marriage, apprenticeship, and gift, and occupied a very important position in the structure of town government. As distinct from the aldermanic council, which had responsibility for administration, the common hall controlled general policy, and the actions of the council would appear to have required its confirmation.

Together with presiding over the leet court and the aldermanic council, the portreeve also presided over the vestry, the nerve centre of the parish, which had been selected by the Tudor sovereigns and their ministers as the basic unit of local civil administration. Furthermore, he appointed and swore in the churchwardens, so that in the government of the parish the vicar appears to have been a mere cipher and his name is never more than casually mentioned in the parish and corporation records. The vestry consisted of all the parishioners, though in many places a 'select vestry' of twelve to fourteen, holding office for life, and filling vacancies by co-option, had come to represent the parish and to manage its affairs. The responsibilities of the vestry at Swansea have been discerned in several directions: in the maintenance of highways, the relief of maimed soldiers and the prisoners in the county goal, in payments to the muster master and the house of correction, and finally in the destruction of vermin.

Until the Tudor period, little attention had been paid by Parliament to the maintenance of roads, and the medieval obligation of keeping them in repair had attached itself to particular persons or corporations owning property and, in some cases, to guilds and monasteries. But the Tudors, bent as they were on commercial regeneration, could hardly afford to neglect the arteries of commerce and an act of 1555 had provided for the repair of highways, the parish being made the responsible unit. The justices of the peace were empowered to inquire into all failures to observe the law and to inflict, in Quarter Sessions, fines for default. It would appear that the vestry at Swansea frequently defaulted where the roads were concerned, since it was regularly presented in the Great Sessions Court on the ground of its 'insufficiency'. In September 1590 the parishes of Swansea, Llangyfelach and Llandeilo were presented for an unsatisfactory highway between Swansea and Pontardulais, while in September 1591 the parish of Swansea was again in trouble over its failure to maintain a satisfactory road running from Swansea to Neath and known as 'Crymlyn Water'. In the spring of 1595, as also in the spring of 1596, the town was presented on no fewer than four occasions altogether for defaulting in this respect. The distressing state of the roads in Swansea and the neighbouring parishes might well, in the main, have been attributable to the frequent and heavy loads of coal being conveyed over them to the port, though much of this would have been transported by boats down the Tawe as well.

Another responsibility of the vestry at Swansea was the relief of maimed soldiers and the prisoners in the county gaol. The justices of the peace were authorized by statute to assess upon each parish within their jurisdiction a sum of money for this purpose. Swansea's contribution toward the relief of soldiers disabled in the wars was 3s.8d. a quarter and, in the common attorneys' accounts, entries are found relating to the payment of this amount. The following are a representative selection of them:

> 1618 Item paid the petty constables towards the maimed soldiers          iiis. viiid.
> 1619 Item paid to the petty constables towards the maimed the 13th day of July          iiis. viiid.
> 1624 Item paid the 3 day of April to the high constable for the maimed soldiers          0-3-8

The town's contribution toward the relief of the prisoners in the county gaol at Cardiff, on the other hand, does not appear to have been a fixed annual sum, but fluctuated from year to year and may have been related to the number incarcerated there. These fluctuations are highlighted by the following entries taken at random from the accounts of the borough treasurers, the attorneys:

> 1617/18 Item paid the high constable by a warrant towards the relief of prisoners          0-xd.
> 1619 Item paid to the constables towards the prisoners of Cardiff          is.
> 1622/23 paid the high constable towards the relief of the poor of Cardiff Gaol          xvid.

Again, the responsibilities of the vestry may be discerned in the payments made to the muster master and the house of correction. Swansea's contribution toward the payment of the wages of the muster master was 7s.3d. annually, while the governor of the house of correction was in receipt of 4s.10d.

These houses of correction were a response to the passing of the Poor Relief Act of 1576 by which justices of the peace in Quarter

Sessions were empowered to build such establishments so that both the needy poor and those who went about begging might be put to work. The cost of erecting and 'furnishing' them was to be met by a tax levied by the justices on all the inhabitants of their several jurisdictions.

Finally, the responsibilities of the vestry may be observed in its encouragement of the destruction of vermin such as rooks, choughs, crows, foxes, and wild cats. These would have abounded during this period and, because of their numbers, represented a serious threat to corn crops and livestock. As early as 1532 it had been enacted in consequence of the 'innumerable number of rooks, crows and choughs' that every parish, township or hamlet was to provide itself with a net for their destruction, to maintain it for 10 years, and to present it annually before the manor court steward, 2*d*. to be paid for every twelve old crows, rooks or choughs by the owner or occupier of the manor or lands. In 1566, in an act for the preservation of grain, it had been provided that the act concerning rook nets should be renewed. It was further provided that the churchwardens, together with another six parishioners, should assess holders of land or tithe for the destruction of 'noyful fowls and vermin', and provide a fund to reward every person bringing 'any heads of old crows, choughs, (mag)pies or rooks, for the heads of every three of them a penny, and for the heads of every six young crows etc a penny, and for every six eggs of any of them unbroken, a penny, and likewise for every twelve star(lings) heads a penny'. The heads and eggs were to be brought before the wardens and assessors at least one a month, and an account was to be kept of the money paid for them, together with the sums paid for 'the heads of such other ravening birds and vermin'. This act was renewed in 1572 and yet again in 1598. At Swansea, the churchwardens' accounts are littered with records of payments for the destruction of such pests. The following items are typical of the payments made:

| | |
|---|---|
| for casting down of rooks nests | iii*d*. |
| paid for killing of three dozen of rooks | vi*d*. |
| to Richard Johns for the killing of a brock | xii*d*. |

| | |
|---|---|
| to one of Kilvey for the killing of a brock | xii*d*. |
| for killing of two foxes | xvi*d*. |
| paid to Morgan David for killing of a wild cat | iiii*d*. |

In the late sixteenth and early seventeenth centuries the borough became increasingly exclusive. The government of the town was in the hands of a comparatively few and, presumably, better off families who adopted a proprietorial attitude towards the other inhabitants. The burgesses and burgesses alone could fill municipal offices so that to the rest of the little community the corporation presented the appearance of a closed shop. This growing exclusiveness of the corporation was reflected in several directions: in the preoccupation of the council with the more profitable aspects of town life—the port, market and corporation estates—and in the defence of the revenues accruing from them; in the greater self-consciousness of the corporation; in class conflicts, and finally in the attitude of greater independence which the corporation adopted towards the lord by the early decades of the seventeenth century.

To understand the conduct of local affairs by a body constituted after the manner of the corporation at Swansea, it is necessary to disabuse our minds completely of modern conceptions of the nature of local government. There is but little evidence in its operations of any sense of responsibility to the population of the town as a whole, and membership of the corporation was regarded more as a privilege to be enjoyed than as a duty to be performed. Thus, only the minimum of provision was made for such essentials as public health and education. On the other hand, it has already been seen how zealous the burgesses were in promoting and regulating the business of the port and market, and how concerned they were in the defence of the revenues received from them and the corporation estates. The adverse effect of this was emphasized by the fact that the corporation wielded authority over a very wide area, for the boundaries of the borough embraced the district bounded by the Brynmill stream, the Burlais Brook, and the river Tawe, although the town itself, until the nineteenth century, was confined to a cluster of houses at the mouth and along the bank of the river. But one very valuable service provided by the corporation related to the administration of justice; for two civil courts, the court baron and court of pleas, were held on every third Monday. The first had jurisdiction over causes under 40s., while the jurisdiction of the second was unlimited. Such institutions were very useful for the settling of actions of debt, but the non-burgess who wished to sue a burgess might well be suspicious of courts which recruited the presiding judges, the juries, and the court officers from members of the corporation.

Perhaps one should not be too severe in condemning the corporation for failing to some extent in its responsibilities towards the townspeople because a study of the corporation accounts reveals that it had only a limited amount of money at its disposal. The corporation had four main sources of income. These were rents, payments on admission of burgesses, profits of the port, and fines for breaches of municipal regulations. In a typical year, like 1629-30, the receipts from all these sources only amounted to £18.8s.1d. The disbursements in this year were for repairs or other essentials, and for the relief of the poor, and amounted in all to £14.11s.

Again, the growing exclusiveness of the corporation in the late sixteenth century can be discerned in its greater self-consciousness. Considerably more emphasis was placed on the dignity and decorous behaviour of its members. In 1569 it was laid down that if a burgess participated in any unlawful games, or kept prostitutes or vagabonds in his home, he was to be fined 12d. Again, when in 1583 two Irishmen were made burgesses, it was agreed in common hall that if they got involved in any street brawls, then they should be disfranchised. A new importance was also attached to 'pomp and circumstance'. In 1573, two maces were purchased for the town and it was agreed by the portreeve and aldermen 'that the commons should pay for one mace and the xii men for the other', and on 2 February on the occasion of the Feast of the Purification of the Virgin Mary, the maces preceded the portreeve and, presumably, the other aldermen and burgesses walking in procession.

Both these maces suffered damage and so, in 1615, a new pair, 'larger and fairer than those old ones', were ordered from a Bristol goldsmith by the portreeve Walter Thomas. The new pair continued to represent the dignity of the corporation and presence of Mr Portreeve until the reign of George III. The greater emphasis on pageantry is also reflected in the purchase in 1639 of four halberds and a staff for the crier. For these items the corporation paid £1.2s. Finally, at the close of the sixteenth century considerable quantities of crescloth were imported into the town. It is just possible that at this time the members of the town council were beginning to clothe themselves with scarlet or purple.

Another indication of the growing exclusiveness of the corporation is to be found in the class conflicts which occurred in the town in the latter half of the sixteenth century. It would appear that these struggles had arisen between the narrow oligarchy of wealthy ruling families on the one hand, determined to mulct the non-burgesses of as much as they could, and on the other, the general body of poor inhabitants. A letter from William Somerset, the third Earl of Worcester, to his brother-in-law Sir Edward Mansel, the father of Sir Thomas, dated 31 August 1570, is of great relevance and value in this respect. It reads as follows:

> Brother Mansell, being careful how the inhabitants within those towns of mine which are franchised with liberties, may peaceably enjoy their common quiet, as also by government be reformed, if amongst them happen occasion of any disorder, hearing that my tenants in Swansea (of whom I had lately conceived some cause of liking) are not now adays so conformable amongst themselves as co-brethren ought to be, by mean whereof many times they have overthrown such orders as for their benefit have been devised (the chiefest cause of this altercation rising (as I take it) partly through the wilful disobedience of the meaner sort towards their superiors, and partly also by the wealthier sort meaning to suppress their inferiors by ravin for that I wish them to be brought into a better trade, and that their several outrages may be reduced into an union of desire for the common profit of the town, I have

thought good to pray you to bestow some time of abode and dwelling in Swansea amongst them to the end that by your presence residing, advice and direction, you may help to restore them to that which quiet townsmen and honest burgesses ought to embrace. Thus with my hearty commendations I end from Raglan the last day of August 1570.

The town records have been most unhelpful in casting further rays of light on the nature of these tensions between the haves and have nots in the borough community which had obviously surfaced and been brought to the attention of Somerset.

And finally, the growing exclusiveness of the corporation can be observed in the attitude of greater independence which it adopted towards the lord in the early decades of the seventeenth century. That the control of the Earl of Worcester over the town had been perceptibly weakened by this time is admirably illustrated in a letter which Henry Herbert, the second son of the fourth earl, wrote to the portreeve and aldermen in January 1622 entreating them not to admit one Turberville, a brewer, as a burgess without first consulting his father's pleasure. Underlying the earl's concern was his fear that such a move would prejudice the profits which he received from his mill there:

> I understand of one Turberville a brewer, that is a very earnest suitor, to be by you admitted burgess of your town who (as I am informed) by his trade is like to prove very prejudicial to my lord father in respect of the custom of his mill there & which if it be so, as I know that you have a special care to preserve as well his privileges as profit so let me entreat you, not to admit him a freeman amongst you until his lordship's pleasure be first known in that behalf, or at leastwise until you give his lordship (or myself in his behalf) good satisfaction, that his said admittance be not anyway forth prejudicial or hurtful unto us. So not doubting of your friendly and respective care herein, I betake you to God, and will ever remain.

The tone of Henry Herbert's letter is milder and less commanding than that of any such letter would have been a generation or two earlier. One can hardly imagine Sir George Herbert entreating the burgesses to conform to his wishes in so gentle a manner, or the burgesses of his day venturing upon such an assertion of their own independence. The weakened authority of the Worcester family, together with being an outward manifestation of the town's increasing exclusiveness—which doubtless owed a very great deal to the rapid economic progress being made there—may also have reflected a clash of religious views between the corporation and the lord, for whereas the corporation in the late sixteenth and early seventeenth centuries was acquiring something of a Puritan complexion, the Earls of Worcester had, despite the changes of the times, continued to cling to the Catholic faith.

It is certain that a greater willingness to admit burgesses indiscriminately was not characteristic of the corporation's own attitude. Some years earlier in 1613 it had sought to limit the number of burgesses by raising the composition fees payable by freemen on their admission. At one time these had been trifling and uncertain. Now they were fixed at 20s. It would appear that the more relaxed policy had led to persons of little means being admitted to the freedom, and their poverty was such that they were unable to serve any office adequately.

This regulation was not strictly adhered to for more than a few years and in Michaelmas 1636 three burgesses were admitted, one paying £5 and two 1s.2d. each. Those admitted by right of birth or apprenticeship were required to pay the smaller sum. Moreover, in 1613, it had been made increasingly difficult for those burgesses who had been disfranchised for behaviour inimical to the good of the corporation to be restored to the freedom. Whereas previously payments for re-admission had varied a great deal, and had been usually small—in one case submission alone had been sufficient—now they were fixed at 20s.

As was to be expected, the loosening of the shackles of lordly control was not something that had been achieved overnight but by a process of historical evolution which had been going on over a considerable period of time and found outward expression at least as early as 1565/6. From a letter written then by William Somerset, the third Earl of Worcester, to Edward Mansel, it would appear that the town had been wilfully guilty of some act prejudicial to the lord's best interests which had led to his instituting legal proceedings that had the effect of extracting from the town an admission of its guilt. The significant portion of the letter reads as follows:

> And also concerning the burgesses of Swansea I do think their answer very slight, and not worthy of any favour to be showed them for fair words make fools vain.
>
> And where you write to me that they will be certain of the town of Swansea, with a submission of their fault and that three of them that I sued doth come in number with them to that point.
>
> I do thereto full answer you if they come I will not deal with them . . .
>
> And as for the corporation I had as live a throw it to the fire almost, as to deal with them for they that will bear their money against me in any suit, I think they might as well come to cut my throat as they were ready to bear their money against me. Therefore I am lothe to deal with them any kind of way for I take them to be careless but only to serve their own turn.

This was certainly a letter written by the hand of a very disillusioned and embittered man. But that the action of the corporation which had so angered the lord was not, at this stage, tantamount to an assertion of independence appears not only from the letter itself—the general attitude assumed by the lord had been one of superiority, while the burgesses, on the other hand, had made a submission of their guilt—but also from another letter which, as has already been shown, was sent by Somerset to Mansel in 1570. In this letter the reality of the lord's control over the town is further confirmed. Not only had the corporation ingratiated itself once more in his favour since he had 'lately conceived some cause of liking' towards his tenants in Swansea, but Somerset had also directed Mansel to reside personally there so that by his presence he might help to restore a better relationship between the various social groups which were at loggerheads.

Despite the exclusiveness of the corporation, the town could not exist in isolation. It was part of a wider jig-saw and had to relate to national as well as county politics. At county level the town has already been discerned contributing to the relief of the maimed soldiers and the prisoners in Cardiff gaol, and making payments to the muster master and the governor of the house of correction. But, within the county of Glamorgan, Swansea was also called upon to help alleviate the distress caused by natural calamities, such as floods, and to contribute towards the repair and maintenance of vital organs of commerce like bridges. On a wider plane the town responded to the requirements of national legislation, and major political events were celebrated by the ringing of church bells and the reading of proclamations in the market place.

In 1607, a pamphlet was published, with the title of 'God's Warning to his People of England, by the great overflowing of the Waters or Floods, lately happened in South Wales and many other places Wherein is described the great Losses and wonderful Damages that happened thereby by the Drowning of many Towns and Villages to the utter undoing of many thousands of People'. The deluge, which had apparently been caused by a strong south-west wind that raged for three days without intermission, had taken place at about nine o'clock on the morning of 20 January 1606 when 'they might see and perceive afar off, as it were in the Element, huge and mighty hills of water, tumbling one over another, in such sort as if the greatest mountains in the world had overwhelmed the low valleys or marshy grounds', and upwards of 500 men, women or children are said to have been drowned in south Wales. Swansea is mentioned as one of the places at which 'many great harms were done'. In the corporation records, however, there is no mention of the town having sustained any damage and the only entry in them relating to the event appears in the Book of Orders. This entry reveals that considerable damage was caused to the sea-walls of Aberavon and the corporation made a contribution of 20s. towards their repair. In the porch of the church of St. Bride below Newport, there is a mark which shows that the waters rose to a height of five feet above the floor, and it was the same flood which destroyed the church of St. Mary at Cardiff.

By mid-sixteenth century the bridge over the river Taff at Cardiff was in such a dangerous state that it endangered life and had, of necessity, to be rebuilt. However, great dissension had arisen between Cardiff and the county respecting the onus of rebuilding it, the inhabitants of the county maintaining that the county town had always been responsible for its repair since it lay within the borough liberties. In an attempt to resolve the matter finally, Parliament, in 1581, passed an act for the rebuilding and repairing of the bridge. The act acknowledged that repair properly appertained to Cardiff, but since the 'poor state' of the town made it impossible for it to bear so great a charge, the cost should be shared between town and county in the ratio of one part to five. All boroughs in the county of Glamorgan were to contribute with the county towards the charges. Furthermore, it was laid down that Cardiff and the county were to be jointly responsible for the maintenance of the bridge after its completion. The accounts of the common attorneys at Swansea contain several references to the amounts contributed by the town towards the work. The following items are typical of these entries:

> 1621 Item paid the xxth day of August towards the decayed bridge of Cardiff iiiis.ii*d*.
> 1622 paid the high constables the 15th of August towards the bridge of Cardiff iiis.vi*d*.
> 1623 paid to the high constables towards the turning of the water under Cardiff bridge iiiis.i*d*..

This last entry seems to imply that the construction of the new stone bridge had been completed, and subsequent entries in the accounts relate to payments towards its repair which fell on both the town and county. In 1624, 1s.8*d*. was contributed, while in 1635/6, £1.0s.8*d*. was paid to 'William Wybbarne high constable the xvii of February towards the repairing of Cardiff bridge'.

But Swansea had to fit itself into a framework of national as well as county politics. The impact of central on local politics can be discerned at the town not only in the effects of legislation like the

Acts of Union, but also in such activities as the ringing of the bells on special occasions, and in proclamations read in the market place. In March 1603, 5s. was paid to the ringers of St. Mary's 'for ringing the coronation day', while in the market place, on the last day of the month, the proclamation announcing James I to be King was read. The entry in the Book of Orders relating to this event is of considerable intrinsic interest and runs as follows:

Anno domine 1603
being the xlv[th] year of her reign
Elizabeth Queen of England departed out of this world the xxiiii[th] of March 1603 and in the afternoon there was proclaimed at London James the sixth of that name King: King of England, Scotland, France and Ireland and then after was proclaimed here in our town of Swansea by Sir Thomas Mansel Knight & Lison Evance Esquire & William Price Esquire there then present the last of March 1603.

In 1625, on the decease of James, his son Charles Stuart was proclaimed King in the market place by Henry Flemyng, the portreeve.

Occasionally, the town is found having to acknowledge a wider framework than even that afforded by British politics, for in 1565 Swansea was fortuitously brought into touch with the stormy beginnings of French colonization in America. When the attempt made by Jean Ribaut and René de Laudonnière to establish a French colony at Fort Caroline in Florida in 1565 was stamped out by the blood-thirsty ferocity and treachery of the Spaniard Menendez, it was at Swansea that the few who escaped massacre (including Laudonnière himself) were landed. Its merchants, together with the gentlemen of the county, especially one Morgan, did all they could to 'succour the poor sea-worn fugitives with the horrors of a fiendish slaughter among the lagoons and sand dunes of Florida still fresh in their minds'.

Between 1485-1640 the town had taken considerable strides along the road to prosperity and the quickening of the economic pulse had in turn stimulated further municipal development. The growing volume of business transacted by the town authorities became reflected in an increase in the number of existing officers and the creation of entirely new ones. In 1635 the number of constables was increased from four to six because it was considered that four constables 'were too few to manage the affairs of the said town & franchise'. This development had also become necessary because these officials were often recruited from the ranks of merchants or seamen who transacted their businesses outside the borough limits and consequently could not attend to their civic duties. In 1609 a new officer had been created known as the overseer of the quay. Four years later, in 1613, he was described as the overseer of the quay and mount.

The character of municipal government at Swansea had been moulded by two sets of circumstances, one internal and the other external. It had responded to the rapid expansion of the town's economy and reacted also to the central legislation of the times. By 1640, though the actual framework of civic administration at the town was not markedly dissimilar from what it had been at the end of the Middle Ages, subtle changes had taken place in the working of that administration. Supreme power and authority had become increasingly concentrated in the hands of a few of the wealthier and more prominent among the town families, so that to those outside the exclusive circle, the non-burgesses, the corporation had acquired increasingly the appearance of a closed shop. The oligarchical aspect of town government at Swansea was to remain one of its most characteristic features right down to the nineteenth century.

# Chapter Five

## THE REFORMATION AND THE EMERGENCE OF PURITANISM

The religious life of Swansea during the Middle Ages revolved around three institutions: the Chapel of St. John, the Hospital of St. David and the parish church of St. Mary. Though nothing much can be said with certainty about the religious beliefs of the townspeople, they probably differed little from those of most of the people of Wales at this time. While there is no evidence of open hostility to the church, or serious criticism of its teaching, it should be remembered that Swansea was one of the few parts of Wales that would be less immune to the infiltration of Reformation ideas than most of the country. It was in the towns of south Wales that some slight evidence of anti-clerical and even heretical tendencies, has been discerned during the fifteenth and early sixteenth centuries. Certainly, the only two cases of heresy occurring in the pages of the episcopal registers of St. David's both relate to south Pembrokeshire. In one instance, an Irish priest, Sir Roger Burley, had, in 1486, spoken words of an heretical nature concerning the mass while in the other, a layman of Pembroke, one Stephen Hall, had expressed heretical opinions concerning the Trinity. Again, in Tenby, as early as 1535, one of William Barlow's servants had possessed a copy of the New Testament in English while Barlow himself who, at this time, was prior of Haverfordwest, delivered anti-papal orations from his pulpit. The reason for these tendencies in the towns of south Wales may be found in the fact that conditions there were not entirely unpropitious for the reception of changes in religion. Their inhabitants were in commercial contact with other larger trading centres, notably Bristol and London, where Protestant opinion took root. They were also better able to buy and to read the English Protestant writings than the mass of the rural population of Wales. These towns ultimately became centres of Puritan worship, but what anti-clerical or Protestant sympathies there were among Swansea's merchants and craftsmen have left little trace in the town's archives. The effect of the Reformation changes as revealed by contemporary records is confined very largely to externals. Most of these changes carried with them tremendously important implications for religious beliefs, but it can only be conjectured what the reactions of the townspeople were. The most spectacular changes undoubtedly were those which swept away some of the most familiar features of the medieval religious scene. The first of these was the dissolution of the religious houses in Henry VIII's time. This was followed shortly afterwards in Edward VI's reign by the destruction of other monuments of medieval piety, notably chantries, hospitals and other institutions. Though there was no monastery in Swansea, there were two institutions of a quasi-monastic nature which had important interests in and near the town. They were the Chapel of St. John belonging to the Hospitallers and the Hospital of St. David. The former was the first to be affected when the Order of St. John was dissolved in 1540.

During the early Middle Ages the Order of St. John, partly as a result of the wave of enthusiasm that had swept over the country during the period of the Crusades, had acquired considerable possessions in Gower. At Swansea these acquisitions had comprised one burgage from Henry de Newburgh (c.1156-1148); another burgage and 12 acres of land from Einion and his brother Goronwy, sons of Llywarch (*ante* 1198); the third part of the fee of Brictric, one acre of meadow and 30 acres for the construction of the Chapel of St. John from Robert, son of Walter (c.1165); the House (c.1180-1200) and Hospital of St. John the Baptist (*ante* 1214) from John de Penrice; the manor of Millwood from John de Breos (1220-1232), and finally all the lands of Robert Bured in Cwmbwrla (*ante* 1241).

By the sixteenth century the Order was showing unmistakable signs of decay, the roots of which can be traced far back into the medieval period. This decline is attributable to several factors. First, the wars against the Turks had been a constant drain on the resources of the Order both in men and money. Furthermore, these conflicts, by involving the Order increasingly in the profession of arms, had led to combatant duties assuming an importance above that of charitable works. It was thus inevitable that there should have been a decline from the former high standard of asceticism, and from the objects for which the Order had been established. Despite the efforts of the masters, it was difficult to check the growing tendency to luxury. Again, the waning of the crusading spirit had seen a steady dwindling in the stream of donations and, finally and most important of all, as the crusading age passed away, the spirit of protest against the medieval church had increased, ultimately to break in the Reformation.

The various Hospitaller estates in west Wales continued, in the main, to be held by the Order until the time of the Reformation, though by that time the rents were much reduced in value, and the courts of Slebech yielded only £4.7s. A comparison of the later lists of the Slebech estates with those of earlier days seems to reveal certain discrepancies which would suggest that, during the intervening period, some lands had been lost. These lands could have disappeared as a result of the maladministration of an easy-going prior, but it is more probable that they had been lost because of the pressure that was being brought to bear on the Commandery, especially in the early sixteenth century, by greedy and unscrupulous laymen, conscious of the weakened power and authority of the Order. Foremost among these was Sir Rhys ap Thomas who was, to all intents and purposes, the King's viceroy in south Wales. It would appear that he had anticipated Henry VIII's onslaught on the religious houses as early as 1520. In this year, Sir Clement West, head of the Commandery, presented a bill of complaint in the Court of Requests against Sir Rhys, his son Sir Griffith, Harry Cadarn, and David ap Rhys. From the bill it appears that the Commandery had been let to farm to Sir Griffith and that he had failed to pay the rents, or to maintain it in an adequate state of repair. Also, even after the termination of the lease, the defendants had continued to receive the profits of large areas of lands belonging to the Order. More important than this, however, was the implication that the defendants had, without any colour of legal right, seized some of its lands for their own use. The extent of the decline of the Commandery by the sixteenth century can be estimated from the fact that while in 1338 the revenues accruing from the entire bailiwick from all sources, lay and spiritual, had amounted to £303.1s.10½d., on the eve of the dissolution the gross revenue had fallen to £211.9s.10½d.

In 1540, like all religious orders, as well as the monasteries and other houses connected with the church, the Hospitallers found the doors of their Commandery at Slebech closed against them. At the time of the dissolution (7 May) the estate at Slebech was already being leased by Roger Barlow at an annual rent of £125.15s.10½d. The Slebech possessions in Gower and Kidwelly, on the other hand, were purchased from the Crown by the Herberts and the Mansels and by other families in the neighbourhood. The manor of Millwood passed to Sir Thomas Mansel. From a survey of the manor made in 1641 it becomes apparent that by that time the property had descended to Bussy Mansel, a minor, the son of Arthur Mansel.

The next monument of medieval piety to be swept away was the Hospital of the Blessed David, which had been founded by Henry de Gower, bishop of St. David's, in 1322 for the aged and infirm priests and laymen of his diocese. Gower had provided the Hospital with considerable endowments and he had, furthermore, settled two-thirds of the tithes upon the warden and the remaining third upon the vicar of St. Mary's. It had become an established custom in the twelfth and thirteenth centuries and, to a lesser extent, in succeeding generations for patrons to attach the revenues of benefices to religious houses. This had been done, however, on the more or less explicit understanding that the religious house would, in return, provide a vicar to serve the parish. Consequently, from 1332 until the dissolution of the Hospital in the reign of Edward VI, the history of St. Mary's was closely bound up with it. In 1403, during the reign of Henry IV, it had been ordained that the vicar should be a secular priest and not a member of any religious house, that he should be a vicar perpetual and not removable at the caprice of the religious house, and that he should be canonically instituted and inducted and sufficiently remunerated. Hence, there were coexistent rectors and vicars of St. Mary's until the reign of Edward VI. In his reign, with the dissolution of the Hospital, the connection was finally severed.

But despite the quite considerable possessions which the Hospital had acquired at its foundation in 1332, and subsequently in grants from pious lay donors and from Henry de Gower himself, by the fifteenth century it was in a state of decay. One indication of this decline is to be found in the non-residence of some, at least, of the wardens. A rule of the Hospital had been that the warden was to reside personally within it, or within the parish in which it stood. David Martin would certainly not have been able to observe this injunction because after 1357 he combined the office of warden with that of Archdeacon of Carmarthen, and the chances are that he would have devoted most of his attention to the latter office. Again, in September 1402, John Fayrewode, another warden, had been granted by the Pope a licence to enable him to be absent from the Hospital for seven years to study Civil Law at an university. For his maintenance there he was permitted to enjoy the 'fruits' of the Hospital. Non-residence might also have been encouraged by the medieval practice of appointing to ecclesiastical offices for political reasons. At Swansea, in the late fourteenth century, there is evidence of this demoralising spectacle when, on 24 July 1361, Edward III appointed his clerk, Richard de Thorn, to the office of warden of the Hospital. For Edward this was a very convenient way by which he could reward Thorn for his work as a civil servant.

Another indication of the decay of the Hospital is to be found in its impoverishment by the fifteenth and early sixteenth centuries. It has already been demonstrated how, during the fourteenth century, its revenues had been greatly diminished by plagues with the result that it had been found necessary to reduce the number of chaplains from six to four, and to appropriate to it certain churches.[1] By 1403 the Hospital had entered on better times because in this year the full complement of six chaplains was restored. However, between this date and 1546, when the chantries in both England and Wales were surveyed under the provisions of an Act of Parliament, the number of chaplains had been reduced to two. Furthermore, from this survey it appears that whereas the Hospital should have been supporting ten poor men— though in the original charter of foundation the number had been

[1] Supra, p. 30.

*The Reformation and the Emergence of Puritanism* 163

indeterminate—at the time of the survey the number being maintained was only four. In 1548/9 another survey of the Hospital was made, by which time the number of poor there had fallen to two. These considerations argue for a decline in prosperity and this poverty would have increased the difficulties of the Hospital in fulfilling its duties as laid down in its foundation charter and later injunctions.

By the winter of 1545 a depleted treasury had forced King Henry VIII and his ministers to seek new sources of income, and they found that many patrons of chantries and other religious institutions of a similar nature had converted their revenues to their own use; that some priests or wardens had sold or let manors and lands belonging to them, and that many chantries and similar promotions had been dissolved by these or other means. The actions of the patrons, priests or wardens may, to a very large extent, be accounted for on the grounds that in the 1530s there were rumours that the dissolution of the monasteries would shortly be followed by spoliation of the parish churches. By selling or leasing lands belonging to their respective institutions they were, in effect, anticipating possible confiscation. At Llandaff, the canons residentiary had made provision for themselves by breaking up and distributing among their own number the gold, jewels and other valuables which had been accumulated for centuries in the Cathedral. Happenings of a similar nature had occurred at St. David's during the years 1547-8. It would appear that the warden and chaplains of the Hospital of St. David at Swansea had also resorted to these practices because prior to the dissolution they were not only letting out the hospital lands but they had, furthermore, granted away *in toto* certain rectories, advowsons, and possessions belonging to it. In 1544 Richard Rawlins, warden of the Hospital, had leased to Morgan ap John ap Hopkin one parcel of land at 'Kregenyth' and one-tenth of the fish taken in the sea as well as in a weir on the west side of the river Tawe within the parish of Swansea. The rent was 18s.4d. yearly, 13s.4d. for the land and 5s. for the tenth part of the fish. In the 1540s Rawlins was involved in a dispute, eventually to be taken for settlement to the Court of the Council of Wales and the Marches, with the burgesses of Swansea

The Despoiling of the Monasteries

over the possession of a piece of land near Cadle in Fforest-fach. It appears that Rawlins had leased part of the Hospital's land there, adjoining the Portmeade of the burgesses, to one John Henry Gruffyth Benett. Benett, however, under colour of this lease, had encroached on the Portmeade and enclosed part of it. The dispute was submitted to arbitration on three separate occasions. On 30 April 1550 the arbitrators appointed by the Council in the Marches gave judgment that the land in question belonged to the burgesses but that they should lease it to Benett for 99 years at an annual rent of 4s. and 2 capons.

It is well established that long before the dissolution there was considerable lay interference in the internal affairs of the religious houses. The patrons, high stewards, bailiffs, receivers, surveyors, farmers, and other officers of monasteries were being recruited increasingly from the ranks of the gentry and, consequently, exercised a considerable influence on their affairs. On the eve of the dissolution the actual share which the religious themselves had in the management of their own estates was but small. This situation enabled the gentry 'to become well acquainted with the monastic estates and to feel at home within the monastic walls: and this was one of the causes which contributed to the success of the dissolution. When the monastic estates came into the market, the

*The Reformation and the Emergence of Puritanism* 165

squires knew not only to whom they should address themselves, but knew also what particular estates to ask for: thus they easily selected the most profitable portions for themselves'.[2] The Hospital of St. David was certainly not free from lay interference. Not only was a pension paid to Sir Edward Carne, who had acquired Ewenny priory on its dissolution, but the steward of the Hospital was none other than Sir George Herbert, undoubtedly the most powerful and influential man in Swansea at this time. The bailiff, one Morgan John ap Hopkyn, was also a layman. It is not really surprising that Sir George should be steward of the Hospital because his family was one of three (the other two being the Somerset Earls of Worcester and the Devereux) which between them had possession of nearly all monastic stewardships in south Wales on the eve of the dissolution. On 4 April 1550 Sir George had secured from the warden and chaplains the grant of the rectories, advowsons and possessions of the vicarage of Swansea, Oystermouth and Llangiwg. It may well be that the Hospital was in debt to him and that this represented its way of honouring that debt. On the other hand, and this perhaps is the more likely explanation, it may well have been an arrangement of mutual benefit to both sides by which, anticipating dissolution, they had divided the spoils, Sir George obtaining possession of the coveted Hospital lands while the warden and chaplains received some financial recompense. There is no positive evidence to support this conjecture, but it could well be true since it is known that the stewards generally had been taking care to protect their own interests.

On 22 November 1550, as reward for the loyal services which Sir George had rendered against the rebels in the west, the King, Edward VI, confirmed him in his possessions. To Sir George the acquisition of these possessions came as a release from a weighty annual charge for the support of one of the chantries of St. Mary's imposed upon him by the will of Sir Matthew Cradock, whose heir he was. Sir Matthew, anxious to perpetuate the chantry in the chapel of St. Anne founded by his ancestor, had left instructions in

[2] A Savine, 'English Monasteries on the Eve of the Dissolution', *Oxford Studies in Social and Legal History*, Vol. 1 (Oxford, 1909), pp. 259-60.

his will that his heir 'George Herbert and his feoffees shall appoint lands and tenements of the yearly value of xx nobles for the maintaining and repairing of the said chapel, and to find a priest to sing there for evermore for my soul and my wife's soul, my ancestors' souls and all Christian souls'. By virtue of these acquisitions also, Sir George became the patron of St. Mary's and the first lay rector. Furthermore, the rectorial tithes were secularized and transferred with the temporalities to him. From the survey of Gower taken on 9 September 1583 it appears that these lands had descended to William Herbert and that he held them by suit of leet court.

On 12 April 1550 the warden, Richard Rawlins, and the vicar, William Price, had released the parishioners from their Easter offering of ½d. each, which had been collected annually by them at Midsummer (21 June), provided that the King or his council or parliament did not re-grant it, in which case the remission would become null and void. It has been suggested that this concession was a kind of goodwill offering on the part of the warden to the parishioners before the final transfer of the possessions of the Hospital to Sir George. However, it may be nearer the truth to suggest that the release implies that something from the original establishment had been reserved for the warden even after the final transfer had taken place.

Finally, the effects of the Reformation on the parish church of St. Mary have to be considered. Basically, the changes were of two kinds: those which affected the fabric of the church, and those which affected the services conducted within it.

The Reformation led to considerable changes being effected in the physical appearance of the parish church at Swansea since, during the reign of the boy King, Edward VI, when Protestantism replaced Catholicism as the religion of the Church of England, the altars were replaced by wooden communion tables; the rood, with its attendant images, was removed; and finally, the church plate and vestments were confiscated.

The demolition of the altars had begun as early as 1548, when those of the dissolved chantries had been destroyed; but the first general attack on them had been made at Carmarthen in the summer of 1549, the most populous town in Wales, lying within the diocese of St. David's. That the initial onslaught, where Wales is concerned, should have taken place in this diocese, was not entirely unexpected since a dynamic Protestant bishop of the see, William Barlow, between 1536-48, had been doing his utmost to disseminate Protestant opinion there, and he had been succeeded as bishop by another zealous Protestant, the Yorkshireman Robert Ferrar. In 1550 Ridley, who was to die a martyr's death at the stake in Mary's reign, ordered the removal of all altars in the diocese of London. This policy was finally adopted by the Council and applied to the whole Kingdom. On 24 November 1550 an instruction was sent in the King's name to every bishop 'to give substantial order' that 'with all diligence all the altars in every church or chapel . . . within your said diocese to be taken down, and instead of them a table to be set up in some convenient part of the chancel within every such church or chapel, to serve for the ministration of the blessed communion'. Mary, as an ardent Catholic sovereign and champion, had the altars restored but with the accession of the Protestant Elizabeth, they were once again removed. Though there is no evidence of this before Elizabeth's reign, these kaleidoscopic changes must have been observed at Swansea. The Churchwardens' Accounts have survived only from 1558, but it is most significant that in this year they record the removal of two altars from the

Sketch of St. Mary's Church

church, for which William the mason was paid 2s.4d. That they were replaced by a wooden communion table is indicated by an entry in the disbursements for 1559 when 14d. was 'paid to John Thomas for v posts for to make the table of the communion'. Among Protestants generally there was considerable uncertainty as to the position which the communion table should occupy in the church. In the diocese of St. David's, by far the most extensive in Wales, the few adherents of that faith had certainly not been able to agree among themselves on this point. In St. Peter's, Carmarthen, the table had been moved a dozen times within a very short space of time. Unfortunately, neither the church nor corporation records of Swansea provide any indication as to whether there was any wrangling or uncertainty in the parish church there. If there had been such unseemly scenes, it could have had nothing but a debilitating effect on the growth of Protestantism in the town.

Again, the Reformation resulted in the removal of the rood and its attendant images. In 1547, injunctions were issued which instructed the clergy to take away and destroy 'all shrines, candlesticks, pictures, and all other monuments of feigned miracles, pilgrimages, idolatry, and superstition . . .' Consequent upon the issuing of these orders the rood would, in all probability, have been removed from Swansea's parish church though no record of the event has survived. In Mary's reign, however, with the undoing of Edward's work, the rood would have been restored. In 1558, following the succession of Elizabeth, the rood was finally removed from St. Mary's, and the Churchwardens' Accounts of that year record the payment of 4d. to 'William Johns the smith' for performing this work. But despite the establishment by Elizabeth of a Protestant Anglican church, old customs died hard in Wales, and from Bishop Middleton's visitation of 1583 it appears that Catholic practices persisted strongly among the people of the diocese of St. David's. The host was still elevated in the communion service, crosses placed on graves, holy days observed, and prayers said for the dead, while in the great majority of the churches images, pictures, altars, and rood lofts were still very much in evidence. At Swansea, even though the rood had been removed, the loft had been left untouched—probably owing to its continued use as a singing gallery—and it figures quite frequently in the accounts since money was expended on its cleaning and maintenance. In 1558 6d. was paid to William Lewis for washing the rood loft, a cleaning task possibly made necessary and very desirable by the operations of the smith when removing the rood. A fair amount of attention had to be devoted to the loft in 1586, and 7s.8d. was disbursed 'for making up the window over the rood loft, for a new desk and for pointing over the rood loft'. These items of expenditure could have represented much-needed repair to an ageing fabric, or it could be that the church had suffered some degree of storm damage because in the same year 7s.4d. was paid to the glazier for eleven feet of new glass for the window situated above the loft. The amount of glass required would point to the window, which would have provided light for the loft, being a very substantial one. However, this stubborn adherence to the past did not proceed from any deep-seated conviction; rather was it the product of ignorance and dislike of change.

Finally, the effect of the Reformation on the fabric of St. Mary's may be seen in the confiscation of the church plate and vestments. In the 'Act for the Dissolution of the Chantries, 1547' it was stipulated that 'our Sovereign Lord the King shall have and enjoy all such goods, chattels, jewels, plate, ornaments, and other moveables as were or be the common goods of every such college, chantry, free chapel, or stipendiary priest, belonging or annexed to the furniture or service of their several foundations'. The following items of church property belonging to St. Mary's were presented in 1549 before Sir George Herbert, the King's commissioner appointed for the viewing of such goods:

> First one chalice of silver weighing xv ounces
> Item another chalice of silver weighing xxiii ounces
> Item a suit of vestments of blue velvet
> Item an old cope of vestment cloth of gold
> Item an old suit of vestments of white damask and a cope of the same
> Item an old cope of black velvet

Item a vestment of tawny velvet with a cope for the same
Item ii pair of vestments of Bruges satin, one red & one blue
Item iii corporases³ and ii cases of velvet
Item iiii altar sheets
Item another vestment of blue Bruges satin
Item iii bells by estimation xxiiii$^c$ weight or thereabouts
Item one small bell by estimation xl$^{li}$ weight or thereabouts
Item xiii candlesticks by estimation xxiiii$^{li}$ weight
Item a censer of brass by estimation ii$^{li}$
Item ii brazen crosses by estimation vi$^{li}$
Item a lamp of brass by estimation iiii$^{li}$
Item a canopy of cloth of gold and velvet
Item a case for relics of brass by estimation ii$^{li}$
Item a holy water pot of brass by estimation vi$^{li}$
Item a standard of brass for a candlestick by estimation xxx$^{li}$ weight
Item the steeple covered with lead
Item a chapel of Sir Matthew Cradock covered with lead.

This is a much fuller list than is available from most parishes in Glamorgan and it is only in Glamorgan that the inventories of church goods are at all complete. A comparison of these church goods with those of other churches in the county reveals that, apart from town parishes like those in Cardiff, none of them could vie with St. Mary's in their wealth of ornaments and vestments. In 1553, among the goods which it was alleged had been taken away from the church at Barry by Edward VI's commissioners, the following were enumerated:

A cross of copper gilt
ii candlesticks of brass
A cope of blue satin of Bruges
A pair of vestments of green damask
A pair of vestments of green silk
A pikes of brass
A holy water pot of brass
A censer of brass.

³Cloth, usually of linen, on which elements were placed.

Other churches were to show considerably less even than this. In the church at Whitchurch, near Cardiff, there were only 'four candlesticks of brass price vi$s$. viii$d$.'.

To plunder the churches was to plunder the parishioners since all, rich and poor alike, worshipped in them. Moreover, much of the social life of the parish was centred in and around the church. If life was drab and lonely for many, here at least was a place which was common ground for everyone, for worship, business and pleasure. It was natural that the parishioners should have lavished their gifts on making their churches as attractive as they could to enhance the dignity and beauty of its services. For Swansea, as far as is known, no pre-Reformation wills have survived. Consequently, it has not been possible to ascertain the extent of the generosity of the parishioners in this respect. Judging, however, solely on the wealth of ornaments, it must have been considerable.

At Swansea the endowments of the church and the religious orders had been acquired by the local gentry. This policy of dividing the landed possessions of the church among the squirearchy had been pursued by Henry VIII and his son, Edward VI, mainly to replenish depleted royal coffers and to reward their servants for political services rendered. It had been done also in order to establish the Reformation on a basis of vested interest though, indeed, it had not always worked out that way as gentry families, like the Carnes of Ewenni and the Morgans of Llantarnam, had battened on monastic spoils without abandoning their allegiance to the Catholic faith. It was these lands, acquired as a result of the dissolution, that enabled the gentry families in the neighbourhood of Swansea, which were already well established, to extend appreciably overnight their broad acres.

Together with the effect on the fabric of St. Mary's, the Reformation also bore witness to the introduction of far-reaching liturgical and doctrinal changes, while the vernacular replaced Latin as the medium in which the services were conducted. To the Protestants, doctrine could be absorbed by each believer from the reading of a self-authenticating scripture. Furthermore, the sacraments did not confer grace, but were rather the means of strengthening and confirming saving faith. To them the church, and its ministrations, now played a less important part in religion, for the church was not the only authoritative interpreter of scripture, and the sacraments, though still important, were not as significant as in medieval times. Consequently the aims of the Protestant liturgical reformers were two-fold. First, they wished to eradicate from the church services those things which seemed to them to inculcate false ideas, and secondly, so to simplify and alter the forms of worship as to make them both more intelligible in themselves and also expressive of the ideas they considered true. This involved the transformation of the sacrifice of the mass into a commemorative service—this was the real meaning of the substitution of a wooden communion table for the stone altar—and a fairly radical revision and simplification of all the other services including their translation into everyday language. In 1537 the 'Great Bible' or Mathew's Bible was published, while in 1549 the first Prayer Book, enforced by an Act of Uniformity, appeared. It is doubtful how far the Prayer Book was understood in Wales outside the market towns and anglicized areas like south Pembrokeshire, for few of the priests, and almost none of the people, knew English. William Salesbury consequently undertook the task of translating into Welsh the epistles and gospels appointed to be read in the communion service on Sundays and Holy Days, and these appeared in 1551 with the title *Kynniver Llith a Ban*.

In 1552 the second Prayer Book, more markedly Protestant in complexion than the first, appeared and its use enforced by another Act of Uniformity. It is quite possible that the Prayer Book was used in St. Mary's, since an appreciable number of the inhabitants of the town were English in speech, but what their reactions were to its introduction, one can only conjecture. It can only be speculated also what their response had been to the return to the old faith under Mary, or to the Protestant Anglican Settlement of Elizabeth. In all probability their attitude would not have differed greatly from that of the rest of Wales, where these changes were accepted with relative indifference. Certainly, as far as is known, there were no Protestant martyrs or Catholic recusants in Swansea. The absence of records does not preclude the possibility that Protestants had been burnt in the town, for it is well known that the martyrdom of

## The Reformation and the Emergence of Puritanism

Thomas Capper at Cardiff in 1542, presumably for his denial of transubstantiation, would have passed into complete oblivion had not the bailiffs of the town recovered from the corporation the sum of 4s.4d. spent in purchasing the firewood used to burn him. It might be that at Swansea such chance entries have not survived. As far as Catholic recusants are concerned, a study of the gaol files of the Great Sessions Court for the Glamorgan circuit has not revealed the presence of any in the town. It is doubtful whether this evidence again should be regarded as conclusive, for these files suggest very strongly in other directions—in the fewness, for example, of the number of transgressions presented from Swansea as compared with those from Cardiff and Cowbridge—that the justices in west Glamorgan were very lax in the execution of their duties. However, it is as well to remember that since conditions in the town were not unconducive to the reception of Protestant ideas, that some sections of the populace, even in the mid-sixteenth century, might have sympathized with, and even welcomed, the movement away from Roman Catholicism.

From some of the ancient books in the possession of the corporation, it is possible to reconstruct in part the framework of administrative church life at Swansea during this period. From them, information is gleaned about the organ, bells and pews of St. Mary. The main sources of church income and the chief outlets for church expenditure, are also discerned. Finally, an introduction is provided to the more prominent of the church officers.

Church organs had been introduced into England at least as early as the dawn of the eighth century. By degrees it came about that the ordinary parish churches became possessed of these aids to vocal music until at last their adoption was practically universal. An organ had certainly been installed in St. Mary's by 1558 because in that year it is recorded that 'a pennyworth of colours' were purchased for it. In 1562 there was 'paid for a pennycord for the organ 1d.'; in 1564 another 1d. was spent for a 'candle to have light to mend the organs'. But there were other items of expenditure in connection with the organ to be met in this year for the following purposes: 'paid John Keru' for the mending of the bellows of the organs and for foot stools for the communion table xxd.; paid for glue v*d*., and paid for leather to mend the bellows iii*d*.'. It is also clear that the organ was housed in a loft, and since the instrument was a treasured possession, the door to the loft was kept locked when the organ was not in use. In a list of pews drawn up in 1587 there are mentioned 'the pews under the organs'. Three years later, in 1590, 13*d*. was paid to one Bartleye 'for twists & viii spikes and a lock to the door of the organ loft'. By 1627 this lock had apparently become defective because a new lock and key were purchased for 6*d*. The organ at St. Mary's was a source of continuous expense, and in 1631 further work had to be done to it and the repair was entrusted on 15 April to John Hayward, an organ maker from Neath. The reference to it in the corporation papers makes interesting reading:

> Memorandum that I, John Haywarde, of the city of Neath, organ maker, have had & received of Mr John Daniell & Lewis Johns churchwardens for the town of Swansea the sum of seventeen pounds being in full payment & satisfaction for the finishing, fitting, & tuneable making of their organs in the church at Swansea, & making the gallery & painting work there done of which said sum of xvii[li] I do acknowledge myself fully satisfied & paid, & if that there happen any defect in any of the pipes of the said organs within this two years, or bellows, or any part of the said organs, that the same shall not be sufficient & tuneable, I do hereby assume & promise that upon & after a month's notice given me by the said wardens, or any their successors, to come & repair & amend any defect or fault that shall or may come or happen to the said organs. In witness whereof I have hereunto put my hand the day & year above written.

Happily, then, for the churchwardens the repair work was guaranteed for two years, the only condition attached being, that in the event of any further malfunctions, he should be given a month's notice before coming to see to them.

The organist, or as he was described in the Churchwardens' Accounts, the 'organ player', was not extravagantly paid, nor was his stipend, such as it was, always paid regularly for in 1562 there was 'paid to William organplayer for his wages that was unpaid at the last year by John Ryde & William Watkins xiii*s*. iiii*d*.'. Two years later, William was still organist and was paid 13*s*.4*d*. for his wages, so that professional services were not very well requited. However, there were certain perquisites attaching to the office, for although his salary was paid by the churchwardens, the corporation had undertaken to clothe him. The accounts of the common attorneys for 1618 record the following disbursements: 'paid for stuff to make the organist a suit xviii*s*. iiii*d*.; paid to Thomas Phillip for making his clothes iii*s*.; paid for a pair of shoes to the organ (player) ii*s*. vi*d*.; paid for stockings to the organ player ii*s*.'. A complete suit, no less, and all for £1.5*s*.10*d*. From these accounts it also appears that the organist was provided with an assistant to operate the bellows, and various entries relate to payments being made 'for blowing the organs'. In 1610 a William Harry was paid 8*s*. for performing this function and for keeping the church clean.

The bells were the most valued possession of St. Mary's and, from the inventory of church goods compiled in 1549, it becomes evident that there was a peal of four—three large and one small in the tower, which, incidentally, was surmounted by a spire. One of the bells bore an inscription indicating that it had been donated to the church by Sir Matthew Cradock. In 1558 these bells were still there, for a payment was made 'to William carpenter for mending the four bells iii*s*. iiii*d*.'. There is a further charge in 1559 of 1*s*. to the carpenter for work upon the bells and ½*d*. was expended 'for black soap to noint the bells'. William was paid an additional 3*s*.4*d*. in 1562 for 'the mending of the great bell in the stocks', while in 1564 nine shillings were paid 'for mending of the frames & wheels of the bells'. In 1583 considerable repairs were made, either to the bells, or to the bell-chamber, and it is probable that, during their progress, the bells were temporarily hung in the churchyard in a house erected for that purpose. It must be remembered that these were days when the warning and call of the curfew were strictly observed. The Churchwardens' Accounts for 1583 contain charges of 7*s*. 4*d*. for 'planks for the bell house', and 6*d*. for 'carriage in the planks to the bell house'. Other items of expenditure incurred in the same year are those for mending the bell loft and for 'lath nails' for the same. Later, in 1586, there are indications of the work being completed and 11s. 4d. was spent in 'repairing of the steeple windows & for fastening of the bells in the stocks'. After all these repairs, however, the small bell appears to have been damaged since 2s. 6d. was paid 'to the smith for working the bands for to bind the small bell & for iron'. Despite the smith's attentions, the small bell was apparently still of no use and so, in 1619, the decision was taken to have it recast and the operation was entrusted to a Roger Purdue of Bristol. The entry in the corporation papers reads as follows:

> In primis Owen Price, Hopkin Davies, Griffith Penry and Walter Thomas is to deliver, or cause to be delivered, unto the said Roger Purdue, his executors, or assigns before the last day of May next at, or upon the Back, in Bristol aforesaid, one old bell now remaining and being in the steeple of Saint Mary's church at Swansea aforesaid called the treble bell to be newly cast and made by him the said Roger.

Together with recasting the small bell, Purdue was also commissioned to cast a new bell to replace another of the bells in the steeple of St. Mary's, which must have been considered in some way defective. Bells could crack either from metal fatigue or because of an inherent flaw in the casting, and at Swansea experience had taught that binding a flawed bell with iron was no answer to the problem. In 1626 the new bells were probably placed in position, for there are entries relating to the payment of 1s. 8d. 'for iii pound and a half of rope for the treble bell' and of 7d. for a 'rafter for the wheels of the second bell and for nails'. The costs attending the repair of the bells must have been considerable about the year 1631 for the town council—which appears at this time to have largely dominated the church, vicar and wardens—decided that peals rung at the request of individuals or strangers should be paid for by the persons concerned. The resolution runs as follows:

> In regard that the town and parish bath been at an extraordinary charge towards the repairing of the bells, in consideration thereof it is agreed upon these orders as followeth concerning the safety of them. In primis the ringers for their part is to have

for every peal ringing of half an hour long the sum of eight pence. Also it is ordered that no double knell is to be rung for any single body unless they do pay to the churchwardens towards the bells two shillings and eight pence. And, as for strangers, if there be any that will have any knell rung, that they do likewise pay unto the wardens towards the bells two shillings eight pence, so that they do not exceed above six peals, and if they will have any more rung, it is agreed upon that they shall likewise pay towards the said bells 2s. 8d. more.

These were the bells which rang out over Swansea, its bay and its hinterland and which, whenever they were tolled, conveyed some message, whether a summons, a farewell salutation to the dead, or good tidings.

The Churchwardens' Accounts establish with certainty the presence of pews in St. Mary's. These were a new development in the sixteenth century and in this early period they were usually arranged around the church in the aisles, the nave being reserved as an open space. In all probability, the early general rule for a congregation had been to stand when not kneeling. Stone bench tables against the walls or round the piers would have sufficed for the aged and infirm. The custom of providing wooden seats for the congregation would appear to have originated with patrons and founders of chantries causing seats to be fixed within their parcloses or screens, and this practice was then gradually extended to the body of the church. Pews were doubtless intended for those parishioners whose circumstances enabled them to secure sittings by payment of a rent. The earliest record relating to pews in the Churchwardens' Accounts of Swansea relates to 1560 and reads: 'An order made by John Thomas Fleming, portreeve of Swansea, and by Iankyn Phillip & John ap John Thomas Sadler, proctors of our lady church of Swansea, as concerning the pews of the said church in the year of our Lord God 1560 as every man & woman may know their pews without any variance or strife'. The churchwardens at Swansea then were determined to guard against any unseemly proceedings and therefore allotted the pews to those who had applied for or claimed them. This was a very wise procedure, as disputes over pews were very common occurrences in the sixteenth century. However, despite the efforts of the wardens, it appears that they were not entirely successful. In 1601 William John Harris of Swansea and Robert ap Morgan of Pontardulais were called upon to arbitrate between John Moris and Joan his wife, plaintiffs, and Edward Morgan and Mary his wife, defendants, concerning the occupancy of a pew in St. Mary's. Their determination was that both parties should be lovers and friends, that they should both forthwith cease to pursue actions against each other in the ordinary court, and that they should jointly occupy the same pew.

In 1560 there were five pews in St. Mary's, four of which were occupied by the most prominent and affluent of the town inhabitants who also, by virtue of their wealth and standing, filled the most prestigious borough offices. It was natural and understandable in these circumstances that the first pew on the left hand side of the church should have been allotted to the portreeve. There was a fifth pew but it was apparently unappropriated. At this time there is no mention of rents, but two years later the number of pews had been increased considerably and payments were charged for the sittings. 'The names of them that had taken pews' now numbered 27 and each paid 4*d*. The grievous evil of seat-rents, from which the Church of England was to suffer so bitterly for centuries by making it the very centre of class distinctions based on wealth, had begun from comparatively innocent motives in early days. The idea originated in the fifteenth century with the supplying of seats for women only and these, probably, of an aged and delicate nature. The Reformation gave a great impetus to the seat-letting movement with the result that the church became parcelled out into ranges of pews or seats in accordance with the position or wealth of the occupant. In 1586 more pews were installed, since money was spent on 'making & mending of the new pews & for nails to the same'. The following year a list of the pews was drawn up together with their situations. There were six pews under the rood loft, two new ones in the southern 'yeld', eleven others in the same place, seven before the pulpit, two under the organ and, quaintly, five under the organ 'where the men were'; in the Glovers' Chapel there were three pews, seven by the Glovers' Chapel, a similar number next to the northern 'yeld', and two by the west door. It would appear, therefore, that by 1587 there were 52 pews in St. Mary's church, a reflection possibly of the increasing population and prosperity of the town in which the church was situated.

St. Mary's had two main sources of income. These were rents—from lands and houses, pews, and standings at the three fairs held annually in the town—and knells for the dead. That the church finances were simple and modest in scale appears from the fact that in a typical year like 1611-12 (May to May) the total receipts from all sources only amounted to £4. 10s. 3d. Of this sum, rents accounted for £3 15s. 3d., £3 4s. 4d. from lands and houses, 9s. 3d. for standings in the fairs, and 1s. 8d. for pews. The remainder came from such miscellaneous sources as collections for the poor (10s.), knells for the dead (4s.), and the previous year's surplus (1s.). Against this low income the largest items in a total expenditure of £3 4s. 5d. were for the maintenance and repair of the church fabric and goods, and for administration.

The church officers included the wardens, the beadle, and the clerk. The wardens, the guardians or keepers of the church, whose office dated back to the fourteenth century, and whose duties comprised the provision of necessaries for divine service and the assignment of seats to parishioners, were four in number at Swansea, two for the town and two for the parish. They were chosen and sworn in by the portreeve at a meeting of the vestry. No information is available as to how the beadle was appointed but, in all probability, he was selected in much the same way as the wardens. The accounts of the common attorneys, however, reveal that he was clothed and paid by the corporation. Among the disbursements for 1622-23 are the following items:

| | |
|---|---|
| paid for Evan the beadle's clothes | vis. id. |
| paid to Hopkin Morgan as long as he was beadle | viiis. |
| paid to Evan the beadle | xvs. |

The duties of the beadle are not recorded in the town muniments, but from other sources it can be established that he was responsible for summoning the parishioners to the parish meeting, impounding stray cattle, and driving out of the church any dogs, which had doubtless followed faithfully in the wake of their masters, but whose presence could disrupt services; but his main duties were punitive in nature.

The clerk was appointed by the portreeve, aldermen, churchwardens, common attorneys, and burgesses, with the consent and approbation of the vicar. His assistant appears to have been appointed in much the same way.

During the latter half of the sixteenth century there emerged at Swansea trends seemingly indicative of Puritan sympathies. It has already been demonstrated how conditions in the town in the early part of this century had not been unconducive towards the reception of Protestant ideas. Not only had there been a strong merchant group in the borough in contact with such large trading centres as London and Bristol, where Protestant opinion took root, but the inhabitants had also been favourably placed to buy and read the English Protestant writings if they were so inclined. Even though there is no positive evidence to that effect, there might well have been present in the town those who had welcomed the religious changes introduced in the reigns of Henry VIII and Edward VI. These propitious conditions still prevailed in the reign of Elizabeth, and would have facilitated considerably the implantation of the Puritan seed which was being introduced into Wales, by sea as well as by land, from the English border counties. That the town might have acquired a mild Puritan complexion by the late sixteenth and early seventeenth centuries is indicated in three directions: in a demand by the parishioners for the divine services to be conducted in Welsh; in payments made by the corporation to itinerant preachers; and, finally, in the baptismal names given by some of the parishioners to their newborn.

Realization of the importance of instructing the people in their own language had in 1563 prompted the introduction into Parliament of an Act by which a complete translation of the Prayer Book and Bible in Welsh was to be prepared by 1 March 1567 and a copy of each placed in every parish church. The responsibility for seeing that the work was accomplished was placed on the shoulders of the four Welsh bishops and the bishop of Hereford. The time was too short for the completion of the work, but in 1567 there appeared the Prayer Book and the New Testament, translated very largely by William Salesbury. Further translation was brought to a standstill by a quarrel between Salesbury and Bishop Richard Davies and it was not until 1588 that a complete translation of the scriptures in Welsh, the work of William Morgan, appeared. It had been enjoined by the Act of 1563 that once the scriptures had been translated, the services were to be celebrated in Welsh 'where that Tongue is commonly spoken or used'. At Swansea it is quite possible that a very large element in the population at this time was Welsh in speech but, despite this, the vicar, John After, a 'preacher of God's word', continued to conduct the services entirely in English. Though John After was a married man, his son, Francis (d.1646), was not to take the cloth; rather, he became a prosperous shopkeeper living in a substantial house containing two halls, one large and one small, a kitchen, five chambers, cellars and a shop. In 1632 he was selected to become portreeve.

On 18 January 1592/3 Morgan Rosser and Roger John Hopkin, on behalf of themselves and the parishioners, presented articles against their vicar in the Consistory Court of the Archdeacon at Carmarthen on the grounds that he had not celebrated divine service in Welsh (*in Wallica*). The court attempted to reach a compromise, for in a decree issued on 6 February 1592/3 After was, on the following Sunday, to celebrate the service in Welsh. Furthermore, he was subsequently to conduct divine service in Welsh on every third Sunday. He was also to be provided with a curate who was conversant with the Welsh language. On 28 June 1593 further articles were presented against the minister by Hopkin John and Thomas William. Their proctor, Rees, alleged that After had also not conducted the burial services in the maternal language, namely Welsh. The vicar, however, through his proctor, Morgan, contended that he had observed the previous injunctions diligently.

The demand for the services in Welsh may have arisen for more than one reason. It almost certainly reflected the presence in the parish of a substantial number of Welsh speakers. It might also have been an insistence on the use of Welsh, less for the sake of the language itself, than as a means of attacking an unpopular vicar. But on the other hand, it may well have been indicative of the emergence of Puritan sympathies, as insistence on the individual reading and interpretation of the scriptures was of the very essence of Puritanism.

Perhaps a stronger suggestion that there may have been a Puritan element in the town is to be found in the attention given to sermons. That the corporation had caught something of the prevailing mania for them is indicated in the payments that were made to itinerant preachers. The following items selected from many others of the same kind in the accounts of the common attorneys will serve to illustrate this:

1617/18 Item paid the 21st of December for a sermon viis. od.
paid Mr Holsegrave for a sermon iiis. iiiid.
Item paid to the preacher of Carmarthen xs.
1623 Item paid Mr. Edwards first quarter the 2 day of January for reading of morning prayer 0-10-0
1624 Item paid Mr Rogers for a sermon 0-6-8
1634 paid to Robert Guy, for preaching a sermon on the 2 of December 1634 vs
paid to Mr Hodges for two sermons the 3rd of August xs
1639/40 Item paid to Mr Parsons for a sermon 0-06-08
Item paid Mr Lowe preacher for his sermon 0-06-08.

Though it has not been possible to identify the greater number of the itinerant ministers who preached at Swansea, it has been possible to identify two positively and a third with a reasonable degree of certainty. The two whose identification is certain are Evan Williams and Lewis Thomas, both men whose strong Puritan sympathies were to be exemplified in their later careers. Evan Williams, during the Propagation period, appeared as an itinerant whose particular field of activity was Glamorgan and Carmarthen, while Lewis Thomas not only became a member of John Miles's Baptist church at Ilston in Gower (27 November 1650), but he was also one of the two upon whom devolved the responsibility of supervising the Baptist cause in the Swansea area after Miles had

*The Reformation and the Emergence of Puritanism* 183

departed for America. The third preacher whose identity it has been possible to ascertain with a reasonable degree of certainty is (Christopher) Jackson who, during the period of the Propagation, was active as an itinerant in Pembroke, but who later was settled as minister at Lampeter Velfrey. It is significant also that many of the preachers who delivered these sermons in St. Mary's were described as having come from Carmarthen or Monmouth, both areas where Puritanism had made considerable progress by the late sixteenth and early seventeenth centuries.

Finally, the names chosen for their children by some of the townspeople may also have some bearing on religious trends. It is well-known that those who sympathized with Puritan teaching tended to give their children biblical names. In the Swansea parish register a number of such names begin to appear in the 1630s. In so far as the fathers' occupations can be established, they appear to have been mostly craftsmen, many of whom, moreover, had been admitted to the freedom.

It has been possible to collect, from the register, the following list of biblical names given to their children by some of the parishioners. For purposes of clarity the child's name has been placed in one column, the father's in a second, and the father's occupation in a third.

| Child's name | Father's name | Father's occupation |
|---|---|---|
| Ruth | John Roberts | Miller |
| Rebecca | Hugh William | Tanner |
| Sara | Richard George | Vintner-burgess |
| Mathew | William Vaughan | — |
| Moses | Thomas Arnalt | — |
| Debora | Rees Bevan | — |
| Joseph | William Granford | — |
| Isaac | Thomas David | — |
| Samuel | Roger Williams | — |
| Emanuel | John David | — |
| Hester | William Bayly | Burgess |

In the early decades of the seventeenth century Puritanism was emerging not only at Swansea itself but also in the neighbourhood of the town, and may be discerned in the activities there of such young Puritan ministers as Marmaduke Matthew at Penmaen and Ambrose Mostyn at Pennard.

The son of Matthew ap John of Nydfwch, Llangyfelach, Marmaduke Matthew was an M.A. of All Souls College, Oxford. In 1636 he was vicar of Penmaen near Swansea where he preached 'against the keeping of all holy days'. Following episcopal censure of his behaviour, he fled to New England. His activities are clearly indicative of the district's new mental and spiritual outlook because the denunciation of holy days was an important element in early Puritanism.

Ambrose Mostyn was the son of Dr Henry Mostyn of Calcott, Flintshire. Born in 1610, he had matriculated at Brasenose College in 1629. It has been maintained that he started ministering in south Wales after he had finished his education at Oxford. In 1642 the parishioners of Pennard, 'having never had more than four sermons a year in their parish church, and those by a man of a very scandalous life', prayed for the nomination of Ambrose Mostyn 'a Lecturer, a man of goodly sort, and one who can preach in the Welsh and English tongues'. This petition received the favourable attention of the House of Commons and on 30 April it was ordered 'That Ambrose Mostyn, a godly and faithful preacher, be at the Desires of divers of the Parishioners of Pennard, in the County of Glamorgan, recommended to the said Parish to be their Lecturer at their own proper costs and charges; to preach every Lord's day in the forenoon and afternoon'. He could not have remained there for long because, on the outbreak of the Civil War he, together with other Puritan divines in Wales, was constrained to flee and seek safety in England.

In this survey of the religious history of Swansea between 1485-1642 it has been shown how, during the reigns of Henry VIII and Edward VI, some of the monuments of medieval piety had been swept away never to be restored. It has also been demonstrated that Swansea's attitude towards these and other changes effected by the Reformation would not have differed greatly from that of the remainder of Wales. However, even though the religious changes of the early sixteenth century had been accepted with apparent indifference, conditions in Swansea were far more propitious than in most areas of Wales for the reception of Protestant ideas. In the Elizabethan and Jacobean periods, on the other hand, distinctive pointers appear to indicate the emergence of Puritan sympathies both within the town and its hinterland. Though by 1642 the number of Puritans in Swansea would not have been great, by 1660 the town had become the very mecca of south Wales Puritanism. It was, of course, the events of the Civil War and Commonwealth periods which determined that this should be so.

# Chapter Six

## SWANSEA DURING THE CIVIL WAR

On 22 August 1642 King Charles I raised his standard at Nottingham. The first Civil War had begun. Richard Baxter, the eminent Puritan divine, classified the supporters of King and Parliament in the war thus: 'A very great part of the Knights and gentlemen of England, and also most of the poorest of the people, whom the others called the rabble, did follow the gentry and were for the King. On the Parliament's side were the smaller part of the gentry in most of the counties, and the greatest part of the tradesmen and freeholders and the middle sort of men, especially in those Corporations and counties which depend on clothing and such manufactures'. This economic factor was one of the most important considerations which determined the loyalties of both persons and corporations. During the period 1540-1640, the great rise in prices, consequent upon such factors as the influx of gold and silver bullion from the new world into the old, and the considerable increase in the population, had resulted in the Crown, which was dependent for much of its revenue on fixed rents, becoming impoverished. On the other hand, the same causes had given a great stimulus to industrial activity which had taken place outside the old corporate boroughs and thus outside the controlling influence of the guilds. Most of the capital for these industrial developments had come from the merchants in the towns but a great deal had also come from the landowners. Furthermore, during this period there had been a revolution in the use of land. As a result of the price revolution, rents had risen, enclosures had taken place, and capitalist methods had been applied to land exploitation. The people who stood to benefit most from the changed economic climate, and the unparalleled opportunities presented by these one hundred years, were the progressive gentry[1] and merchant groups. The older

---
[1] Professor Tawney had maintained that the gentry had risen as a class at the expense of the aristocracy and on the profits of agriculture. Professor R.H. Trevor-Roper, on the other hand, held

aristocracy, on the other hand, the heirs of ancient wealth, dispersed rights, and large responsibilities, found it increasingly difficult to keep their heads above water. The balance of social forces, on which the stability of a constitution depends, was upset. The early Stuarts failed to appreciate this and, consequently, did not realize that a modification of the constitution, to correspond with the new conditions, was necessary. In this failure may be found one of the main causes of the Civil War.

Together with economic considerations, religion also played an important part in the struggle. Indeed, it may be doubted whether there ever would have been an actual outbreak of hostilities but for the influence of, and the bitterness engendered by, religious differences in what was probably the most religious age in British history. The Stuarts had tried to use the established church to strengthen the cause of monarchy, and this policy had made the Church of England vulnerable to attack from both those who wanted to supersede it and those who wanted to strengthen the Protestant element within it. The claims which were made by the church on its own behalf, and on behalf of the Crown, had become more widely embracing, and this had made it difficult for the clergy and laity within the church to propose changes in a Protestant direction. In the consequent inability of the church to accommodate the growing forces of religious dissent may be found another very important cause of the hostilities.

The attitude of Wales towards the struggle was largely determined by four main considerations. In the first place, the 'middle sort of men' had few representatives in the country. Again, the gentry, with a few exceptions, were loyal to the Crown, while their tenants, in turn, were loyal to them. The squires had been intensely loyal to the Tudors, partly through gratitude for past favours, and partly through a lively expectation of more favours to come. This loyalty they had transferred to the Stuarts, but in the process of transfer this allegiance had undergone an important

that it was a section of the gentry, those connected with the Court, trade, and who held office, who were the ones to rise. The other gentry, whom he described as the 'mere' gentry, found themselves in difficulties. Hard hit by the price revolution, slow to redeem their losses by good 'husbandry', heavily taxed, they felt themselves to be a depressed, declining class and grumbling, consoled—or armed—themselves with religious dissent.

change. No longer did it attach itself merely to persons—but for this it could hardly have survived the neglect and misrule of Charles I— rather did it embrace the whole complex of institutions through which the monarch acted: parliament, the law, and church establishment. Support for an arbitrary despotism, therefore, was no part of their creed, but any sympathies which they may have felt for the parliamentary cause were soon swept away by the growing violence of the opposition and, above all, by its attack on the church. Another factor which may help to explain the attitude of Wales is to be found in the language in which the parliamentary appeals were made. Of all the hundreds of pamphlets that appeared in the years before and during the civil wars, not one tried to explain the parliamentary standpoint in Welsh. The bards, balladmongers and clergy, on the other hand, who were, at this time, perhaps the main agents for the dissemination of news—and propaganda—in Wales, were unswervingly loyal to the Crown and the episcopate. Finally, as far as Wales is concerned, Puritanism had not as yet made any great impact.

Most parts of Wales, then, were royalist in sympathy. Only in those limited areas which had commercial contacts with London or Bristol, or which had felt the influence of border Puritanism, did parliamentary supporters gain the upper hand. The nucleus of parliamentary strength in south Wales lay in the towns of Pembroke, Tenby and Haverfordwest, boroughs whose English-speaking populace and close connections with London and Bristol had always tended to make them less immune to radical influences than most of the Principality. Conditions in Swansea were not dissimilar to those in the south Pembrokeshire towns. Not only was there a thriving trading and merchant community there, which had commercial contacts with London and Bristol, but the evidence also seems to suggest that by 1642 the town was harbouring a pocket, if not of Puritans, certainly of people showing unmistakable Puritan sympathies. But it was, in fact, for the King that Swansea declared itself. The loyalty of the town to the Crown may, perhaps, be explained on three grounds: first, a business background did not of necessity breed parliamentary sympathies; again, the influence of the Worcester family, though weakened by this time, was still not negligible; and finally, there were the royalist sympathies of the neighbouring gentry.

That a business background did not of necessity breed parliamentary sympathies is admirably illustrated in the career of Walter Thomas, a Swansea mercer and merchant. A descendant of Einion ap Collwyn and a cadet of the Prices of Glyn Nedd, he had twice occupied the office of portreeve, in 1615 and again in 1625. On the decease of Sir Thomas Mansel in 1631, he was appointed deputy-steward, an office which he held until 1645, when he was displaced by Philip Jones. From 1620 onwards he occasionally appears in the Port Books as an exporter of iron and agricultural by-products, such as skins and feathers, to that great entrepôt of trade, Bristol. His strong royalist sympathies received recognition when, in 1644, he was appointed governor of the town. As a result of the triumph of the parliamentary forces, his fortunes were later to suffer two severe setbacks: his estates were sequestrated and he was deprived of his aldermanic status.

An important factor which may have helped to determine Swansea's loyalty to the royal cause was the influence of the Earls of Worcester. Though the control which the family exercised over the town had been weakened by the early decades of the seventeenth century, it had by no means been completely removed. It was not in the best interests of the town to sever all connection with its lord, for he, and especially one like the Earl of Worcester who had considerable influence at Court, could do much to promote the prosperity of the borough. Thus, on the eve of the Civil War, the wishes of the Worcester family—especially as they would have been made known to the town through the deputy-steward, Walter Thomas—while not a decisive force, perhaps, would certainly have weighed heavily in the determinations of the corporation. In 1642 the lord was Henry Somerset, the fifth earl and first marquis. He was a Catholic and the staunchest royalist in south Wales. The full weight of his influence, therefore, would have been thrown in the scales in favour of the King.

Even more important, perhaps, in determining the attitude of the corporation was the influence of the local gentry. That the greater number of these were royalist in sympathy, and exercised a considerable influence in the town, is indicated by the fact that when in 1644 Swansea was called upon to surrender by a parliamentary ship stationed at Milford Haven, the letter in which the demand was rejected was subscribed to 'by the High Sheriff and most of the Gentlemen of Glamorganshire'. Unfortunately, the names of those who subscribed, or who would have subscribed, are not appended to the letter. Consequently, their number, and the degree of influence which they could have exercised in the town, are not known. Nevertheless, it is probably safe to assume that among the subscribers would have been that eminent barrister and judge, David Jenkins of Hensol, who, indeed, is credited with its compilation, William Thomas of Dan-y-Graig, and Bussy Mansel of Briton Ferry. Jenkins and Thomas were particularly staunch in their allegiance to Charles, which led to Jenkins being imprisoned by Parliament from 1645 to 1660, while William Thomas, a relative of Walter Thomas, was not only deprived of his status as alderman but his estates were sequestered as well. Bussy Mansel, on the other hand, the youngest son of Arthur Mansel and Jane, the daughter and heiress of William Price of Briton Ferry, proved to be of an entirely different kidney. He averted possible imprisonment and confiscation of his property by deserting the royal cause some time between September and November 1645. It is quite possible that among the subscribers there were many others who, like Bussy, were not unprepared to change sides.

Since, however, there were in operation at the town factors conducive to the growth of parliamentary sympathies, it is not surprising that there existed in Swansea what may well have been a considerable minority of disaffected. Most prominent among the laity were Philip Jones, Rowland Dawkin, John Price, Ienkin Francklin and Mathew David. Philip Jones was the son of one David Johnes, and it is thought that he was born c.1618 on a freehold known as Pen-y-Waun in Llangyfelach, a property of the annual value of £17 to £20. That he was a Puritan, and that his disaffection in all probability sprang from this source, would appear from the fact that his name is entered on the register of John Miles's Baptist church at Ilston in Gower. Further indications of his Puritan sympathies may be found in his efforts, particularly after 1645, to

Colonel Philip Jones

establish Congregationalism in the Swansea area and his presentment, in 1662/3, on three separate occasions before the Consistory Court of the Archdeacon at Carmarthen for failing to attend church. Puritan leanings may also have been an important determining factor in the loyalty of Rowland Dawkin. The eldest son of George Dawkin of Kilvrough (Cilfrwch) in Gower, he was a gentleman of good connections and considerable landed wealth. His wife was Mary, the daughter of George Bowen of Langrove, and he had by her three sons and three daughters. He was commissioned in the parliamentary army—he held the rank of Colonel—and served on various parliamentary commissions and committees. His Puritanism may be adduced from a consideration of the following significant circumstances. His home lay in the parish of Pennard, which, on the eve of the Civil War, had acquired a strong Puritan complexion; again, his three daughters were all given biblical names, a fairly common practice among Puritans generally. The eldest was named Rebecca, the second Priscilla, and the youngest Ruth. And finally, in 1662/3, he was on four separate occasions presented before the Consistory Court for failing to have his children baptized in the parish church, a more certain indication perhaps of his Puritan sympathies. In the case of John Price, the eldest son of William Price of Gelli-hir, any Puritan views which he might have held would have been reinforced by family connections, for his eldest sister, Jane, was married to Philip Jones, the leading parliamentarian in south Wales. Again, the loyalties of Ienkin Francklin (gentleman) and Mathew David (mercer and shoemaker) may well have been largely determined by Puritan beliefs, for the names of both appear on the register of Miles's church. Furthermore, in the case of Mathew David, his presentment on two separate occasions before the Consistory Court in 1664 for failing to attend church is a signal confirmation of his Puritan outlook. But together with these religious and family considerations, the loyalties of some, at least, of these men may have been determined by a desire to hold high office, which they could hardly have hoped to occupy but for the lavish scale on which Parliament rewarded its servants. Indeed, it was in accordance with the victorious Parliament's policy of filling the most important municipal offices with its own nominees that Mathew David, in company with Philip Jones and two others, was appointed an alderman of the town on 19 August 1650. The restoration of monarchy in 1660 resulted in his exclusion and he remained in the political wilderness until 1682.

It does not do to over-emphasize the differences between the adherents of King and Parliament because the lines of demarcation between them were rather blurred, and there is plenty of evidence to suggest that, in many cases, the partisans of both sides were very lukewarm in their support. It was with deep distaste that most men had embarked on what the parliamentary general, Waller, writing to the royalist Hopton, called 'this war without an enemy'. It was never a war between geographical areas or rival classes, and men took up arms from all manner of motives, and sentiment weighed as heavily as logic or law. The absence of clear-cut issues is aptly demonstrated at Swansea in the conduct of Rowland Dawkin and Bussy Mansel, for the former, before joining the parliamentary forces, had compounded for his delinquency to the royalist Commissioners of Array, while the latter had long been a royalist stalwart before finally going over to the parliamentary side.

In addition to the lay supporters of the parliamentary cause, there were also some notable Puritan ministers in the Swansea district. Included in their ranks were stalwarts like Marmaduke Matthew and Ambrose Mostyn. All these parliamentarians and Puritans were, however, at first overwhelmed by the strong royalist tide. It was only later in the wars, when the fortunes of battle had turned in their favour, that they came into their own.

The first indication of approaching troubles is to be found in the Common Attorneys' Accounts for 1642 when some expense was incurred 'in making of the new magazine in the lower town hall'. From the nature of the disbursements it becomes clear that the room was stone-built and, since weapons and gunpowder were to be stored there, the floor was strengthened and the door provided with two strong locks. The walls were plastered on the inside and, as a finishing touch, given a coat of whitewash made from lime. Since mention is made of masons building one wall, and 1s. only was expended on the provision of new stones, it would appear that what probably happened was that an area in the town hall, possibly beneath it, was converted into a room by the simple device of constructing one wall, and access to the magazine was then provided by the insertion of a door in the new wall.

The outbreak of hostilities drove some of the leading Puritans and their sympathizers out of the area. The Puritan ministers fled in haste to safer and more congenial quarters in Bristol or London, while laymen like Philip Jones and Rowland Dawkin joined the parliamentary forces. The goods of the more prominent among the disaffected were appropriated. Thus, on 26 July 1643, Bussy

Mansel and William Thomas were ordered by the Commissioners of Array for Glamorgan to sequester the estates of all 'Convicted separatists, fugitives and other disaffected persons within the several hundreds of Swansea, Neath and Llangyfelach'. Their movable goods were to be sold, and their lands and tenements set out to rent. In conformity with this order, on 15 September 1643, they took custody of the goods of Rowland Dawkin of Pennard and Ienkin Francklin of Ilston 'as separatists and persons disaffected unto his Majesty, the laws and constitutions of this Realm'. Rowland Dawkin and Ienkin Francklin, however, conformed, with the result that the goods which had not been disposed of by Bussy Mansel and William Thomas were restored to them. From this it would appear that it was some time after this date that Rowland Dawkin fled to join the parliamentary forces.

At this stage in the wars, Swansea was firmly under the control of the royalists. In 1643, the lord of the town, himself the greatest and most ardent royalist in south Wales, came in person to Swansea, for there is recorded in the accounts: 'There was paid in April last 1643 for my Lord Marquis of Worcester his servants' diet & horse meat 10li. 09s. 04d. and 19s. 2d. more was paid for one night's entertainment to Sir Marmaduke Lloyd, all being 11li. 08s. 06d./3li whereof we had received out of the contribution moneys, for making up our magazine, & the other 8li. 8s. 6d. we paid out of the town moneys—08li. 08s. 06d.' Worcester had undoubtedly visited the town to exhort the townspeople to make the utmost effort on behalf of their King, and to ensure that the borough was put in an adequate state of defence.

Swansea was of value to the royalist cause in many ways during the early campaigns of the war: it was a garrison town; a port of entry, and a storage place for arms smuggled in from the Continent; it supplied contingents of men for the King's armies; and finally, it was a source of revenue.

As a result of the war, Swansea was constrained to assume once again its medieval status as a garrison town, a role which it had discarded after the Acts of Union. The town was of importance to the King as a military centre since it enabled him to provide—as far as in his power it lay—for the defence of west Glamorgan against any seaborne attack by the parliamentary forces from Pembroke. In a report submitted to Colonel Charles Gerard some time in 1644 by the Commissioners of Array for Glamorgan on the state of that county, the strategic importance of the town in this respect is emphasized. The report declared that two garrisons had, of necessity, to be kept in the county, one at Swansea and the other at Cardiff. But in addition to these garrisons, 'at least 24 special creeks upon the sea-coast, which extends itself upon this county between 40 and 50 miles in length, ought to be defended continually with strong guards and watches'. The evidence is too slender for any estimate to be made of the numerical strength of the royalist garrison at Swansea. However, it would not appear to have been particularly formidable in view of the King's pressing needs in other spheres of the war, and, since on the two occasions that they occupied the town during the first Civil War, the parliamentary forces were allowed to do so unopposed.

Again, it is apparent that Swansea during the early years of the conflict was a port of entry for arms purchased abroad, particularly in France. On 24 July 1643 the Commissioners of Array for Glamorgan entered into an agreement with two Frenchmen, Hammon le Baut and Francis le Milbeau, whereby they were to procure and deliver at the town the following munitions:

> 200 hundred barrels of powder whereof 2 parts must be musket powder and the third cannon at 18*d*. per pound, the one with the other
> 1000 pound of match at 6*d*. per pound and 500 li. muskets and bandoliers of the best at 18*s*. musket & bandolier.

In the agreement it was provided that if any miscarriage should happen then the said Hammon and Francis were to receive compensation. The mischance referred to was doubtless the possibility that the arms would fall into the hands of the parliamentarians. The navy had defected to Parliament—'the ghost of Raleigh pursued the House of Stuart to the scaffold'—and the chances, therefore, of the ship or ships carrying the arms being intercepted were great. However, on this occasion, the French vessels successfully evaded the patrolling parliamentary warships and the arms were brought safely to their intended destination, whereupon the commissioners ordered Robert Donnell of Swansea to deliver 'all such muskets as lately were landed', together with one barrel of powder and the whole quantity of match, to William Thomas of the same town. The latter, after due trial of the arms, was to distribute those muskets which he regarded as serviceable, with the assent of Sir Edward Thomas and the rest of the western commissioners, among the trained bands of the five western hundreds of Glamorgan in order to supply their deficiencies. What remained of the arms and the match were to be sent to Cardiff to be disposed of by the commissioners of the eastern parts among the trained bands of the five eastern hundreds as they thought best. It is quite apparent that the King's attempts to arm his Welsh levies by importing arms from abroad were beset with difficulties. Not only did these arms have to run the gauntlet of the parliamentary blockade but many of them were also defective. Corroboration of the King's problems in providing weapons may be adduced from the fact that he was driven to resort to the expedient of borrowing arms from private persons. An entry in the Register of the Commissioners of Array, dated 18 August 1643, contains a list of the arms lent by certain gentlemen, including William Thomas of Swansea, for the King's service. It reads as follows:

A perfect list of all such arms as have been lent by the gentlemen underwritten; for his Majesty's service to be either satisfied, (for) them in money or the like arms to be promised and judgements in that behalf/

| Lent By | Muskets | Powder | Bandoliers Glaives |
|---|---|---|---|
| Sir Nicholas Kemys | 14 and | 4 & | 10 |
| Sir John Aubery | 6 | 30 & | 24 |
| Marmaduke Mathew Esq. | 15 | 21& | 15 blackbills |
| William Thomas Esq. | 06 | 10 | 00 02-2 and 2 clubs |

Swansea, however, was not only a port of entry for arms. The indications are that it was also a storage place for them. The corporation had been busily employed in 1642 in erecting a magazine, and the town was undoubtedly an important royalist arsenal. In the report on the state of Glamorgan presented to Gerard, the arms of the trained bands in the ten hundreds of Glamorgan were estimated at 800. Of these, 784 were housed at Swansea.

A further service rendered by the town to the royalist cause during the opening campaigns of the war was that it supplied contingents of men for the King's forces. Indeed, this was a vital contribution made by Wales as a whole, which has been described as the 'nursery of the King's infantry'. In August 1643, Bussy Mansel, Walter Thomas and William Thomas were ordered by the Commissioners of Array to raise in the three hundreds of Swansea, Llangyfelach and Neath, sixty, twenty, and forty able men respectively, all well armed, and to despatch them under the chief constable of each hundred to Cardiff.

There was, however, some natural reluctance on the part of these men to serve in the King's levies. On 13 August, William Thomas wrote to Sir Anthony Mansel to protest against this order. He indicated that it would impose a great hardship on the hundred of Swansea since 'their whole band is already in service and so long continued under your command in the garrison'. He desired that Llangyfelach should be spared as well. The answer from Cardiff was not encouraging. The forces to be raised in the hundreds of Swansea and Llangyfelach were ordered to proceed to Cardiff with all possible speed. There was some delay in despatching them because, on 15 August 1643, the commissioners again wrote to the 'Western Gentlemen' urging them to greater speed. Mansel, Walter Thomas and William Thomas, replying on the same day, explained that in the hundred of Swansea they had been unable to raise more than forty men. These, together with the twenty from Llangyfelach, had been delivered over into the hands of the high constables. However, the impressment of these men, probably farm labourers, had left the area 'so gleaned of all spare people with those several occasions of late that the husbandmen will be hardly able to manage their tillage, and thereby not only a scarcity of grain will ensue but also an inability to maintain any necessary charge that shall be imposed upon them'.

From this letter it appears also that the men were poorly armed, just as the Welsh contingents at Edgehill in October 1642, the first battle of the Civil War, had been badly equipped: 'We received xii bill staves from Mr. William Gybbs which are carried by some of these men; more arms we could not get together upon so short summons. Neither do we conceive that the country will afford any worth the showing in the field'. From an order dated 18 August 1643 it becomes apparent that Swansea had failed to provide even the forty men, for it is stated that 'George Bath and William David chief constables of the hundred of Swansea hath disbursed the sum of 13li. 5s.: over and above vili by them formerly received towards the advancing of 30 men sent out of the said hundred'. The gentlemen commissioners of the Swansea hundred were ordered to take the necessary steps for the repayment of this sum. This reimbursement had still not been made by 25 August because, on this day, the Commissioners of Array, in order to repay the money and to spare the county a general rate, ordered William Thomas of Dan-y-Graig to 'reserve and keep in his hands so much of the personal estate of the separatists and indicted persons within those two hundreds as shall satisfy the high constables of Swansea'. The fact that the expenses incurred in conducting the men to Cardiff were to be met from the sequestered estates of the supporters of Parliament is a clear enough indication of the policy of making the enemy, as far as was possible, pay for the war.

These men were needed for the siege of Gloucester. In 1643 the King, while the initiative still remained with him, had planned a threefold attack on London. One thrust was to be directed down the Thames valley; another from the south-west; and a third from the north. The capture of the three great strongholds of Gloucester, Bristol and Hull was an essential prerequisite for the success of this strategy. Of particular importance was Gloucester, as its seizure would provide the King with complete control of the Severn and open the road to Wales. An army was raised by Lord Herbert of Raglan to lay siege to it but, on 24 March, this force was taken by surprise by Waller at Highnam in the Forest of Dean and surrendered without a blow being struck. The King himself then proceeded to invest the city, and it was to strengthen the attacking forces that the troops raised in the hundreds of Swansea and Llangyfelach were required.

Finally, at a time when Charles I's financial needs were extremely pressing, Swansea assisted his cause by contributing to the war chest. On 18 October 1643, £1000 were levied upon the county of Glamorgan, and the town's contribution towards the raising of this sum was assessed at £120.16s.8d. Comparable figures for the other nine hundreds were as follows:

|  | £ | s. | d. |
|---|---|---|---|
| In Kybbor besides Cardiff | 58 | 6 | 8 |
| Cardiff Villa | 29 | 03 | 4 |
| Dinas Powis | 120 | 16 | 8 |
| Llantrisant | 100 | 00 | 00 |
| Cowbridge | 112 | 10 | 00 |
| Caerphilly | 100 | 00 | 00 |
| Newcastle | 112 | 10 | 00 |
| Ogmore | 87 | 10 | 00 |
| Neath | 87 | 10 | 00 |

For purposes of assessment, each of the hundreds of Glamorgan had been rated separately and Swansea's rate, together with that of Dinas Powis, was again the highest. This, in itself, is a positive indication of the relative wealth and prosperity of the town and its hinterland.

The King's main problem in the conduct of the war was the raising of money and Charles was prepared to adopt almost any expedient in order to replenish his coffers. Since the beginning of Elizabeth's reign, and owing mainly to the rapid diminution of the timber supplies, coal had acquired a new importance. Charles was not blind to the possibilities of making this commodity meet his financial needs to some extent and, at Swansea, this fuel could be found in abundance. Consequently, when the estates of John Dorington were sequestered on account of his delinquency, the King, on 1 February 1643/4, granted to Walter Thomas the right to mine the coal to be found on those parcels of his lands which lay within the parishes of Swansea and Llangyfelach. For every wey of coal that was mined and sold, Thomas was to pay the King 18d.

By 1644, when the parliamentary forces were vigorously pressing the war into former strongholds of the royalists, there was need to put the town of Swansea itself into a state of greater military preparedness, and the rather paltry sum of 16*s*.6*d*. was spent on repairing the turret of the castle. It is quite possible that this tower was the only readily defensible part left since the castle, by this time, was in a ruinous condition. In 1583 the castle buildings were described as being in 'great decay', and in Cromwell's survey of Gower (1650) mention is made of 'an ancient decayed building called the New Castle' valued at £2.10*s*.0*d*. and 'a piece of ruinous building called the Old Castle' which, with an adjoining cottage, was valued at 10*s*.

The turret referred to undoubtedly belonged to the New Castle which had been built in the late thirteenth or early fourteenth centuries immediately to the south of the Old Castle, a stone fortification that had occupied the site of an earlier motte on a natural scarp overlooking the river Tawe. From the slender documentary and archaeological evidence still extant, it appears that the earth and timber castle, sitting astride what is now called Worcester Place, was rebuilt in stone sometime in the thirteenth century. It has been a generally held view—a tradition clearly started by the antiquary Leland—that the New Castle was built by Bishop Henry de Gower and that it became an episcopal palace. With good reason, the arcaded parapet, which is the crowning glory of the south block, can be attributed to the influence of the bishop, since the episcopal palaces at St. David's and Lamphey, both built by him, provide the only British parallels for this embellishment at Swansea. However, the available evidence would seem to suggest that the New Castle, a self-contained unit, was built by the lord of Gower, John de Mowbray (1331-61). Although seldom resident in Swansea, he could still have taken advantage of the rare skills possessed by Henry Gower's masons, engaged in building the Hospital of St. David in such close proximity to the castle.

Together with the repairs to the castle, a governor was chosen whose loyalty to the Crown was unquestioned. This was Walter Thomas, a substantial mercer and merchant, and a person of considerable local standing and influence since he had occupied the prestigious offices of portreeve and deputy-steward.[2] The reason for these measures may well be found in the justifiable fear of the corporation that a parliamentary attack from Pembroke was imminent. There, in the early months of 1644, Parliament had gained considerable success. Rowland Laugharne, the young and energetic parliamentary leader, had proved a far better soldier than the royalist Earl of Carbery who, instead of concentrating his forces, had mistakenly dispersed his strength in small garrisons. These Laugharne had proceeded to overcome one by one. By a combined land and sea assault, he had captured the fortress which the royalists had been constructing at Pill to dominate the Haven. He had then proceeded to occupy Haverfordwest and Tenby. After the fall of Tenby (9 March 1644) he had advanced against and occupied Carmarthen. Having thus broken Carbery's power, he was free to move further afield. That his next thrust might well have been in the direction of Swansea would appear from the fact that its capture would close the last loophole in south-west Wales for a possible landing of royalist troops from Ireland. Considering the military background, it was not to be wondered at that consternation was felt at Swansea, an anxiety that was reflected in hurried preparations and in the failure of the corporation, 'by reason of the troublesome times', to hold the spring leet. The imminence of the danger must have further impressed itself upon the town when, in May 1644, it was called upon to surrender. The order was signed by Robert Moulton on board the frigate *Lion* at Milford. The text of the summons is of some interest and reads as follows:

> To the Mayor and Gentlemen of Swansea
> Gentlemen,
>   These are to will and require you, in the name of the Right Honourable Robert, Earl of Warwick, Lord High Admiral of England, Wales, and Ireland, and his Majesty's Navy Royal at Sea, that you forthwith yield the town and garrison into the obedience of the King and Parliament, and in so doing you shall be received into the protection and the associated Covenant, and

[2] Supra, p. 189.

shall be defended against all Irish rebels, Papists, and those who seek to subvert liberties, and to destroy religion, which, at this time, all the Papists and rebels in the three Kingdoms are in arms to overthrow. Therefore, consider of it, and submit; for if you shall be obstinate, and spill any blood in resisting, you may not expect such favour as your neighbours have had. And this is the advice of your friend, who endeavours to preserve you, if you accept of his proffer; if not, I shall endeavour to keep you without trade till your forced obedience bring you to the mercy of him that tendereth you grace and favour. I shall expect your answer by the bearer.
Rob(ert) Moulton

To this order an answer was sent so sharp in its terms that it is attributed to the hand of the famous David Jenkins of Hensol, 'The Judge of the Mountains'. It ran as follows:

To Robert Moulton, subscriber to the Paper directed to the Mayor and Gentlemen of Swansea.

We cannot understand how we may, with any justice or loyalty, return you the name of gentleman to your rude and rebellious paper, in the front whereof you have the boldness and presumption, in the name of the right honourable (as you term him) (whom we do and must account a dishonourable and most insulting rebel) Robert, Earl of Warwick, (by you styled) High Admiral of England, Wales and Ireland, and his Majesty's Navy Royal at Sea (the which we do and ought to protest he hath most traitorously betrayed and rebelliously possessed) to will and require us forthwith to yield the town and garrison of Swansea into the obedience of the King and Parliament (a most foul treason, masked under a fair and specious show of a most loyal and just adherency and subjection to his Majesty and his Parliament at Oxford), in defiance of which, your traitorous summons, we send you this our fixed resolution, that we will neither yield town or garrison, nor any the least interest we hold of life or fortune (under the protection of his Sacred Majesty) but will defend the same and our county against any your proud and insolent menacings (wherein your proper trade is exhibited), and in the account of a rebel and traitor we leave you to your fearful destruction.

Subscribed by the High Sheriff, and most of the Gentlemen of Glamorganshire.

No action appears to have been taken by Parliament following the refusal of the town to surrender, and Swansea celebrated the defeat of Sir William Waller at Copredy Bridge near Banbury at the end of June by ringing the church bells, for which the ringers were paid 5s.

The reason for the parliamentary forces' failure to follow up their successes in Pembrokeshire may be found in the appointment of Sir Charles Gerard, a very able professional soldier, to replace Carbery. Gerard immediately proceeded to reduce west Wales. At the head of a troop of horse, he landed at the Black Rock, near Chepstow in Monmouthshire, and advanced to meet Laugharne. He passed through Cardiff, took Kidwelly, and on 18 June occupied Carmarthen, Cardigan and Newcastle Emlyn as well as the castle at Laugharne; and Roch had also been quickly reduced. On 22 August he took Haverfordwest. Pembroke was then besieged. However, as a result of the ill-fortune which had beset the King's forces in England—Charles had been defeated by Cromwell at Marston Moor on 2 July—Gerard was recalled with his work unfinished.

In April 1645 the bells were again rung at Swansea. Though the recall of Gerard had enabled Laugharne to recover all his losses in west Wales, his triumph was short-lived. Early in 1645 Gerard returned. From Chester he marched through mid-Wales by way of Llanidloes, ravaging as he went. On 23 April he encountered Laugharne at Newcastle Emlyn and completely defeated him. It was to celebrate this victory that the bells tolled out so joyously over the town.

Swansea was not to remain for very much longer in royalist hands, however. In view of the King's pressing needs in England, Gerard was yet again recalled, and Laugharne proceeded to move against the local royalist leaders. These he defeated with great loss of life at Colby Moor, some three miles from Haverfordwest, on 1 August. He quickly cleared the royalists out of Pembrokeshire and on 12 October occupied Carmarthen. Advancing into Glamorgan, he took Swansea, and the accounts of the common attorneys record the expenditure of £1.0s.4d. 'for wine & beer for entertainment of General Laugharne'. The custody of the castle was taken from Walter Thomas, and Richard Donnell was installed in his place. He did not hold it for long, as on 17 November 1645 Philip Jones was appointed by Parliament to this office. On this day, also, Bussy Mansel, previously a royalist stalwart in the Swansea area, was promoted commander-in-chief of the parliamentary forces in the county of Glamorgan. It is rather surprising that he should have received this appointment because he was only 22 at the time. This would seem to indicate that he was either precociously experienced and capable or that he was possessed of powerful influence in high quarters. In a letter written on 13 September 1645 to Sir Jacob Astley, Baron of Reading, he appears to have been still a royalist though wavering, perhaps, in his allegiance. It was between this date, therefore, and 17 November that he apostatized from his allegiance to the King. His motives for doing so are not known, but since in 1658/9, when the cause of Charles II was gradually becoming more hopeful, he changed sides once more, he would appear to have been nothing more than a 'trimmer'.

In the *Mercurius Academicus,* a royalist journal, there appeared on 28 February 1645 a dispatch from Raglan, dated 10 February, which stated that the King's troops were 'endeavouring to block up Cardiff', and were 'already in actual possession of Swansea'. Among the charges of corruption and neglect brought against Philip Jones in 1650, by a person or persons unknown, was one to the effect that, while he was governor of Swansea, he had allowed a troop of 38 horse, commanded by one Edward Gwyn, to enter the town and seize the magazine and barks there. The result was that the enemy 'did then get the advantage of sending horse-loads thereof to the siege which was then laid by them before Cardiff'. Unfortunately, it is not now possible to ascertain the degree of truth in this allegation. The charges were obviously intended to discredit Philip Jones, and consequently they would have been presented in the way most likely to achieve this end. Rowland Dawkin's evidence, on the other hand, in which he categorically rebutted these charges—he declared that Jones had not been present in the town at the time of the incident—would have been biased in his favour because he and Jones were comrades of long standing. What is certain, however, is that a royalist force did occupy the town. At a common hall meeting held on 10 January, new common attorneys, of whom one was Leyson Seys, were appointed, and this Seys, who in the following year was disfranchised for his loyalty, was on 20 January made an alderman. The royalists could not long have remained in possession of the town, for on 19 February they were routed at Cardiff by Laugharne and he most probably reoccupied Swansea without opposition at about the same time. A common hall on 27 April was held before 'Patrick Johns portreeve and Phillip Johns steward and governor of the town of Swansea', and there is nothing in the corporation books, apart from a few trifling charges for candles for the main guard, to indicate a state of warfare or that the late changes were attended by any hostilities or confusion.

It is of considerable significance that Swansea had never once offered any resistance to the entry of the parliamentary forces. Rather had they been permitted peaceful possession of the town. This submissive behaviour on the part of the inhabitants may perhaps be explained on three grounds. In the first place, the burgesses were more intent on the physical preservation of their borough than in defending the majesty of the King. They were merchants, traders and craftsmen. What they craved was peace and continuity to enable them to pursue their commercial and business activities without impediment. To them, the town was a means by which their wealth was created; it was also a symbol of their prosperity. Its destruction, on the other hand, would have spelt disaster, economic and otherwise, for them. In their attitude there was nothing of the chivalrous abandon of the true cavalier who would willingly choose ruin and exile rather than abandon his prince. At Swansea the military commanders and traders were never prepared to play the role of a Basing House.[3]

Again, there was a Puritan element within Swansea and some, at least, of the townspeople who had supported Parliament had been

[3] The Catholic defenders of Basing House in Hampshire were prepared to die to the last man rather than surrender to the Roundheads. The House was taken after a bloody assault on 14 October 1645.

motivated by this factor to do so. Even if the greater number of the Puritans there had not actively espoused the parliamentary cause, it is reasonable to assume that they would, in all probability, have had considerable sympathy with it. Moreover, the papist allegiance of the ardently royalist lord of Swansea may well have aroused the suspicions of some inhabitants who, by no stretch of the imagination, could have been described as Puritans.

Finally, it is possible that some of the former royalist gentry in and around the town were, like Bussy Mansel, not unwilling to change sides. The fact that the number of royalists who were obliged to conform was so very small may well be attributable to the operation of this factor.

Both King and Parliament pursued the policy of removing from municipal appointments the other's most active supporters, and this was again exemplified at Swansea on 6 January 1646 when Walter Thomas and Leyson Seys, on account of their attachment to the royalist cause, were declared by a resolution of the common hall to be 'incapable of the places and privileges of aldermen and immediately and henceforth be disenabled thereof and debarred to serve as aldermen of the said town'. In their stead were appointed William Bayly and Richard Jones, both, doubtless, parliamentary sympathizers. Walter and William Thomas had also suffered sequestration of their estates, though both had compounded for their delinquency. Walter Thomas had done this on 9 April 1646. He had been appointed one of the Commissioners of Array for the King and 'ingeniously confesseth that, being made governor of Swansea, he did arm and array the inhabitants'. His submission to Parliament had been made before 1 December 1645. Because of his great weakness and age, being unable so much as to stir in his bed without the assistance of two, he had begged to compound by another. On 7 August 1646 his fine had been assessed at £400, but it was stipulated that if he declared under the hand of the county committee that he surrendered according to the rules of the Committee for Compounding, then the fine was to be reduced to £313. He appears to have heeded this advice because, on 31 October, his fine was determined at that sum.

William Thomas had compounded for his delinquency earlier on

7 April 1646. He had been made sheriff of Glamorgan by the King when the royal forces under Colonel Gerard had gained the ascendancy so that, according to his own account, he had been obliged to execute the office. On 25 February 1646 he had surrendered voluntarily to Major-General Laugharne and had begged that he might compound through his agent. His fine was fixed at £786 on 26 September. However, he settled £50 *per annum* of his impropriate tithes of Llandeilo-tal-y-bont (Pontardulais) on the maintenance of the minister there, with the result that his fine was reduced by quite a considerable amount to £336.

A policy generally pursued by the victorious Parliament was that of destroying the royalist strongholds. It was hoped, in this way, to diminish the chances of success of any royalist insurrections against the parliamentary regime. On 3 March 1647 Parliament ordered that 'Swansea castle be disgarrisoned and the works slighted'. It can only be conjectured what damage was done, since the castle was already in a ruinous state, but it has been claimed that the north and west curtain walls were razed.

In 1647 Oliver Cromwell became the new lord of Swansea. The estates of the Lord Marquis of Worcester had been confiscated in 1646, and on 5 May 1647 all his lands in Gloucestershire and Monmouthshire were settled on Cromwell by a grateful Parliament. By a subsequent order his estates in Glamorgan were added to the grant. Thus began Oliver's lively interest in the town, which was later to lead to far-reaching changes being effected in its administrative framework.

The victory of the parliamentary armies was no less a victory for the Puritan ministers. Many of those who had fled from Wales early in the Civil Wars lost no opportunity in returning again along with the parliamentary forces. On 27 July 1646 Ambrose Mostyn, a member of a north Wales gentry family, who, in 1642, at the request of the parishioners, had been nominated by Parliament to minister at Pennard but who, on the outbreak of the Civil War, had been constrained to flee to safer quarters, was appointed by the Committee of Plundered Ministers to officiate at Swansea. For a stipend of £50, 'he was required to preach and officiate as well in

Oliver Cromwell

ye parish church of Swansea, as in ye parishes and places thereto adjacent'. It would appear that he was not there for long, because on 20 July 1648, he, Morgan Llwyd and Vavasor Powell were named as 'Itinerant Ministers for North Wales'. It is quite possible that it was in this period (1646-48), during his short stay in the Swansea area, that he became instrumental in establishing there the first gathered church although Henry Maurice, writing in 1675, suggests that he might have done so earlier in 1642 or shortly after.

The triumph of their cause, however, brought to a head the latent dissensions in the ranks of Puritans and parliamentarians. These quarrels led, in 1648, to the outbreak of the second Civil War. South Pembrokeshire, once the stronghold of the parliamentary cause in south Wales, was now dominated by Puritan dissidents who were willing to draw the sword on behalf of their former enemies. Most prominent among these were John Poyer, his brother-in-law Rowland Laugharne, and Rice Powell. In order to suppress the rising, Colonel Horton was despatched to south Wales by Fairfax. After considerable skirmishing with Rice Powell, in the course of which Colonel Fleming—whose replacement of Poyer as governor of Pembroke had originally sparked off the revolt—accidentally shot himself (27 April), Horton was forced to retire to Brecon. Powell then advanced into Glamorgan and occupied Swansea. In another of those charges brought against Philip Jones in 1650 it was declared that 'Colonel Rice Powell in February last, with a brace of pocket pistols singly forced the said Jones his sentinels from their standings at Swansea, he being then personally in the garrison, and not making the least resistance, but permitted the said Colonel Powell to place sentinels of his own there when he first appeared against the Parliament, and so immediately Jones quit the Town and fled to Haverfordwest'. Colonel Rowland Dawkin, in Philip Jones's defence, declared that it was true that Powell had come to Swansea and quartered two or three companies of foot there. He also admitted that Powell had appointed his own sentinels, pretending 'that it was not safe for them to lay there unless they might put a guard of their own men'. However, he denied adamantly that Philip Jones had been in the town at the time. In view of the inevitable limitations attached to statements of this kind, it is best not to elaborate too much on them.

After taking Swansea, Powell passed through Neath and proceeded to negotiate with the royalists of the Vale of Glamorgan and the governor of Cardiff castle. Meanwhile Laugharne, who had been called to London to answer to Parliament on charges of conspiring with the King's agents, slipped away and joined Powell on 4 May. It was probably while he was on his way to join Powell that he also passed through Swansea, for the accounts of the common attorneys record the payment of £4 'for grass that Major General Laugharne his troopers did make use of to Mr Walter Thomas'. Swansea was not to remain for long in the hands of the royalists for, on 8 May, Horton met Laugharne and Powell at St. Fagan's, outside Cardiff, in what was to prove the biggest and bloodiest battle of either Civil War in Wales. He decisively defeated them and they retired hastily to south Pembrokeshire. Powell now installed himself in Tenby where he was soon besieged by Horton who, on his way there, had entered Swansea, as in the Common Attorneys' Accounts for 1648 there is entered the following item of expenditure: 'paid by Mr Portreeve his order for the expense of ten horse of Colonel Horton—00li.-15s.-00d.'. On 19 May Cromwell himself came to Swansea, and it was recorded in the Minute Book of the common hall that:

> At which time came unto this town the truly honourable Oliver Cromwell Esquire, Lieutenant General of all the forces of this Kingdom of England under the command of the Parliament, lord of this town, the Seignory of Gower, and manor of Kilvey, with the members thereof, who gave unto the poor of this town to be set out at interest for the benefit and advantage of ye said poor the sum of ten pounds and the sum is referred to the portreeve of the town for the time being.

Cromwell was on his way to besiege Laugharne and Poyer. Pembroke castle withstood his investing forces for 48 days but on 11 July it surrendered. The second Civil War, as far as south Wales was concerned, was over.

Soon after Cromwell's departure, on 10 August 1648, a meeting of some of the leading supporters of Parliament in Glamorgan took place at Swansea. Among these were such well known figures as Henry Herbert,[4] Philip Jones, Rowland Dawkin and Bussy Mansel.

[4] He was the eldest son of William Herbert and Elizabeth, daughter of Sir John Claypole, of Northamptonshire. On 31 March 1642 he was elected to fill the seat in the Long Parliament vacated by the death of Sir Charles Williams, Llangibby. Despite the royalist sympathies of most of the family, he chose to support Parliament. His allegiance to the parliamentary cause may, perhaps, be accounted for in two ways: first, his wife was Mary, the daughter of John Rudyard, a London grocer and cousin to Sir Benjamin Rudyard, a leader of the opposition; and secondly, it may well be that he desired the landed possessions of the Worcesters of Raglan. Unfortunately, it has not been possible to ascertain the degree of influence he exercised in the town.

At this meeting it was resolved to advise the Committee of the Army 'that during the present distractions' a monthly assessment of £850 should be raised on the eight southern counties (including the county town of Haverfordwest) to maintain a regiment of 1,000 men 'which in the opinion of the Lieutenant General and Council of War and the well affected in this county, is as little as possible may be, to secure these parts, considering ye dangers not only from within, but from abroad, being that all South Wales borders upon ye sea and towards Ireland'.[5] These activities at Swansea mirror the prevailing nervousness of the Welsh gentry at the prospect of an attack directed from Catholic Spain or Ireland against the exposed seaboard of south Wales. The Spaniards were the *dynion duon* (black men), while in bardic literature *Gwyddel* (Irishman) was a traditional term of abuse. Ireland was also looked upon askance as a competitor in the cattle trade, and as the battleground which took such heavy and constant toll of Welsh money and men.

It would appear that the normal tenor of life had been little disturbed at Swansea by the two Civil Wars. The town had suffered no physical damage, and the townspeople would have performed their daily routine in very much the same way as they had done before the wars broke out. On the economic side, however, the hostilities must have considerably disrupted the trade of the town; markets were closed, ships had to be convoyed, while taxation upon coal cargoes became a recognized source of revenue of great value. The closure of markets and the need for the proper convoying of vessels become evident on several occasions. In July 1643 the Commissioners of Array for Glamorgan drew up orders whereby the officers of the port of Swansea were not to grant passes to any port of England in rebellion against the King. Again, the disaffection of Milford Haven meant that the parliamentary fleet stationed there could keep a very close surveillance over the shipping bound to or from the town. Robert Moulton, when he had called upon the town to surrender to Parliament in 1644, declared that if it failed to comply with the request, he would 'endeavour to

[5] Towards the raising of this sum the eight counties were assessed as follows: Monmouth (£192 9s. 1d.), Glamorgan (£132 15s. 10d.), Pembroke (£116 4s. 3d.), Carmarthen (£150 15s. 6d.), Cardigan (£122 9s. 10¾d.), Brecknock (£103 6s. 11d.), Radnor (£73 2s. 7½d.), and Haverfordwest (£10 2s. 6½d.).

keep you without trade till your forced obedience bring you to the mercy of him that tendereth you grace and favour'.[6] That the parliamentary blockade had been to some extent successful is demonstrated by a report in 1645 that the parliamentary ships had taken 'many of Swansea boats, and some from Cardiff'.

But the closing of markets and the need to convoy vessels were not the only factors that had disrupted the trade of the town. Equally important was the heavy taxation on coal exports. In 1644 the foreign exporter paid 13*s*. 2*d*. export tax on each Newcastle chaldron (then 52 cwts) and the English trader 11*s*. 6*d*. per chaldron on coal shipped abroad. Unfortunately, it is not possible to provide statistical data for the decline which must have occurred, as Port Book evidence for this, as for the Commonwealth period, is not available.

By the end of 1648 the wars, as far as Swansea was concerned, were finally over. The royalists were defeated but by no means entirely eliminated from public life; the new men among the parliamentarians and the trimmers had come to the top, and most of them were to remain there even after the Restoration. Puritanism, already rooted in the area before the war, now basked in the sunshine of official favour and recognition, and could be expected to grow and prosper. Economically, though the export trade of the town had suffered dislocation, it would not appear to have been as great as it could have been, because in 1649—as later events were to prove—the town was poised on the brink not only of a revival but also of an expansion of prosperity.

---

[6] Supra, p. 202.

# Chapter Seven

## SWANSEA UNDER THE INTERREGNUM, 1649-1660

On a cold and frosty afternoon, on 30 January 1649, the King, Charles I, was beheaded outside the Banqueting Hall, Whitehall, London, and the country entered upon the Interregnum or, to give it a more popular designation, the Commonwealth period. During the ensuing eleven years, Swansea experienced many changes. The most spectacular were those in the field of religion and education; hardly less sweeping, but certainly less permanent, was the remodelling of the administrative framework of the town. Least obtrusive, but much the most long-lasting, was the revival of economic prosperity which consolidated still further the foundations for the remarkable industrial development of the town and its hinterland during the eighteenth and nineteenth centuries.

By this time, Puritanism was becoming deeply implanted in the area, and this was very evident even in the period preceding the final capture of the town by the parliamentary forces in 1645. Young, ardent Puritan ministers like Marmaduke Matthew and Ambrose Mostyn were active there; the town was the spiritual home of such eminent Puritans as Philip Jones and Rowland Dawkin; itinerant Puritan divines were being entertained and actively sponsored by the corporation; Puritan influences had undoubtedly contributed to the readiness with which the town capitulated to the enemy forces, and accounted also for the rapidity with which, when provided with an opportunity to do so after 1645, it became the very centre of Puritanism in south Wales. It is only against this background of significant Puritan development there before 1649, that the religious history of Swansea during the Interregnum can be understood.

In 1646 Ambrose Mostyn had returned to minister at Swansea and the neighbouring parishes. Towards the close of the decade, however, a new personality appeared on the scene. This was none other than John Miles, a native of Newton Clifford in the Welsh-speaking part of Herefordshire. After having, in all probability, served as a chaplain with the parliamentary forces in south Wales during the second Civil War, he made his home in Gower. In the spring of 1649 he travelled to London and, having been baptized by immersion at a Baptist church—The Glass House, in Broad Street— he returned to Gower and established at Ilston, 'according to the primitive pattern', the first Particular Baptist church in Wales. Miles was an organizing genius, possessed of enormous energy and drive, and the new sect soon spread. Other churches were shortly established at Hay, Llanharan, Carmarthen and Abergavenny, and local arrangements were controlled and, to some extent, supplemented by the 'General Meeting' of representatives which also had the difficult task of arranging for ministerial supplies and maintenance.

Miles's activities were to embrace a considerably wider field than Ilston, for not only was he nominated as one of the Approvers under the terms of The Act for the Better Propagation and Preaching of the Gospel in Wales (1650) but, on 31 July 1656, he was also appointed 'Lecturer' in Llanelli parish church at an annual stipend of £40. His chief care, however, was Ilston though it was not until 29 September 1657 that he received official recognition of his status as minister there, at a stipend of £40 per annum. A month or two later, this sum was augmented by £20 from the tithes of Whitchurch, near Cardiff.

Between 1 October 1649 and 12 August 1660, 261 members joined the church at Ilston. Of these, by far the greater number came from Swansea (33); next, in numerical order, came Ilston and Margam (26 each), Llanelli (18), Llannon (14), Llangennech (12), Cadoxton (10) and Llandeilo (9). Naturally, most of his supporters were recruited from Gower, Swansea and neighbouring districts, though some came from parishes as far distant as Hay in the north, Llantwit Major in the south, Abergavenny in the east and Rhosili in the west. A few members even came from English parishes such as Mansfield (4), Berwick (5) and Barnstaple (2), though these appear to be exceptional and were obviously people who had moved into the area. The greater part of his congregation was made up of women. They accounted for 153, while the men only numbered

108 of the total membership. A factor which must considerably have facilitated the growth and development of Miles's church at Ilston was the support that it received from the very commencement from the powerful group of Puritan sympathizers among the local gentry, led by the radical squire Philip Jones. They joined Miles's congregation and became, furthermore, some of the leading parliamentarians and Cromwellians in south Wales. A striking characteristic of the church was the intensity of the conviction of its members, which was exemplified later in the careers of young men who had been grounded in their doctrines during the first year of the Republic. These included Lewis Thomas, who taught a conventicle at Newton Nottage and who, on 30 September 1672, was licensed to preach at Swansea, and Morgan Jones upon whom, in conjunction with Lewis Thomas, devolved the supervision of the cause in the Swansea area after the departure of Miles for America in 1663.

But in Wales as a whole, despite the powerful preaching of eloquent Welsh Puritan ministers, and the missionary zeal of the London churches which brought new men to the border, Puritanism made only slow progress. Important among the factors accounting for this situation were the spiritual inertia and ignorance of the mass of the Welsh people, their subservience to the gentry, and the continuingly firm grip of the unejected royalist clergymen. Those who exercised supreme authority in England were not oblivious of the peculiar claims of Wales and, in July 1649, Major-General Thomas Harrison, a convinced millenarian, and one of Cromwell's best cavalry officers, was appointed to the south Wales command. His impressions, together with the persuasive arguments of that most dynamic of crusaders, the Cornishman, Hugh Peter, the perceptive advice of the courageous and mercurial activist, Vavasor Powell, the impact of a cascade of petitions emanating from both north and south Wales calling for church reform, and the readiness of the Rump Parliament to listen sympathetically, led to the passing, in February 1650, of the Act for the Better Propagation and Preaching of the Gospel in Wales. This legislation was to remain in force for three years. By its terms, a body of 71 commissioners was appointed, any five of whom, acting together, could examine ministers and, if they thought fit, eject them from their livings. Within three years they had removed in all 278 clergy; 82 in north Wales, 151 in south Wales, and 45 in Monmouthshire. Among those turned out of their parishes was Hopkin Morgan, vicar of St. Mary's, Swansea, on the ground of 'insufficiency'.

To plug the gaps left in the ministry by the activities of the commissioners, a body of 25 Approvers, among whom were Walter Cradock, John Miles and Vavasor Powell, was established by the act. Any five of these could 'approve' preachers who would receive a salary, not to exceed £100 a year, to be drawn from the sequestered revenues of the church. On 17 March 1652/3 Morris Bidwell was appointed by them to minister in the town of Swansea. This action so infuriated Richard Seys, a royalist living in High Street and the lay rector of St. John's, and, by virtue of that office, owner of the chancel of the church, that he caused his father's bones to be disinterred from St. Mary's and reburied in St. John's.

But the commissioners soon discovered to their mortification that it was much easier to destroy an old structure than to erect a new edifice. While trumpet blasts could reduce the walls of old Jericho to dust, the fiery tongues of impassioned Puritan missionaries could not as easily build the walls of the new Jerusalem on Gwalia's green and pleasant fields. The problem was that while the harvest could be plentiful, the labourers were few. There was a great dearth of suitable ministers, and the commissioners' remedy for the 'famine of the word' in Wales lay in the continued use of itinerant preachers, some 90 of whom, on salaries of £100 *per annum*, were active in Wales during the Propagation years. It appears that the spiritual needs of the Swansea Puritans, even at this time, could not adequately be met by one minister, because Bidwell's efforts were supplemented by those of an itinerant, David Walter, variously dubbed a 'weaver' and a 'common country thatcher'. Though his particular patch was the Swansea and Neath district, he delighted at times 'to exercise his faculty in Llandaff Cathedral'.

During the period of the Interregnum, and indeed since 1645, the corporation at Swansea would appear to have stopped making its own specific contribution towards the preaching of the word, for the accounts of the common attorneys contain no references to any payments being made for sermons as had previously been the practice. This situation probably arose because, after the final capture of the town by the parliamentarians in 1645, the demands of the Puritans there for sermons could be met by the ministers, resident or itinerant, officially appointed to preach in the town and district, first by the victorious Parliament and later by the Commonwealth authorities. After 1660, on the other hand, with the re-establishment of the Anglican ascendancy, payments for sermons are once again recorded in the corporation books, though far less frequently than during the period preceding 1645, a situation which may well be accounted for by the considerable number of nonconformist ministers who continued to preach in the town. In 1660/1 the corporation paid £2 to a Mr Band for preaching, and 15s. to a 'Mr Thoumstone for preaching 3 sermons'. No further payments for sermons are recorded until 1669/70 when 10s. was paid to a 'strange minister that preached by Mr Portreeve's order'. In 1678/9 ten shillings was 'paid unto Mr Thomas Lewis being a poor minister for preaching in our church in November by the consent of the aldermen etc', while on 3 June 1683 a like sum was paid to a Mr Dinnam 'for preaching'. That these could well have been sermons delivered by Puritans or Puritan sympathizers would appear likely from a consideration of the following circumstances. During the period 1660-2 the situation from the religious viewpoint was very fluid, and consequently it would have been comparatively easy for the corporation to subsidize, on occasion, sermons of this nature. Furthermore, it is doubtful whether the Penal Code was ever rigidly enforced in Swansea, because Marmaduke Matthew, after his ejection from the living of St. John's, had continued to preach in the town 'by connivance of the magistrates'. Again, it is questionable whether Swansea, as it was only a contributory borough, really came under the terms of the Five Mile Act, for this act only applied to cities, towns corporate or boroughs 'that send burgesses to the parliament'.

The blindness of the magistrates, the loophole possibly provided by the terms of the Five Mile Act, together with the sizeable number of Puritans in the town, may well explain how, during the period of persecution, there were five nonconformist ministers at work in Swansea. In addition to Marmaduke Matthew, there were: Daniel Higgs, ejected from the livings of Rhosili and Porteynon, Stephen Hughes, the deprived minister of Meidrym; William Thomas, ejected from St. Mary Hill; and Lewis Thomas. It is interesting to speculate whether the Thomas Lewis who preached in the town in 1678/9 was one and the same person as the Lewis Thomas upon whom had devolved the supervision of the Baptist cause in Swansea after Miles's departure for America. He was certainly preaching in the town after the Restoration and on 30 September 1672 was officially licensed to do so.

Together with the appointment of ministers, the commissioners under the Propagation Act, as part of the government's efforts to puritanize the country by dispelling 'ignorance and profaneness', established schools in Wales. Though the objective was predominantly religious, there was a political motive as well, since spreading the Puritan gospel was regarded by Hugh Peter and others as the most effective means of winning political support. The Approvers were to select suitable men to act as schoolmasters, at a salary not to exceed £40 a year, and to be drawn, as in the case of the ministers, from the sequestered revenues of the church. Sixty-three schools were established in the larger towns of Wales, 37 in the south and 26 in the north. The schools were free, open to both sexes, and the medium of instruction was English. That their curriculum was more akin to the ordinary grammar school of the time than to the modern primary school is indicated by the commissioners' specificiation of the subjects to be taught, by the employment of 'master' and 'usher' and, finally, by the phraseology of the act itself. The schools naturally had a strong Puritan bias, devoting much attention to the Bible and books of devotion, and having a particular regard for the classics as representing the most effective means of acquiring a better knowledge of the original scriptures and the early Christian church.

On 17 March 1652/3 Moor Pye, the ejected minister of Llanfable in Monmouth, was appointed schoolmaster at Swansea, and James Williams as usher. Pye received £38 *per annum* and Williams £26.

The salaries of both were drawn from livings in Carmarthenshire: the former's wage of £38 was made up of £22 from the rectories of Llanfynydd, Llangadog and Llanddeusant, together with £16 from the rectory of Llanarthne; the latter's remuneration of £26, on the other hand, was drawn entirely from the rectory of Llandysilio.

The commissioners incurred some expense in arranging for the new schools, and at Swansea there was an outlay of the very large sum of £59 15s. 7d. on repairs, for which a certain 'Ensign Thomas Williams' was made responsible. Regrettably, there is no indication at all in the town records as to the nature of these renovations, though it is evident that an existing building or room was being converted for the purpose. On the question of the location of the new school, the town records are again silent.

It would appear that Pye remained at his post as master of the school at Swansea until 1654. On 16 April 1655, however, Colonel Philip Jones reported that Pye had left that sphere 'in the beginning of January last', evidently to take up his new pastoral duties at Bishopston. In most cases where masters turned ministers, the schools fell into decay. At Swansea, on the other hand, Peter Meyrick was appointed to replace Pye on the very day that the colonel made his report. At the Restoration, because of their narrow Puritan outlook, lack of tradition and the disappearance of the revolutionary authorities that had created and sustained them, the Commonwealth schools closed their doors.

This was not the only school established at Swansea during the Commonwealth period, because another ejected minister, Hugh Gore, had opened a private school in the town. Born in 1613 at Maiden Newton, in Dorset, he was the eldest son of John Gore, archdeacon of Lismore in Ireland. He received his early education at Lismore grammar school but in 1628, when he was fifteen years of age, he entered Trinity College, Oxford, and remained there for a few terms. After leaving Oxford, he proceeded to Trinity College, Dublin, and graduated there as a B.A., B.D. His first preferments are believed to have been the living of Nicholaston and the rectory of Oxwich, both in Gower, which he owed to the patronage of the Mansels. It was after his ejection from Oxwich by the Puritan authorities, on the grounds of his delinquency, that he moved to Swansea and opened a school there. After the Restoration he returned to Ireland and became, in 1666, bishop of Waterford and Lismore. Doubtless it was his experience as a schoolmaster, together with his great affection for the town and its inhabitants, that inspired him in September 1682 to establish a free grammar school there in a house in Goat Street. He endowed his foundation with 600 acres of mountain farmland at Cwm-y-Fuwch in the Vale of Ogmore. The master, who was to be 'discreet and well learned', was to provide instruction in Latin and Greek, in virtue and good literature, to 'twenty poor children and youths, sons of the poorer sort of the burgesses that were the burgesses of the said corporation and burgh of Swansea, and in case the corporation happen to be dissolved and to cease, then to instruct as aforesaid twenty poor children and youths, sons of the poorer sort of the inhabitants or that were the inhabitants of the said town of Swansea'. To qualify, the children had to be at least eight years of age and able to read English perfectly. It was in this fashion that the school, later to be known as Bishop Gore grammar school, was founded.

Bishop Hugh Gore's Residence

In 1652, when the Propagation Act was fully operative, an attack in the form of a petition emanating from south Wales and Monmouth, and reportedly signed by 15,000 hands, was made on it in the interests of 'well-affected' but disillusioned Puritanism. The petition was presented to the House of Commons on 10 March 1652. The chief sponsors were William Thomas of Brecon, John Gunter of Tredomen in the same county, and Colonel Edward Freeman, attorney-general for south Wales and Member of Parliament for Hereford. In one passage reference is made to 'rents and divisions' among the Puritans at Swansea, Merthyr, Bedwas and Mynyddislwyn. This statement, however, cannot be accepted at face value, since the petitioners, and especially the sponsors, were motivated by personal animus. They were out to shipwreck the act.

The Propagation Act lapsed in 1653 and the place of the commissioners was taken by a body generally known as the Triers. The old appointments to livings were practically all confirmed, and among the new appointments was that of Marmaduke Matthew to the chapel of St. John at Swansea. It has already been shown how, in 1636, following episcopal censure of his denunciation of Holy Days, he had fled from his vicarage of Penmaen to America.[1] However, from the very outset there were minorities of 'enthusiasts' who had refused to toe the line drawn by the dominant orthodoxy in New England and, within a year of his arrival, he was involved in a dispute about a fast which delayed his election as a full freeman of the colony. When, with the establishment of the Protectorate, the latitudinarian religious policy of the new authorities appeared to offer more scope for spiritual adventure, he returned to Wales, and it was through the agency of his old neighbour, Philip Jones, that, in 1655, he was appointed to the living of St. John's.

At this time, also, the Quakers became particularly active at Swansea. Despite the fact that they were, undoubtedly, only a very small sect, their activities loom large in the religious history of the town, partly because they were so vocal a minority—they delighted to shout their message from the rooftops—but even more because of the care with which their records have been preserved. But, in

[1] Supra, p. 184.

recounting their activities and particularly their 'sufferings', it is important to remember that knowledge of them comes almost entirely from Quaker sources and is, in all probability, more than a little biased in their favour.

In October 1655 John ap John, a Ruabon yeoman, and a leading Quaker missionary—he came to be known as the 'Apostle of Quakerism in Wales'—arrived at Swansea and his activities there soon brought him into disfavour with the Commonwealth ministers. He interrupted Morris Bidwell, the Puritan minister of St. Mary's church, asking him whether he was a minister of Christ. The Quaker was removed and, after being kept in custody overnight, was brought before the magistrates the following day. It would appear that the offended preacher and a colleague demanded that the magistrates should 'have the devil whipped out of' John ap John and, whenever he tried to explain his conduct, they either struck him or stopped his mouth with their hands. Apparently, John ap John had waited until after the sermon before putting his question, and since the law provided punishment only for those who maliciously disturbed ministers during the sermon, the Quakers claimed that the proceedings were illegal. However, like so many other Friends, he had refused to provide security for a subsequent appearance in court, and on 8 October 1655 the magistrate, Robert Dawkins, committed him to the Keeper of the Common Gaol at Cardiff. Though there is no record of how long he remained there, it would appear to have been at least three months. Before his arrest John ap John had succeeded in making a few converts, the most notable among whom was William Bevan, a prosperous merchant. Bevan's wife and sons also accepted the Quaker message and members of the family were to attend the Swansea meeting for over a century. It was this William Bevan who gave the Quakers the site for their Swansea meeting house.

Despite difficulties, the number of Friends in Glamorgan, and especially Cardiff, grew steadily. Particularly successful was the aggressive propaganda of the Quakers when directed against the Baptists in the county, a success which provoked the latter, at a meeting of their sect at Brecon in the summer of 1656, to order John Miles to write a pamphlet as an 'antidote against the infection of the times'. No south Wales Quaker attempted to write an answer to this challenge and it was left to George Fox himself, the Quaker leader, to reply to Miles after a lapse of three years. This attack by the Baptists may have influenced Fox to visit south Wales in 1657. He travelled to Swansea, where he records that a meeting had been established. However, the only people who are known to have been convinced about this time are the brothers Thomas and Daniel Hopkins of Pontardulais.

In 1658 the most concentrated persecution ever to have fallen to their lot was brought to bear on the Quakers. It is quite possible that Fox's visit had encouraged the Quakers to make their testimony more public at a time when the decease of Oliver Cromwell in September had made local authorities more determined than ever to deal very severely with cases of extraordinary behaviour and disturbances which might aggravate still further the unsettled state of the country. John ap John was again in the vanguard of the sufferers. After having been imprisoned in Cardiff for a few days he was released, and he moved on to Swansea only to be removed from the town on several occasions for preaching. Eventually, on account of his public opposition to one of the ministers there, he was brought before the magistrates' court, where Morris Bidwell struck him and pulled him by the nose, without incurring any reproof. His release came only after he had spent a further twenty weeks in gaol.

At the time John ap John was detained, two of the Swansea Quakers, Margaret and Rebecca Thomas, criticized the 'fighting priests' for their conduct towards him. The sisters were subjected to much abuse and, after a period of detention, were evicted from the town. When the well-heeled William Bevan went in his boat to Mumbles to bring them back, he, too, was imprisoned and chained by the leg. They were, however, not the only ones to suffer at this time, because two other Swansea Quakers, Thomas Shaw and Roger Colebeach, were also detained; the former spent twenty days in the town goal for criticizing Marmaduke Matthew, while the latter was incarcerated through the malicious information of one William Bayly, a prominent local parliamentarian who was twice portreeve, in 1648 and 1654, and Mayor in 1657.

Possibly the most outspoken Quaker in Swansea at this time was Elizabeth Holme, the wife of Thomas Holme, the Kendal weaver. She, together with her companion, Alice Birkett who, on one occasion, was pinched so spitefully by Marmaduke Matthew, that he drew blood, spent some time in Swansea's infamous 'dark house' for testifying against the Commonwealth ministers. In the event they were soon released without being brought to trial. Elizabeth was quite undeterred by the experience for, after her release, she proceeded to St. Mary's to address the congregation before the commencement of the service. The arrival of the minister led to her removal and imprisonment again. On this occasion not only was she chained at a distance from the door of the gaol to prevent her from berating the ministers as they passed by, but, apparently, she was also denied necessities. Practically as soon as she was released, she encountered the minister, Morris Bidwell, in the street and spoke to him, for which indiscretion she spent another day and night in prison. On her release she transferred her energies to Monmouth where she again came into conflict with the authorities. Despite her privations at Swansea, before the end of the year she had returned there and, after speaking in Marmaduke Matthew's church of St. John's, was detained in prison until the following year. Francis Gawler, the Cardiff Quaker and hatter, took this opportunity to denounce the people of Swansea as drunkards and swearers, saying that they were truly worthy of the ministers and magistrates there.

After a disastrous encounter with the minister and his wife on Easter Monday 1658 in the churchyard at Llandaff, when he had suffered the misfortune and indignity of being struck on the head with the key of the tithing barn, Gawler came to Swansea. His reputation must have preceded him, for his mere presence in St. John's led to his imprisonment. After such cavalier treatment, he obviously thought it wiser to leave the county and he, too, moved on to Monmouth. Not to be deterred, Elizabeth Richard, one of the new adherents at Cardiff, now came to Swansea to question a minister. For her pains she was struck with a Bible by a member of the congregation.

Though there was a marked decline in the intensity of the

persecution which the Glamorgan Friends had to suffer in 1659, Elizabeth Holme was again imprisoned at Swansea. But, together with showing their dislike of the Quakers by their readiness to hand them over to the civil authorities, the Puritan ministers at this time began to refuse to bury them in the churchyards so that it became imperative for the Quakers to have their own burial grounds. The Friends at Swansea had probably used part of the land they had obtained from William Bevan in 1656 for burials, but in 1659 they acquired possession of a plot of ground in Loughor for this specific purpose. It was granted by John Bowen and consisted of about half an acre, known as the New Garden, and situated near the Swansea to Loughor road. However, there is no record of any burials there, and the monthly meeting does not seem to have bothered about the property until the end of the eighteenth century.

By the Restoration period, Swansea had become the mecca of south Wales Puritanism. There were in the area a large number of Independents and Baptists who had grown bold under the patronage of Philip Jones of Llangyfelach, while the Society of Friends had also made many converts there. Indicative of the strength of Puritanism in the town and district were the busy activities of the nonconformist ministers and Quaker missionaries, and the establishment of Quaker and nonconformist meeting houses, in addition to such normal venues for the congregating of Puritan assemblies as the parish churches of St. Mary, St. John and Ilston. It would appear that during the Commonwealth period there were four nonconformist ministers at work in the Swansea district at about the same time. These were John Miles, Morris Bidwell, Marmaduke Matthew and David Walter. Of these, the first three were definitely resident in the district, Morris Bidwell and Marmaduke Matthew in the town itself. Walter, on the other hand, was an itinerant, and since his field of activity embraced Neath as well as Swansea, his home could have been in either place. However, Swansea was a far more fertile place for the activities of Puritan ministers than Neath and hence it is probable that his residence was in the former area. Even John Roberts who, some time before 16 October 1655 had been approved a minister at Loughor, made his home in Swansea. But the propagating efforts of the nonconformist ministers in the town had certainly not been performed without interruption. From 1655 onwards the Quaker missionaries had been particularly active there, and foremost among these had been John ap John, Elizabeth Holme, Francis Gawler and George Fox himself.

Extremely significant also, as reflecting the growth of Puritanism in the area, was the establishment of Quaker and nonconformist meeting houses. The Quakers had obtained from the wealthy merchant, William Bevan, a plot of land in Swansea for this purpose in 1656. On 28 September 1657, a site for a meeting house for the Independents in the High Street of the town was acquired by Christopher Rogers, a mercer. He bought the tenement from Morgan William, a tanner, and Avis his wife, for £20.

With the restoration of the monarchy in the person of Charles II in 1660, the nonconformists could expect nothing but adversity. Among the first to suffer from the return of the 'Merry Monarch' were John Miles and his Baptist congregation at Ilston. Soon after Charles had reached London (27 May 1660), Puritan clergymen were removed to make room for the former incumbents of parishes, or to enable fresh nominees appointed by the King and other patrons of livings to take up their pastoral duties. On 23 July 1660 William Houghton, who, from 25 February 1638/9 until the Commonwealth period, had been vicar of Penmaen, was appointed by the King to the living of Ilston. Since the last entry in the Register is 12 August 1660, it would appear that the Baptists there had already departed and were meeting elsewhere. It has been suggested that the new venue was Trinity Well chapel which was ideally situated for the purpose. Not only was the area secluded, but the land on which the chapel stood belonged to none other than Major-General Rowland Dawkin. However, this conjecture is supported by nothing more than local tradition and it is possible that Trinity Well chapel had already fallen into ruin by this time. A more probable thesis is that after Miles's eviction from Ilston the Baptists had continued to meet, not at Trinity Well as has been suggested, but rather in the town of Swansea itself. Miles gradually withdrew from the public eye and in 1663 he, together with the greater part of his congregation, fled to America, where he founded the town of Swanzey, Massachusetts.

During part, at least, of the period of persecution, which lasted from 1660/1688, it is certain that those members of Miles's church who remained, met in Swansea in the homes of members like Rees ab Ifan (he had joined the church at Ilston on 1 February 1656) and Harry Dykes. Afterwards they gathered at Llodrau Brith farm, about three miles outside the town. In 1698, however, the sect rented from the Presbyterians the chapel which that denomination had built in the town on the passing of the Toleration Act in 1689, but which in 1698 they left for a bigger establishment at the bottom of High Street. For the Baptists of Swansea the renting of this chapel was to begin a new chapter in their history.

Next to feel the effects of the changed religious climate were the Quakers. The devotees of the inner light had suffered great trials and tribulations during the Interregnum, but now their persecution reached new heights of frenzy. Their creed, and frenetic activity, were such that they had incurred the animosity of both the Anglican authorities and the sects; and, in 1660, the situation was exacerbated by their refusal to display their loyalty to the restored monarch by taking an oath of allegiance to him, an objection based on the commandment against swearing found in the Sermon on the Mount. On 15 October 1660, 18 Quakers were committed to Cardiff gaol for refusing the oaths of allegiance and supremacy when required to take them by the justices of the peace. As yet, the oaths had not been administered to the Friends in west Glamorgan, for all 18 incarcerated in Cardiff in 1660 were from the eastern part of the county. During 1660 Thomas Holme reported to Fox from Swansea that all the Friends in the town were safe and well. However, the following year, constraints were placed on their freedom. In February 1661 the high constable issued an order to the constables of Glamorgan urging them to ensure that sufficient watch was kept in their parishes so that 'none of those called Quakers or Anabaptists be suffered to go from one parish to another, or gather together to any meetings or Conventicles'. They were also exhorted to 'have a special care to ensure all the Quakers within your parish until you receive further order from the justices.

Whereof fail not at your peril'. The constables were most diligent in the performance of their duties and 41 Glamorgan Quakers, all again from the eastern districts of the county, were arrested, some in their own homes, a few on the highway, and others in religious meetings. Towards the end of the year the authorities in the western part of the county began to take action against the Friends. Accompanied by officers armed with halberds and other weapons, the portreeve of Swansea, Leyson Seys, a confirmed royalist of long standing, broke up a Quaker meeting in the town and imprisoned all the men. At about the same time, Watkin Richard, David Richard and Robert Thomas were gaoled in an underground cellar for four or five months 'without the common benefit of air allowed to felons', and a poor woman whose husband was blind, and consequently very dependent upon her, was shut up 'in a nasty stinking cockloft for many weeks together'. But despite their rigorous treatment by the Restoration government, the Swansea Friends continued to thrive, and the fact that during 1663-4 several of them, including William Bevan and Roger Coalbeach, were summoned to appear before the Consistory Court at Carmarthen for non-attendance at church and holding conventicles, is ample testimony of this.

In 1662, with the passing of the Act of Uniformity, the Independents in the Swansea area entered upon a period when they were to suffer considerable hardships. By this legislation no one could hold any ecclesiastical office unless he had been episcopally ordained, and communion could only be celebrated according to the rites of the Church of England. Every clergyman in the Kingdom had to accept the Prayer Book in its entirety or, on 24 August, lose his living. Among those ejected as a result of this statute was Marmaduke Matthew, who lost his living of St. John's. His removal, however, did not mean the end of his ministry; for after his ejection, sustained by the goodwill of his family, he continued to preach, with the connivance of the magistrates, 'in a little chapel at the end of the town'. He was a very devout and zealous man who went about from house to house to instruct the people. His conversation was almost wholly about religious matters and he made 'no visits but such as were properly ministerial and received none but in a religious manner'. On market days he would often meet the country people and discuss with them spiritual matters. His reception on these occasions was mixed, since some received him with respect and others with contempt and scorn. He continued in this manner, happily unmolested because of his piety, till his death at a ripe old age in 1683. It would appear that his two sons were not made of such stubborn stuff. Manasseh Matthew conformed to the restored episcopal order and was given first the rectory of Port Eynon and then, in 1670, his father's old vicarage at Swansea. The other son, Mordecai, had been presented by the Triers in 1657 to the living of Llancarfan from which, at the Restoration, he was ejected. However, like Manasseh, he also conformed and, in 1661, was given the living of Reynoldston.

Marmaduke Matthew and his family may perhaps be taken as symbolic of the next phase in the history of Puritanism in Swansea. Those Puritans who, like Marmaduke Matthew, clung to their beliefs despite persecution and social handicaps, continued to live, largely unmolested, in the town and district and formed a hard core of Nonconformists. But many, probably a majority of former Puritans, like Marmaduke Matthew's own sons, conformed, though without necessarily abandoning all their former modes of belief, worship and conduct.

Although the most spectacular changes which had taken place at Swansea during the eleven years of the Interregnum had been those in the fields of religion and education, hardly less sweeping and important were those effected in the field of municipal government and particularly in the administrative framework of the town. It is with the nature and significance of these latter changes, though not to the exclusion of other matters, that particular attention will now be paid.

On 14 May 1649 a leet court was held at Swansea 'In the name of the Commonwealth of England', and shortly afterwards it was recorded that 'By the desire of us the aldermen of this town whose names are underwritten, there was provided for the Right Honourable Oliver Cromwell, Lord Lieutenant of Ireland, and lord of this town, and for all his followers, a dinner in the house of

William Bayly, then portreeve, now to defray the charge of necessaries towards that provision, we have thought fit to take ten pounds out of the town's stock'. Cromwell, as a first step in the reconstitution of the British Empire after the Civil Wars, had decided to subjugate Ireland which was in rebellion. It was while he was on his way there that he stayed at Swansea and was entertained to dinner by the portreeve.

Swansea was of considerable value to Cromwell in his bloody campaigns in Ireland, since it was a convenient terminus for the despatch of both men and supplies there. In December 1649 67 officers and men 'being volunteers entertained for the service of Ireland under the command of Captain Nicholls', were quartered in the town. They stayed for five days and the expense to the corporation amounted to £2 3s. 4d. That provisions were also shipped from Swansea appears from the issue of a warrant on 22 March 1649/50 by the Council of State to the customs officers to permit one Denis Gauden to transport 400,000lb. of oatmeal to Ireland at Cardiff, Swansea or Milford.

On 19 August 1650 Robert Donnell and William Johns, two aldermen of the town, 'by reason of their neglect and absenting themselves from the service of the said town', were deprived of their aldermanic status. On the same day Philip Jones who, in October 1646, had been made a burgess, John Francklin, Thomas Williams and Mathew David were appointed to fill the vacancies. There would appear to be no reason to doubt that the fundamental reason for the dismissal of Donnell and Johns was their attachment to the royalist cause. The purging of royalists from positions of authority in the town and their replacement by supporters of Parliament were natural and logical policies for the victorious party to pursue. They were a means of ensuring that the town remained firmly riveted under parliamentary control.

Though by the middle of August 1650 significant changes had already been effected in the composition of the aldermanic body, the next nine years were to see the acquisition of a 'new look' by that august assemblage. The new men among the parliamentarians gained the ascendancy and eagerly took their places on the council. In 1650 the aldermanic body had comprised seven members who

Major-General Rowland Dawkin

had belonged to the older governing town families (Lewis Jones, Henry Fleming, Mathew Francklin, Patrick Jones, John Benett, John Daniell and John Bowen) and five new men who had risen to the top as a result of the fortunes of war (Philip Jones, John Francklin, Thomas Williams, Mathew David and William Bayly). By 1655, on the other hand, the members of the old guard only numbered five (Lewis Jones, John Bowen, Henry Fleming, John Benett and John Daniell), while the new men numbered seven (Philip Jones, Thomas Williams, Mathew David, William Bayly, William Vaughan, William Jones and Robert Jones). The charter granted by Cromwell to the town at this time made no appreciable difference in this respect, the only changes being the appointment of Philip Jones to the office of High Steward and his replacement on the aldermanic body by his friend and neighbour, Major-General Rowland Dawkin. By 1657, however, the preponderance of the new men had become even more emphatic; while the old guard only mustered three (Lewis Jones, John Bowen and John Daniell), the number of new men had risen to eight (Rowland Dawkin, William Herbert, Thomas Williams, Mathew David, William Bayly, William Vaughan, William Jones and Robert Jones). For some reason or other, the number of aldermen recorded during this particular year was only eleven.

The continued presence on the aldermanic body, during the Interregnum, of persons who had been closely identified with the government of the town in the period preceding its final capture by the parliamentary forces in 1645 is not really surprising because it has been demonstrated that the Commonwealth authorities, in the work of administration generally, aimed at securing the collaboration of those older gentry families which had not been irretrievably compromised. But despite their continued presence, and though they occupied the important office of portreeve and, after 1655, that of mayor, as frequently as the new men, the balance of power and leadership had swung away from them to the latter group. Not only did the new men for the greater part of the period outnumber the representatives of the older leading town families on the council, but the dominant influence behind the whole façade of town government would have been that of Philip Jones, the leading Cromwellian in south Wales.

A close scrutiny of those burgesses who were common attorneys between 1646-59 only serves to corroborate the conclusions drawn above. Thus, of the nineteen burgesses who at various times during these thirteen years appear on the list of common attorneys, eleven were new men who had only been sworn burgesses, or had come into prominence, in and after 1646. These eleven had included Thomas David, Edward Bowen, Walter Thomas, Mathew David, Christopher Hamon, William Gronnoe, Philip David, Thomas Jones Prichard, Walter Paine, John Hughes and William Philip. The remaining eight, on the other hand, had been burgesses before the Civil Wars began. They were David Thomas, John Rowland, John Grandford, John Whithear, David Griffith, Henry

Pickrell, Cradock Rogers and John Bynon. On the whole, therefore, this suggests that in a town like Swansea, where Puritan and parliamentary influences were strong, changes in the personnel of the administration were much more marked than in the counties. Moreover, the ruling body was more compact and concentrated than in the counties and consequently more easily manipulated by new forces.

The new ruling elements, as might be imagined, were not slow to effect improvements. In March 1646 the corporation decided to build a market house. On 20 May 1651 it was concluded 'for that the charge of building the said market house may not be altogether drawn out of the public stock of the said town to the quite exhausting thereof' the sum of £60 should be instantly rated upon the inhabitants, 'care being taken not to lay any part of the said rate upon such poor people as have no subsistence besides their daily labour'. It can only be conjectured whether Cromwell contributed from his own purse towards it. The construction of a new market would appear to indicate that the Civil Wars had not seriously impaired the internal economy of the town, though they disrupted considerably the external trading and commercial activities of its merchant element.

The poor at Swansea certainly benefited from the Protector's close affiliations with the town. In 1648 he had given £10 to be set out at interest for their benefit. He contributed a further 45s. in 1652 and two years later, in 1654, it is recorded: 'more I received by the appointment of the Lord Protector and as a gift from him to be employed to the use of the poor of this town and had for misdemeanours done by Thomas Bowen of Ilston, the sum of five pounds'.

In 1655 Cromwell granted a charter to Swansea. His lack of appreciation of the importance of electoral and other patronage, together with his failure to secure the presence in Parliament of a hard core of experienced front-benchers who could give direction to parliamentary proceedings, had resulted in his being uniformly unsuccessful in his relationships with his Parliaments. In 1654, in order to secure the return of congenial, unorganized, independent county gentry, like-minded with himself, he accepted under a new constitution (Instrument of Government) a new franchise which, while preserving the old property qualifications, notably altered the distribution of membership; the country representation was quadrupled and the borough representation more than halved. Despite the new franchise, however, the first Protectorate Parliament which met in September 1654 was no more successful than its predecessors. Cromwell's failure to utilize the electoral and procedural devices at his disposal resulted in a vacuum of leadership being created; a vacuum which was filled first by the Republicans and then, after they had been purged, by the 'old country party'. Following the failure of this Parliament, Cromwell surrendered entirely to his military advisers and the rule of the Major-Generals was instituted. During this period of direct rule the government radically re-modelled the boroughs and converted them into safe supporters. In general, the new charters granted to the boroughs tended to deprive the burgesses of their political power and to vest it in smaller and more manageable bodies. It was hoped in this way to secure the return to Parliament of members who would not be troublesome to the government. Unfortunately for Cromwell, owing to the new franchise, the boroughs were too few to stem the tide and in the autumn of 1656, from the uncontrollable county constituencies, the critics of the government were returned to the second Protectorate Parliament.

The significance of Cromwell's charter to Swansea in 1655 can only be appreciated if it is remembered that the town was one of the seven contributory boroughs in Glamorgan which shared with Cardiff, the shire town, in the election of a burgess member to Parliament and that furthermore, in 1658, Cromwell granted another charter to it by which it was enabled to return its own member to Westminster. But the charter of 1655 is of importance in two other directions as well: first, it marks the period when the burgesses in general finally lost their right of choosing, within certain limitations, their own corporate officials; and secondly, to fill the vacuum created by the burgesses' loss of power, the lord's influence, which had been perceptibly weakened by the early decades of the seventeenth century, was brought once more into much greater prominence.

The charter recites that Swansea was an ancient port and corporation, to the burgesses of which the lords marcher and the Crown had made many grants in times past. Henceforth, it was to be adjudged, reputed and taken to be a free town and borough, and the burgesses, hitherto known as the portreeve, aldermen and burgesses, should be 'one body politic and corporate in deed and in name by the name of mayor, aldermen and burgesses of the town of Swansea', with perpetual succession. The town was given to the mayor, aldermen and burgesses in 'fee farm'. The burgesses were confirmed in their ancient privileges, while they might also sue and be sued in their corporate name in any court and in that name, hold their land, and lease and purchase land, 'not exceeding the clear yearly value of one hundred pounds per annum above reprises'. They should have one free Guild of Merchants. The mayor and common council were given the power to admit into the guild and burgess body such persons as they thought fit, thus abrogating the claims by birth, marriage, and apprenticeship. Though the charter does not state specifically how the council was to fill vacancies in its own body, the implication is that it should do so by co-option; and corroboration for this, perhaps, may be adduced from the unequivocal establishment of this method as the means of recruitment in the charter granted by James II to the town in 1685. In Cromwell's charter, also, the mayor and council were given the power to disfranchise burgesses. Moreover, the mayor, aldermen and burgesses should have one common seal but they were given the power to 'break, deface, change, alter, and make new the said seal when and as often as to them it shall seem most convenient'. The boundaries of the borough were to be 'from the head of Burlais Brook to the river Tawe to the north, and from the said head of Burlais Brook along by the Weeg House and so by the Cocket by David's Well on the west, and from David's Well along David's Ditch and so by Brynmill to the sea on the south, and by the seaside unto Tawe to the east'. The chief officer, re-named the 'Mayor', was nominated in the charter. This was Lewis Jones, who was portreeve at the time. He was to remain in office for one year and take the oath of office before the high steward or his deputy. For the future, the election of the mayor was to be in the hands of the council; the members were to elect two of the aldermen, of whom the steward was to nominate one to serve as mayor for the following year. Not only was the chief officer nominated but so also was a common council, consisting of twelve aldermen, twelve capital burgesses, the steward and the recorder. The twelve aldermen were to be Rowland Dawkin, Lewis Jones, John Bowen, Henry Fleming, John Benett, John Daniell, William Bayly, Mathew David, Thomas Williams, William Vaughan, William Jones and Robert Jones. The twelve capital burgesses appointed were John Price, Evan Lewis, John Mathew, David Griffith, Ienkin Phillipp, Thomas Philip, David Bailey, John Williams, John Daniell, John Symond, John Wichard and Thomas Dollin. Philip Jones was appointed the first high steward, while John Gibbs was the 'honest able and discreet person learned in the laws of England', appointed to be recorder. He was to hold office during good behaviour. On the decease or removal of a recorder, a new one was to be appointed by the council. The mayor and council had full power to remove any officer or officers guilty of misgovernment, or for any other 'just and lawful cause'. The council could meet at will in their common hall or Guild Hall and make orders for the government of 'the burgesses merchant of the Guild' and the merchants, artificers, and inhabitants of the borough. To that end, they might impose fines and penalties for infraction of such orders, and for the expenses of administration, and the repair of 'the walls, bulwarks, and seabanks', they might assess and levy taxes on the occupiers of land within the franchise. The mayor, high steward, his deputy or deputies, the recorder, the ex-mayor, and one alderman, were to be justices of the peace in Swansea. The mayor should also hold the offices of coroner, escheator, keeper of the gaol and clerk of the market. In the last mentioned capacity he was to regulate weights and measures, and make assize or assay of bread, wine, ale and other victuals. The justices of the peace of Glamorgan were not to exercise any jurisdiction within the town. The council's officers were to be a town clerk and clerk of the peace, two sergeants-at-mace, two chamberlains, two head constables, and one water bailiff. These offices were to be filled by the common council, generally with the consent of the steward. The mayor, high steward, and recorder, or any two of them, were to hold a court twice weekly, on Mondays and Thursdays, in the town hall to hear all manner of pleas whether real, personal, or mixed, and they were to hear and determine pleas of the court of Piepowder.[2] Furthermore, they had view of Frankpledge.[3] They could hold a court leet twice yearly, and enjoy the proceeds of justice other than those for high treason, petty treason, and misprision of treason. Four fairs, each of two days' duration, were to be held annually in the town, on 8 May, 2 July, 15 August and 8 October. In addition, there were to be two markets weekly, on Tuesdays and Saturdays. The mayor, aldermen and burgesses were entitled to all the tolls and customs hitherto levied on goods entering the town, whether by land or sea, and no foreigner or stranger was to trade in the town without their consent. They were also freed from the payment of toll 'within this commonwealth and the dominions thereto belonging' by land and by water. Furthermore, they were exempt from the duty of occupying any office, or of serving on any juries or inquests—with the exception of the Grand Sessions of Glamorgan—outside the borough.

That Cromwell's charter was acted upon immediately appears from a note appended to the proceedings of a leet court held on 1 October 1655 and from an item recorded in the accounts of the common attorneys. The memorandum reads as follows: 'And that Lewis Jones now portreeve, was sworn mayor of this town & borough of Swansea on the eighteenth day of March 1655, in the town hall by Major-General Dawkin, and John Bowen esquires'. The sum of £40 from the Common Attorneys' Accounts, with the consent and assent of the aldermen and burgesses, was also delivered to 'Mr John Bowen & Mr William Baylie the 17th of November 1655 towards the renewing of the charter as per their receipt appeareth'. Further proof that the charter had been adopted is to be found in the fact that in this year, and for four years afterwards, the common attorneys were called chamberlains.

---

[2] A court of justice held at fairs which dealt with disputes between buyers and sellers.
[3] A system in which units or tithings composed of ten households were formed, in each of which members were held responsible for one another's conduct.

On 3 May 1658 Cromwell granted another charter to the town empowering the burgesses to elect 'one able and discreet person of the said town and borough to be a burgess of the Parliaments of us and our successors for the said town and borough'. There is, however, no record of an election except the following which appears in the mayor's account for the year ending at Michaelmas: 'I paid for drawing the indenture between me & the sheriff for our Parliament Burgess, & for the parchment & postage of it to London, 00-08-06'. If Swansea had been visited by the candidate, or if a regular election had taken place, then some notice of the occurrence would, in all probability, have appeared in the corporation books. Since there is no reference to either, and as the return does not appear to have been made in the usual way to the sheriff, it may be queried whether a blank for the member's name was not left in the return for the lord of the borough to fill up. The records of Richard Cromwell's Parliament show that the member for Swansea was William Foxwist, the heir of Richard Foxwist and Ellen, the daughter of William Thomas of Aber. He was born in Caernarfon in 1610. After a period of study at Jesus College, Oxford, he proceeded, on 14 February 1636, to Lincoln's Inn to study law and on 17 May 1645 he was called to the bar.

It appears from Burton's Parliamentary Diary that a Colonel Allured had mentioned in the House of Commons an irregularity in Foxwist's return and it was proposed that an inquiry should be instituted into the matter. The suppression of this investigation may well have been due to an unwillingness to interfere with a nomination borough of the new Protector. From the same diary it becomes apparent that Foxwist was generally a silent member. However, on 11 February 1658/9, he had made a brief speech in which he supported a motion that Richard Cromwell should be allowed to govern by his own will and not be constrained to rule according to the law.

Foxwist was an experienced parliamentarian. He had represented Caernarfon in the Long Parliament in 1647-8, and he had been one of the members violently and arbitrarily excluded by Colonel Pride on 6 December 1648. In 1654 he had been returned for Anglesey to the first Protectorate Parliament. During those periods when he had not been directly involved with politics, he had practised law. In 1645 he had been chosen recorder of St. Alban's and the following year he was made Judge of the Court of Admiralty in north Wales. Between 1655-59 he appeared as deputy-judge for the Great Sessions Court in the Brecon Circuit and, indeed, it was in his capacity as a Welsh judge that he attended the state funeral of Oliver Cromwell.

The Parliament to which he was returned for Swansea met on 27 January 1658/9, and on 5 February he was appointed a member of a committee to consider how north and south Wales and Monmouthshire, 'may be supplied with a learned, pious, sufficient, and able ministry'. This Parliament, however, was dissolved on 22 April. In February 1660 Foxwist took his seat in the Rump Parliament as member for St. Alban's, and on 2 March he was included on a committee to which a bill 'for the approbation of ministers before they be admitted to any public benefice' was referred. He made his peace with the restored monarch in 1660 and, shortly afterwards, made his peace with his maker.

Surprisingly enough, there is no entry in the town records relating to the death of the lord of the borough, Oliver Cromwell. On the other hand, when his son, Richard, was proclaimed Protector, Swansea presented a spectacle of great rejoicing. The bells were rung, for which service the corporation paid 5s. 6d., and a further 16s. 10d. was expended on 14lbs of gunpowder and match, so that the town must have reverberated to the roar of guns firing a salute. Unfortunately, it is not possible to gauge the genuineness of this rejoicing, since the presence of the military would have made some demonstration of loyalty politic.

Before the Restoration, the corporation simply set aside the charter and, at Michaelmas 1659, reverted to the old order of things and bestowed the title of portreeve on William Jones. The proclamation of Charles II as King was accompanied by considerable junketing, and it is recorded that £4. 7s. 0d. was 'paid at Mr Lyson Seyes his house and at the wine tavern in the entertainment of Colonel Freeman and several other gentlemen that accompanied myself [the portreeve] and the aldermen in the solemn proclaiming of his Most Gracious Majesty Charles the 2nd to be King of

England, Scotland, France, & Ireland etc which was performed on the 11th day of May 1660'. The actual proclamation was read by one Edward Landegg, for which he received 5s. The bells were rung, bonfires were lit, and beer was dispensed. The rejoicing on this occasion may have been truly sincere, for by this time there was a wisdespread reaction against the strict moral code of the Puritan regime and military rule, and the country deeply desired a return to monarchy.

On the Restoration, Henry Somerset (1629-1700), third Marquis of Worcester and first Duke of Beaufort, secured the return to the family of those possessions which had been conferred on Cromwell by Parliament. The Marquis's agents now descended upon the town, and in 1660-61, in the accounts of the common attorneys, there are charges 'for wine that was bestowed upon the Marquis of Worcester's commissioners £1. 9s. 8d.; for a loaf of refined sugar containing 4lbs at 18d. per 1lb, 6s. 0d., and for their horse meat, £1. 15s. 6d.'. Further disbursements of a similar nature on the lord's representatives are recorded in the following year. These commissioners effected some changes in the composition of the aldermanic body, for despite the absence of entries in the Common Hall Book relating to dismissals from, or appointments to that body, the ranks of the aldermen in 1662 reveal some significant changes from the position in 1657. In 1662 there are two notable omissions from their number: none other than Major-General Rowland Dawkin and Mathew David, both leading parliamentarians. In their places were restored Leyson Seys and William Thomas, both of whom had been deprived of their status as aldermen in 1647 because of their attachment to the royalist cause. An entirely new appointment was that of Isaac After, a merchant, presumably the son of Francis After, who was portreeve in 1632. His appointment at this time, considered in conjunction with his complete exclusion from active participation in public life during the Interregnum, would point very strongly to royalist sympathies. As a result of these and other changes in the identity of the aldermen during this decade, and the concentration of the office of portreeve after 1660 in the hands of the older governing families and their allies among the new Restoration families, the balance of power and leadership had swung away from the Commonwealth nominees. In 1662, six of the twelve aldermen belonged to the old guard, though three of them had come to terms with the Commonwealth. The six included Leyson Seys, William Thomas, Isaac After, John Daniell, Lewis Jones and John Bowen. The others were new men risen to the top as a result of the triumph of the parliamentary forces but who continued in office despite the restoration of the monarchy. Consequently, this latter group must have executed a complete *volte face*, and their action can be accounted for either on the ground of self-interest, or by a complete disillusionment with a régime with which they had formerly identified themselves. This group included William Herbert, William Bayly, Thomas Williams, William Jones, William Vaughan and Robert Jones. By 1667, apart from the disappearance of Thomas Williams and William Thomas (they had probably died), it would not appear that any further changes were effected in the aldermanic council. However, the following year, three new aldermen were elected: Gamaliel Hughs, David Bevan and William Thomas. In 1668, therefore, the aldermen would have included five who belonged to the old ruling families (Isaac After, John Bowen, John Daniell, Lewis Jones and Leyson Seys), four who had been Commonwealth men (William Herbert, William Jones, Robert Jones and William Vaughan) and three from what may be called Restoration families (Gamaliel Hughs, David Bevan and William Thomas). No further changes were made to the aldermanic body before 1672 although by that date both John Daniell and William Vaughan had departed the scene.

The dominance of the older governing town families and their allies among the new Restoration families in the council was emphasized by the concentration of the office of portreeve in their hands. Between 1660-72 they held that office on no fewer than ten occasions, in the persons of Leyson Seys (1660, 1661, 1662), Isaac After (1662, 1667), Lewis Jones (1666, 1672), Gamaliel Hughs (1669), William Thomas (1670) and David Bevan (1671). On the other hand, the Commonwealth men held the office on three occasions only during the same period—in 1664 (William Vaughan), 1665 (William Bayly) and 1668 (Robert Jones).

A further indication of the ascendancy of the old guard and the new Restoration families may perhaps be found in a scrutiny of those who held the office of common attorney between 1660-72. Of the fifteen burgesses who, at various times during this period held the office, over half were new names, only seven having previously held it. Among the new names were William Thomas, Samuel Hughes, Phillip Jones, Robert Davies, George Bowen, Edmond Whithear and Mathew Jones. The remaining seven had held the office during the Interregnum. They included Walter Paine, John Hughes, John Granfoord, John Whiteard (?), William Phillip, John Rowland and Phillip David.

Symbolic of the failure of a great experiment, and of the return of Swansea to its former condition, were the altering of the seal and the restoration of the town arms. In the Common Attorneys' Accounts for 1661 7s. 6d. is recorded as having been paid 'for cutting the portcullis on the town seal'. The preceding item had been for 'mending the portcullis & for making an S & T to mark the town peck—1s.8d.'.

On the economic side, during the period 1649-60, the corporation continued to devote time and energy to the development of the port and, furthermore, demonstrated a lively appreciation of its financial possibilities. In 1616 Walter Thomas had begun building a new quay at his own expense. This quay was completed in 1619, and the corporation must have assumed responsibility for its maintenance since items in the accounts of the attorneys relate to payments being made for that purpose. The following represent a selection of some of the more interesting of the entries:

1652-3:
| | |
|---|---|
| paid Thomas Griffith for carrying stones to the new quay | 00 02 06 |
| paid for bringing the stones from the mount to make the wall for the new quay | 1 00 06 |
| paid Mr Fraunklen for his boat & men to carry stones to the new quay | 00 01 04 |

1654-55:
| | |
|---|---|
| paid for the carrying of 4 boat loading of stone from the old quay to the new wall | 00 06 00 |

paid for the removing of the stones from the old
quay to the new wall                                    00 04 06

While on the one hand the burgesses endeavoured to maintain the efficiency of their quay, on the other hand they were not blind to the possibilities of letting portions of the riverside to individuals as 'coal places'. In 1658 they leased to Richard Seys 'the coal place by Frances's dock it being the town's land'. The lease was for twenty-one years and was to commence in August 1676. Under its terms the lessee was to pay an annual rent of £3 in two equal portions, 30s. at Michaelmas and 30s. in May 'with one couple capons[4] at Xmas to the portreeve'. A point of particular interest in this entry is the reference to 'Frances's dock', which had evidently come into existence since 1652. Again the lease was not to commence until 1676. There are three possible explanations for this delay: first, that it was an indication of a somewhat timorous disposition on the part of the corporation; second, that the corporation, for some reason or other, did not desire that the coal place should bear rent immediately; and finally, that the site to be leased was already occupied by tenants who could not be disturbed. In 1676 the lease was duly taken up and the common attorneys recorded: 'Received of Richard Seys, Esq (high sheriff of this County) for the coal place at Mill dock which he holdeth by lease from the town at 31i per annum the sum of 45s being part of the last year's rent (the other 15s was received by the old common attorneys from Richard Jones and widow Griffith) received 02li 05s 00'.

The provision of these coal places brought the corporation face to face with the necessity to preserve, exclusively to those who rented them, privileges which the burgesses had long been accustomed freely to enjoy. Consequently, in 1661, the corporation agreed that persons, other than burgesses, must pay dues for dumping coal on the quay or riverside. The order that was now introduced stipulated that 'all persons (except burgesses) that shall lay down any coal upon any part of the land belonging to the town shall pay 2d each wey'. In the event this proved a valuable source

---

[4] A cockerel castrated when young to improve the quality of its flesh for food.

of income for the town and in 1661 it is recorded that the attorneys received £10. 5s. 10d. in dues.

Unfortunately, for the Commonwealth period, it is not possible to provide statistical data as to the condition of Swansea's trade on the export and import sides since there are no Port Books extant. However, it can be surmised that the coal trade from the town, despite the setbacks it had suffered as a result of the dislocation caused by the Civil Wars, expanded considerably for, at the Restoration, Swansea's exports, coastal and foreign, amounted to 10,775 chaldrons, as compared with about 8,712 chaldrons on the eve of the wars. This increase has been ascribed to two factors. First, the growth of industry had led to the discovery of new and highly important uses for coal; and secondly, the rapid development and enlightened exploitation of the coalfields by the new owners—the Mining Adventurers—enabled the sale of greater quantities of coal at lower prices, thus encouraging increased use of the fuel for domestic purposes. Furthermore, it may well be that this expansion was symptomatic of the new drive and energy displayed by a victorious merchant element in the borough. Swansea's trade during the Interregnum had increased despite the activities of Prince Rupert and his royalist privateers. An indication that the shipping of the town had, to some extent, suffered from their depredations is to be found in an order which the Council of State directed to the governor of the Isle of Man on 16 December 1651. By this order the governor was instructed to deliver to Mathew Francklin of Swansea the goods that were in his ship, the *Swansea Merchant*, which had been taken 'by the enemy' but which had been recovered on the surrender of the island to Parliament.

But not only had the volume of the coal trade from Swansea increased during this period; a new orientation was also given to its direction. Before the Civil Wars, most of the coal exported from the town had been transported overseas. At the Restoration, however, by far the greater quantity of the coal was shipped coastwise, 10,100 chaldrons as compared with 675 chaldrons overseas. Futhermore, in the overseas trade, Ireland now replaced France as the principal market. The reason for this change can be found in the high export duties. In 1644 Sir Lionel Maddison had calculated that on every Newcastle chaldron purchased, the English exporter paid 11s. 6d. duty while the foreigner paid 13s. 2d. In view of this, it is a remakable testimony to the demand for coal abroad that the foreigner should have continued to buy coal in England at all. These taxes would have had the result of making him fight shy of trading with the town, and he would have been driven to seek elsewhere for his coal, preferably in Scotland. Furthermore, at the Restoration, an Act of Tunnage and Poundage had discriminated even more sharply against foreign shipping. This act had fixed the tax on coal exported in English vessels at 5s. per London chaldron (about 1⅓ tons) and 8s. per Newcastle chaldron (about 2½ tons), and that on coal shipped in foreign bottoms at *double* these rates. Coal despatched to Ireland, on the other hand, only paid a subsidy of 1s. per London chaldron.

During the Commonwealth period, then, the town had continued to prosper and this increasing wealth had been built up on the export trade in coal. A barometer of the degree of affluence of the town is the size of its population. Adopting the method employed earlier in computing the borough's population, a population figure of 1,690 is arrived at for Swansea in 1662. In this year, greater accuracy was aimed at by counting the number of baptisms, burials and marriages for one year before and after this date and taking the average. On the basis of this calculation, baptism, burial and marriage figures of 39, 57 and 12, respectively, were arrived at. Applying Marshall's multipliers these, in turn, provided figures of 48.477 for births, 68.4 for deaths, and 24 for marriages.

| Year | *According to births* | *According to deaths* | *According to marriages* | *According to average of 3 preceding columns* |
|------|----------------------|----------------------|-------------------------|----------------------------------------------|
| 1662 | 1285 | 2391 | 1395 | 1690 |

Since the town's inhabitants were estimated at roughly 1,638 in the 1630s, it would appear at first glance that Swansea's population had remained fairly static in the intervening years. However, between 1649-62, the town had become the most important stronghold of south Wales Puritanism. The borough harboured a nest of Independents, Baptists and Quakers who had their own meeting houses and burial places. Consequently, they were unlikely to have figured in the parish registers. Perhaps it would be safe to assume that there were at least 300 to 400 Puritans in Swansea in 1662. Certainly in a census taken in 1676 the number of Nonconformists in the town was given as 292, and in this figure only the adults were included. Furthermore, since Archbishop Sheldon who was responsible for this census endeavoured at all times to minimize the strength of the Nonconformists, this estimate itself might well have been too low. Assuming, then, a numerical strength of 300 to 400 to the Puritans, the town population would have been approximately 2,000 to 2,100 at the Restoration and this would not appear to be an unreasonable figure.

It can be seen, therefore, that during the years 1649-60 the seeds of Puritanism which, in an earlier period, had been sowed in soil favourable for their reception, grew and flourished to such an extent under the warm Commonwealth sun that by the Restoration the town was the focus of Nonconformity in south Wales. Against this background of Puritan development, changes, though transient, of a very far-reaching nature were introduced into the administrative framework of the borough which had the effect of placing the town once again firmly under the control of its lord, and reversed a trend towards greater autonomy which had been so conspicuous in the early decades of the seventeenth century. Economically, the town recovered from that contraction of economic activity which was a feature of the external trading and commercial activities of its merchant community during the Civil Wars, and a considerable expansion of the trade in coal, particularly coastwise and to Ireland, took place. It was in this manner that the promise of recovery and development, held out at the end of the wars, was realized in full measure.

# SELECT BIBLIOGRAPHY

Preliminary note

To Colonel George G. Francis the City of Swansea owes an inestimable debt of gratitude for his work in preserving the ancient town records now kept in the library of the local University College. When he first came to examine these books, many had suffered severely from the action of damp. Not only did he successfully combat the ravages done, but he also had the books re-bound in stiff brown leather covers. Moreover, by his numerous publications, he helped to attract attention to their existence and historical value. Another antiquarian who laboured to promote interest in these volumes was L. W. Dillwyn, and much is owed to him as well. The interest displayed by Francis and Dillwyn was later maintained by Mr W. C. Rogers, an Estate Agent for the former County Borough, who catalogued a great deal of miscellaneous material and published in 1981 a pictorial history of Swansea. Currently, this long tradition of responsible care for material relating to the city is being maintained by Dr John Alban, the City Archivist.

A. Primary Sources

Manuscript

1. Charters
   a. William de Newburgh (1158-1184)
   b. King Henry III (8 March 1234)
   c. William de Breos (24 February 1306)
   d. King Edward II (20 September 1312)
   e. King Edward III (18 March 1332)
   f. Henry, 2nd Earl of Worcester (1532)
   g. Oliver Cromwell, Lord Protector (26 January 1655; 3 May 1658)

2. Minute and Order Books
   a. Common Hall Book, 1549-1665
   b. Book of Orders, 1569-1682

3. Corporation Account Books
   a. Common Attorneys' Accounts, 1617-1635
   b. Common Attorneys' Accounts, 1635-1662

4. Church Books
   a. Churchwardens' Account Book, 1558-1694
   b. Book of Benevolences, or Poor Man's Tax or Alms, 1563-1569
   c. Miscellaneous Collection—Borough and Parish, 1545-1844
   d. St. Mary's Swansea Parish Register, 1631-1706

5. Church in Wales Records
Carmarthen Probate, 1586-1652 N.L.W., Aberystwyth

6. Exchequer Port Books (E 190) P.R.O., London

Printed

a. Dillwyn, L.W., *Contributions towards a History of Swansea*, Swansea, 1840
b. Francis, George G., *Charters Granted to Swansea*, London, 1867
Lewis, E.A., *Welsh Port Books*, London, 1927.

Secondary

General
Charles, B. G., *Old Norse Relations with Wales*, Cardiff, 1934
Davies, D.J., *The Economic History of south Wales, prior to 1800*, Cardiff, 1935
Davies, R.R., *Lordship and Society in the March of Wales, 1282-1400*, Oxford, 1978.
Griffiths, R.A., (Ed.), *Boroughs of Mediaeval Wales*, Cardiff, 1978
Jenkins, Geraint H., *The Foundation of Modern Wales: Wales, 1642-1780*, Oxford, 1987.
Nef, J.U., *The Rise of the British Coal Industry*, 2 vols., London, 1932
Phillips, J.R., *Civil War in Wales and the Marches*, 2 vols., London, 1874
Rees, J.F., *Studies in Welsh History*, Cardiff, 1947
Rees, T.M., *A History of the Quakers in Wales and their Emigration to North America*, Carmarthen, 1925
Rees, William, *A History of the Order of St. John of Jerusalem in Wales and on the Welsh Border*, Cardiff, 1947
Rees, Thomas, *History of Nonconformity in Wales*, London, 1866
Richards, Thomas, *A History of the Puritan Movement in Wales, 1639-53*, London, 1920
—— *Religious Developments in Wales, 1654-62*, London, 1923
Soulsby, Ian, *The Towns of Mediaeval Wales*, Chichester, 1983
Williams, Glanmor, *The Welsh Church from Conquest to Reformation*, Cardiff, 1976
—— *Recovery, Reorientation, and Reformation: Wales, C. 1415-1642*, Oxford, 1987

Local

Alban, J.R., *Swansea, 1184-1984*, Swansea, 1984
Evans, Edith, *Swansea Castle and the Medieval Town*, Swansea, 1983
Francis, George G., *Copper Smelting in the Swansea District*, London, 1881,

2nd edition
—— *Old Swanzey*, Swansea, 1840
—— *The Free Grammar School, Swansea*, Swansea, 1849
—— *Henry de Gower*, London, 1876
Harries, Edward, *Swansea: its Port and Trade and their Development*, Cardiff, 1934
Havard, W.T., *The Story of Swansea Parish Church (St. Mary)*, Gloucester, 1932
Jones, W.H., *Swansea Castle*, Swansea, 1879
—— *A brief Account of St. Mary's Church, Swansea: its history and association*, Exeter, 1895
—— *History of Swansea*, Carmarthen, 1920
—— *History of the Port of Swansea*, Carmarthen, 1922
Morgan, W.Ll., *The Town and Manor of Swansea*, Carmarthen, 1924
—— *The Castle of Swansea*, Devizes, 1914
Roberts, Glyn, *The Municipal Development of the Borough of Swansea to 1900*, Cardiff, 1940
Walker, David, *St. Mary's Church, Swansea. A Short History of the Parish Church of Swansea*, Swansea, 1959
Williams, D. Trevor, *Economic Development of Swansea and the Swansea District*, Swansea, 1940

Articles
Davies, J.D., 'Place House, Swansea', *Arch. Camb.*, 5th Series, Vol. 5, 1888
Jones, Ifano, 'Sir Matthew Cradock and some of his Contemporaries', *Arch. Camb.*, LXXIV, 1919
Leeke, S.J., 'Hanes Bedyddwyr Abertawe a'r Cylch', *Y Llawlyfr*, Abertawe, Medi 3-6, 1934
Phillips, D.R., 'Cefndir Hanes Eglwys Ilston', *Cym. Hanes Bedyddwyr Cymru*, Rh. XVII, Trafodion 1928
Rees, William, 'Gower and the March of Wales', *Arch. Camb.*, 1961
Seyler, C.A., 'The early charters of Swansea and Gower', Pts. 1 & 2 in *Arch. Camb.*, 7th Series, 4 (1924) Pt. 3 in *Arch. Camb.*, 7th Series, 5 (1925)
Tucker, Horatio, 'The Dialect Speech of Gower', *Gower Journal*, III (1950)
Williams, Glanmor, 'The Affray at Oxwich Castle, 1557', *Gower Journal*, II (1949)

Unpublished Theses
Evans, B.M., 'The Welsh Coal Trade during the Stuart Period' (MA Aberystwyth, 1928).
Hughes, C.H., 'Wales and Piracy 1500-1640' (MA Swansea, 1937).
John, D.G., 'Contributions to the Economic History of South Wales' (D.Sc. Swansea, 1930).
John, Llywelyn B., 'The Parliamentary Representation of Glamorgan, 1536-1832' (MA Cardiff, 1924).
Williams, Margaret Fay, 'The Society of Friends in Glamorgan 1654-1900' (MA Aberystwyth, 1950).

# INDEX

Act for the Better Propagation and Preaching of the Gospel in Wales (1650) 214, 215, 218, 221
Act of Uniformity (1662) 228
Acts of Union (1536/43) xvii, xviii, 35, 84, 118, 120-4, 155-6, 194
After, John (Minister) 138, 181
Agriculture, animal husbandry xvi, xvii, 10-11, 17, 22, 50-3, 61, 96, 186, 197. *Vide* also Drovers
Aldermen, Aldermanic council xv, xvii-xviii, xix, 24, 85, 101, 103, 129, 138, 139-42, 144, 230-2, 240-1
Approvers 214, 216, 218

Baldwin, Archbishop 27, 31
Barlow, William 158, 167
Basing House 205 + *n*
Baxter, Richard 186
Beadle 179-80
Bells 173, 175-7
Bevan, William (Merchant) 222, 223, 225, 226, 228
Bidwell, Morris (Minister) 216, 222, 223, 224, 225
Birkett, Alice (Quaker) 224
Book of Common Prayer (1549) 172; (1552) 172, 228. *Vide* also Welsh Prayer Book
Breteuil 7
Bridges 154, 155
Bristol 13, 21, 46, 50, 57, 65, 76, 83, 125, 150, 158, 176, 180, 188, 189, 193, 198
Bristol Channel 1, 3, 12, 13, 22, 64, 70
*Brut y Tywysogion* 6
Burgesses, admission of 15, 24-5, 34, 122, 137, 142, 144, 152;
 privileges 8-10, 13, 15-16, 17-18, 19, 50, 79-80, 118, 125-9, 235-7, 238, 243;
 obligations 10, 15, 16, 143-4;
 nature of burgess-ship 24-5, 142-44;
 administration of justice 149;
 financial resources 19, 149;
 elections to Parliament xviii, 120, 121-4, 238-9
Burley, Sir Roger (Priest) 158

Callice, John (Pirate) 74
Capper, Thomas 172-3
Cardiff 4*n*, 22, 36, 37, 59, 62, 80, 83, 120, 122, 146, 154, 155, 170, 173, 195, 196, 197, 198, 199, 203, 204, 209, 214, 222, 224, 227, 230, 234
Carmarthen 15*n*, 21, 31, 59, 62, 80, 81, 162, 166-7, 168, 181, 182, 191, 201, 203, 214, 228
Carne, Sir Edward 165
Castle XV, XVI, 6-7, 11, 19, 20, 27, 79, 89, 200, 204, 207
Charles I 65, 135, 156, 186, 189, 190, 199, 202-3, 213
Charles II 58, 78, 204, 226, 239-40
Charters, general XV, 6-8, 14, 23, 24, 34, 118-9; William de Newburgh 8-11, 17, 24; King John 11—13; William de Breos: to Swansea 15-19, 24, 27, 40, 42-4, 47, 118, 126, to Gower 18, 54; Henry, 2nd Earl of Worcester 53, 118-20, 126; Cromwell xviii, 231, 233-8
Cloth, cloth making xvi, 10, 21, 53, 104
Coal, coal mining xvi, xvii, 15, 18, 37-46, 82, 83, 92-3, 103, 132, 134, 145-6, 199, 243-4
Colby Moor, battle of 203
Common Hall, function of 142-44
Council in Wales and the Marches 42, 51, 129, 134, 163-4
Court Baron 149
Court Leet, functions of 137-8
Cradock, Sir Matthew 22, 41, 73, 88-9, 129, 132-3, 134, 165-6, 170, 175
Cradock, Walter 216
Crier 150
Cromwell, Oliver xviii, 11, 41-2, 78, 130, 200, 203, 207, 210, 215, 223, 229-30, 231, 233-4, 238, 239, 240
Cromwell, Richard 238, 239
Cromwell, Thomas 120
Customs Organisation 22, 35-6

Davies, Richard (Bishop) 85, 181
Dawkin, Rowland 190-2, 193, 194, 204-5, 209, 210, 213, 226, 232, 236, 237, 240

252       *The History of Swansea*

Docks 49, 70, 72-3, 77, 243
Drovers (*Porthmyn*) 125
Dublin 3, 4 + *n*, 219

Edgehill, battle of 198
Education 78, 107-8, 111-12, 148. *Vide* also Schools
Edward I 14, 25, 27
Edward II 7, 25
Edward III 7, 162
Edward VI 159, 161, 165, 166, 168, 170, 171, 180, 184
Elizabeth I 35, 42, 44, 61, 112, 135, 156, 167, 168, 172, 180, 199
English Bible (1537) 172

Fairs xvi, 18, 37, 50, 54-6, 96, 143, 179, 237 + *n*
Fayrwode, John (Warden) 23-4, 31, 162
Ferrar, Robert (Bishop) 167
Ferry 16, 21, 82
Fishing 10
Five Mile Act 217
Fox, George (Quaker) 223, 226, 227
Foxwist, William (Member of Parliament) 238-9
Fulke de Bréauté 12
Furnishings, *Vide* under Housing

Gawler, Francis (Quaker) 224, 226
Gerald of Wales, 27, 31
Gerard, Sir Charles 195, 197, 203, 207
Glamorgan 12, 22, 25, 38, 120, 122, 132, 134, 135, 154, 155, 170, 173, 182, 194, 194-5, 197, 199, 203, 207, 209, 210, 211, 222, 227, 234
Glove Making 49-50, 92, 107
Gloucester 57, 198
Glyndŵr, Owain 23
Gore, Hugh (Bishop) 219-20
Gower 1, 5, 6, 7, 11, 12, 14, 16, 17, 25, 27, 29, 32, 33, 38-9, 41, 44, 50, 52-3, 53*n*, 54-5, 56, 78, 82, 118, 121, 125, 130, 131, 132, 133, 135, 136, 161, 166, 190, 210, 214
Grenville, Richard 74
Griffith, Hugh (Pirate), 73
Gruffydd ap Rhys 6

Hall, Stephen 158
Harrison, Major-General Thomas 215
Harrison, William (Topographer) 91
Haynes, Stephen (Pirate) 75
Henry I 26
Henry III 7
Henry IV xvi, 121, 161
Henry Tudor (Henry VII), 35, 78, 132
Henry VIII 55, 114, 159, 160, 163, 171, 180, 184
Henry de Beaumont, Earl of Warwick 5, 7, 8, 27
Henry de Gower (Bishop) 27, 28-9, 161, 162, 200
Henry de Newburgh 32
Herbert, Henry 210 + *n*
Herbert, Sir George 88, 100, 101, 124, 128*n*, 129, 131-2, 133-5, 141, 152, 165-6, 169
Herbert, William, 2nd Earl of Pembroke 118; 3rd Earl 41
Herbert, Sir William (of Swansea) 41, 75, 85, 128, 136, 139, 143, 166
Holme, Elizabeth (Quaker) 224-5, 226
Horton, Colonel Thomas 209, 210
Hospital of the Blessed David xvii, xviii, 25, 28-31, 34, 79, 80, 134, 158, 159, 161-6, 200
Houghton, William (Minister) 226
Housing 78, 88-91
Hughes, Stephen (of Meidrym) 218

Ilfracombe 22, 57
Iron, ironmaking 46-7, 67, 92

James, I, 62, 65, 135, 156
James II, 235
Jenkins, David (of Hensol) 190, 202-3
John ap John (Quaker) 222-3, 226
John de Acum (Warden) 30
Jones, Philip (Colonel) 189, 190, 192, 193, 204, 205, 209, 210, 213, 215, 219, 221, 225, 230, 232, 236

King John 7, 11, 12, 25
*Kynniver Llith a Ban* 172

## Index

Laugharne, Rowland (Major-General) 201, 203-4, 207, 209-10
Lead 62
Leather, leathermaking xvi, 10, 54, 67, 92, 102, 105, 119
Leland, John 55, 200
Lewis, Dr. David (Judge) 76
Llwyd, Morgan 208
London 50, 55, 58, 64, 158, 180, 188, 193
Lordship of Gŵyr, origin xv, 5; extent 5-6
Loughor 1, 6, 15, 46, 49, 82, 83, 122, 128, 225

Maces 141-2, 149-50
Mansel, Bussy 161, 190, 193-4, 197, 204, 206, 210
Mansel, Sir Edward 74-5, 135, 150, 153
Mansel, Sir Thomas 39, 135, 150, 156, 161, 189
Mareschal, William (Earl of Pembroke) 12-13
Market xv, xvi, 18, 36, 37, 54-5, 96, 108, 115, 125, 128-9, 143, 148, 156, 233, 236-7
Marston Moor, battle of 203
Martin, David (Warden) 31
Mary I, Queen of England 167, 168, 172
Matthew, Marmaduke 184, 193, 213, 217, 221, 223, 224, 225, 229
Maurice, Henry 208
*Mercurius Academicus* 204
Meyrick, Peter (Schoolmaster) 219
Miles, John 182, 190, 192, 213-5, 216, 218, 222-3, 225, 226, 227
Milford Haven 21, 36, 190, 201, 211
Morgan, Hopkin (Minister) 216
Morgan, William (Bishop) 181
Moris, John 85, 87, 89, 90, 96, 105, 127, 178
Mostyn, Ambrose (Minister) 184, 193, 207-8, 213
Moulton, Robert 201-2, 211-12
Mumbles 62, 65, 66, 74, 76, 82, 223

Navigation Acts 35
Neath 36, 38, 46, 57, 60, 62, 64, 67, 74-6, 80, 83, 112, 122, 145, 174, 194, 197, 199, 209, 225

Normans xv, 5-6, 7, 12, 26, 31, 34, 120
Norse xv, 1-5

Occupations 78, 91-95, 104-5
Order and Chapel of St. John 25, 31-33, 38, 39, 158, 159-61, 216, 221, 224, 225, 228
Organ, situation and maintenance of 173-4, 178; the organist 174-5
Owen, George (of Henllys) 44-5, 61, 63, 120

Peter, Hugh 215, 218
Pews, provision of 174, 177-9; disputes relating to 177-8; seat-rents 178, 179
Piracy 22, 35, 73-6
Place House 88-9, 129, 134
Poor, relief of 78, 85, 98-107, 138, 146-7, 149, 154, 179, 223
Poor Law Amendment Act (1834) 105-6
Population xvi, xvii, 3, 4+n, 7, 12, 17, 19, 22, 23+n, 34, 40, 50, 77, 78, 80-85, 121, 124, 148, 179, 186, 245-6
Port, harbour xv, xvi, 3-4, 6, 7, 19, 34, 35, 39, 40, 67-70, 108, 120, 128, 148, 149, 194-6, 242. *Vide* also under Quays and Docks
Portreeves, election of 15, 17, 24, 137; duties 15, 138, 144-5; recruitment xviii, 138-9
Powell, Rice (Colonel) 209-10
Powell, Vavasor 208, 216
Poyer, John (Colonel) 209, 210
Public Health, plagues xvi, 22-4, 30, 34, 84, 107-11, 119, 148, 162
Puritanism xviii, 180-5, 188, 190-2, 193, 205-6, 213, 215, 216-8, 221, 222, 225-9, 233, 240, 246
Pye, Moor (Schoolmaster) 218-9

Quakers 221-5, 227-8, 246
Quays xvi, 21, 68-9, 70-2, 77, 157, 242-3

Rawlins, Richard (Warden) 163, 166
Recreations, sporting: bullbaiting 112-3; cockfighting 112-3; bowls 113; tennis 113; cards and dice 113-5; festive, feastings and junketings 115; entertainment, travelling players 115-6

## 254 The History of Swansea

Rhys ap Tewdwr 6
Rhys ap Thomas 160
Richard III 132
Richard de Thorn (Warden) 31, 162
Roads, maintenance of 145-6
Romans 1

Salesbury, William 172, 181
Sanctuary, rights of: St. Mary 16, 27, 32; St. John 32
Schools 108, 111-2, 129, 218-20
Sermons 182-3
Seys, Leyson 205, 206, 239-40, 241
Seys, Richard 216, 243
Ship-building xvi, 3, 8, 15, 17, 47-9, 92
Smith, Adam 37-8
Somersets: Charles, 1st Earl of Worcester 118, 132, 133; Henry, 2nd Earl 41, 53, 118, 119, 126, 132, 135; William, 3rd Earl 131-2, 150-1, 152-3; Edward, 4th Earl 52-3, 130-1, 132, 135-6, 151; Henry, 5th Earl 41-2, 130, 132, 189, 194, 207; Henry, 3rd Marquis and 1st Duke of Beaufort 240
Star Chamber, court of 113, 114, 116-7, 131, 132, 134-5
St. Fagan's, battle of 210
St. Mary's Church xvii, xviii, 25, 26-9, 32, 34, 39-40, 46, 49, 79, 80, 129, 133, 141, 158, 161, 165-80, 183, 222, 224, 225. *Vide* also under Bells, Beadle, Vestry and Pews
Stewards xv, 8, 15, 17, 24, 53, 101, 119, 123, 124, 129, 131, 132-8, 189, 201, 205, 231, 236
Stradling, Sir Edward (of St. Donat's) 74, 123; Sir John 135
Swein 1-3

Thomas, Hopkin 89
Thomas, William (Dan-y-Graig) 190, 194, 196-7, 198, 206-7, 241

Thomas, Walter (Deputy-Steward) 71-2, 104, 138, 150, 189, 190, 197, 199, 200-1, 204, 206, 210, 242
Toleration Act (1689) 227
Tolls, nature of 125
Town: origins 1-7; liberties xv-xvi, 11, 148-9, 235; perambulation of boundaries 115; government, machinery of xv, 142, 148-53, 157, 235-7. *Vide* also under Aldermanic Council; streets 19-20, 23, 70, 78-9, 96, 108-11, 113, 128-9, 220; walls xv, 19-20, 71, 79
Trade, general xv, xvi, xviii, 13-14, 18, 21-2, 35-7, 38-50, 61-3, 70, 77, 82, 93, 212, 233, 244-5, 246; coastwise 13-14, 21, 38, 40, 46-7, 56-9, 63-5, 188; overseas 4-5, 18, 21, 38, 40, 47, 49, 59-61, 65-7
Triers 221, 229
Tudor, Jasper (Earl of Pembroke) 133

Vaughan, Richard (Earl of Carbery) 201, 203
Vermin, destruction of 147-8
Vestry, responsibilities of 144-48, 179
Vikings. *Vide* under Norse
Villiers, George (Duke of Buckingham) 135

Waller, Sir William 203
Walter, David (Minister) 216, 225
Warbeck, Perkin 133
Wardens, church 179
Wealth, distribution of 78, 85-8
Welsh Prayer Book 180-1
Welsh New Testament 181
Welsh Bible 180-1
William de Breos 7, 14-15, 16-17, 18, 19, 22, 24, 25, 27, 40
William Fitz-Osbern 7
William de Newburgh 7, 8, 13, 17, 24